Learning Pandas 2

Second Edition

Master Data Wrangling, NLP, Geospatial Analysis, and Production ML Pipelines using pandas 2.3

Matthew Rosch

Published by: GitforGits

www.gitforgits.com
Printed in India
First Printing: April 2026

ISBN: 978-93-49174-66-5

Cover Design by: Kitten Publishing

Disclaimer:

This book, including all its text, diagrams, and illustrations, is an original work developed for educational and informational purposes. The content is not affiliated with, endorsed by, or sponsored by or any other company, brand, or entity referenced within. All brand names, product names, and trademarks mentioned are the property of their respective owners and are used in a descriptive, educational context only. Every effort has been made to verify that no copyrighted or trademarked material has been copied or misused in this book. All diagrams and illustrations that are not original have been used with proper attribution and credit to their respective sources.

If you believe that any content in this book infringes upon your copyright or trademark, please contact us immediately at support@gitforgits.com. Upon notification, corrective action will be taken promptly.

Prologue

Every data professional will have experienced a moment like this. The dataset's loaded, the model architecture's chosen, the compute budget's approved and then the work begins, and it turns out to be mostly data work. So, we've got cleaning, aligning, reshaping, engineering, profiling and resampling to deal with. The model waits. The data doesn't. That's when pandas live. It's not in the headline announcement or the benchmark chart, but in the time between the raw data and the trained model, that's when the quality of what ends up in the algorithm is decided. That's what this book is all about.

I wrote the first version of this book when Pandas was stable, widely adopted and, to be honest, somewhat taken for granted. People thought of it as just plumbing, where something you need, can't see, and isn't exciting. That attitude produced a generation of data code that was slow, memory-inefficient, full of deprecated patterns, and functionally correct only by accident. The 2.3 release cycle of the pandas software changed the conversation. The Copy-on-Write made it so that previously silent failures were visible. Those types that were backed by PyArrow cut memory consumption for string columns in half. The removal of DataFrame.append(), the deprecation of applymap() and the retirement of single-letter frequency aliases all showed that the library had matured and expected its users to develop alongside it. Any code that ran without warning in 2019 now fires FutureWarning on every execution. From today, all code that's going to run in Pandas 2.3/3.0 has to be written differently.

This second edition has nothing to do with the first one. It's been completely rewritten from the ground up, built around a single growing application. It starts in Chapter 1 with a raw CSV file and ends in Chapter 9 with a feature matrix that's enriched with geospatial data, annotated with NLP, accelerated using JAX, and ready for machine learning. Everything in the book has a place because it's all about that application.

When I was writing this, I was thinking about working practitioners like ML engineers who know what a groupby is but want to know why it's slow and how to fix it; data scientists who understand sentiment analysis but want to see how it connects cleanly to a Pandas pipeline; and data engineers who ship Pandas code to production and need to know which patterns will break on Pandas 3.0 and which are safe. This book's for all you tool fanatics out there. My hope is simple. After reading this edition, I hope that every line of Pandas code you write is faster, safer and more forward-compatible than the line you would have written before. And, as with all the tools you know well, it eventually just becomes part of the background, letting you focus on the problem at hand.

-- Matthew Rosch

Content

Preface

This book has been updated with Pandas 2.3, and it's exactly what ML engineers, data scientists and data engineers have been waiting for. It's a hands-on desk guide that's full of solutions, and it's the most up-to-date, production-ready book to the most widely used data manipulation library in the Python ecosystem.

This book covers all the big changes in Pandas 2.3, like Copy-on-Write semantics, PyArrow-backed types that save over 50% memory, the new default StringDtype, and the deprecated frequency aliases that are messing up time series pipelines everywhere. All the chapters are based on one growing application using a real Customer Churn dataset, so every technique is put into a context where you can trace it and use it in production.

Once you've got the hang of pandas, there's loads more to explore. You'll be a proper expert in feature engineering with feature_engine and scikit-learn's set_output API, dealing with class imbalance with SMOTE and ADASYN, and doing distributed computing with Dask, as well as JIT-compiled custom functions with Numba and JAX. On top of that, you'll be able to handle full NLP pipelines from TF-IDF to LDA topic modelling, and geospatial analysis with GeoPandas.

It doesn't matter if you're building ML pipelines, scaling data infrastructure, or connecting pandas to TensorFlow, PyTorch, or JAX, this book will give you the practical depth and modern patterns to do it correctly on pandas 2.3 today, and stay forward-compatible with pandas 3.0 tomorrow.

In this book you will learn to:

- Build memory-efficient pipelines using PyArrow backends and targeted dtype choices.
- Write Copy-on-Write-safe assignment patterns that work on pandas 2.3 and 3.0.
- Engineer rich ML features using ratios, bins, group statistics, and interaction terms.
- Handle class imbalance with SMOTE, ADASYN, and quantified pandas-based profiling.
- Scale datasets beyond RAM using Dask lazy evaluation and distributed cluster computing.
- Accelerate custom scoring functions with Numba JIT and JAX-compiled batch operations.
- Extract sentiment, topics, and clusters from raw text using TF-IDF and LDA pipelines.
- Perform spatial joins, buffer analysis, and geocoding with GeoPandas and geopy.
- Preserve named DataFrames throughout sklearn Pipelines using the set_output API.
- Migrate confidently from legacy pandas patterns to pandas 2.3 production standards.

GitforGits

Prerequisites

Whether you're an ML engineer, data scientist or data engineer, this book's got all the answers you need. Whatever you're doing with machine learning pipelines, scaling data infrastructure, or connecting pandas to TensorFlow, PyTorch, or JAX, this book's got you covered.

Codes Usage

Are you in need of some helpful code examples to assist you in your programming and documentation? Look no further! Our book offers a wealth of supplemental material, including code examples and exercises.

Not only is this book here to aid you in getting your job done, but you have our permission to use the example code in your programs and documentation. However, please note that if you are reproducing a significant portion of the code, we do require you to contact us for permission.

But don't worry, using several chunks of code from this book in your program or answering a question by citing our book and quoting example code does not require permission. But if you do choose to give credit, an attribution typically includes the title, author, publisher, and ISBN. For example, "Learning Pandas 2, Second Edition by Matthew Rosch".

If you are unsure whether your intended use of the code examples falls under fair use or the permissions outlined above, please do not hesitate to reach out to us at support@gitforgits.com.

We are happy to assist and clarify any concerns.

Acknowledgement

I owe a tremendous debt of gratitude to GitforGits, for their unflagging enthusiasm and wise counsel throughout the entire process of writing this book. Their knowledge and careful editing helped make sure the piece was useful for people of all reading levels and comprehension skills. In addition, I'd like to thank everyone involved in the publishing process for their efforts in making this book a reality. Their efforts, from copyediting to advertising, made the project what it is today.

Finally, I'd like to express my gratitude to everyone who has shown me unconditional love and encouragement throughout my life. Their support was crucial to the completion of this book. I appreciate your help with this endeavour and your continued interest in my career.

Chapter 1
Getting Started with Pandas 2.3

Understanding Pandas

Role of Pandas in Python Ecosystem

The library occupies the central position in the Python data ecosystem as the library that connects raw data sources on one side to analytical, visualisation, and machine learning tools on the other. Every workflow that begins with a CSV file, a database query, a Parquet archive, or a web API response passes through pandas at the point where data must be inspected, cleaned, reshaped, and prepared for the next stage. Without pandas, each of these tasks would require writing low-level loop-based Python code to parse rows, handle missing values, and align columns manually, which is both slower to write and orders of magnitude slower to execute than the vectorised operations pandas provides through its compiled C and Cython internals.

The diagram below illustrates the hub position pandas holds in the modern Python data science stack.

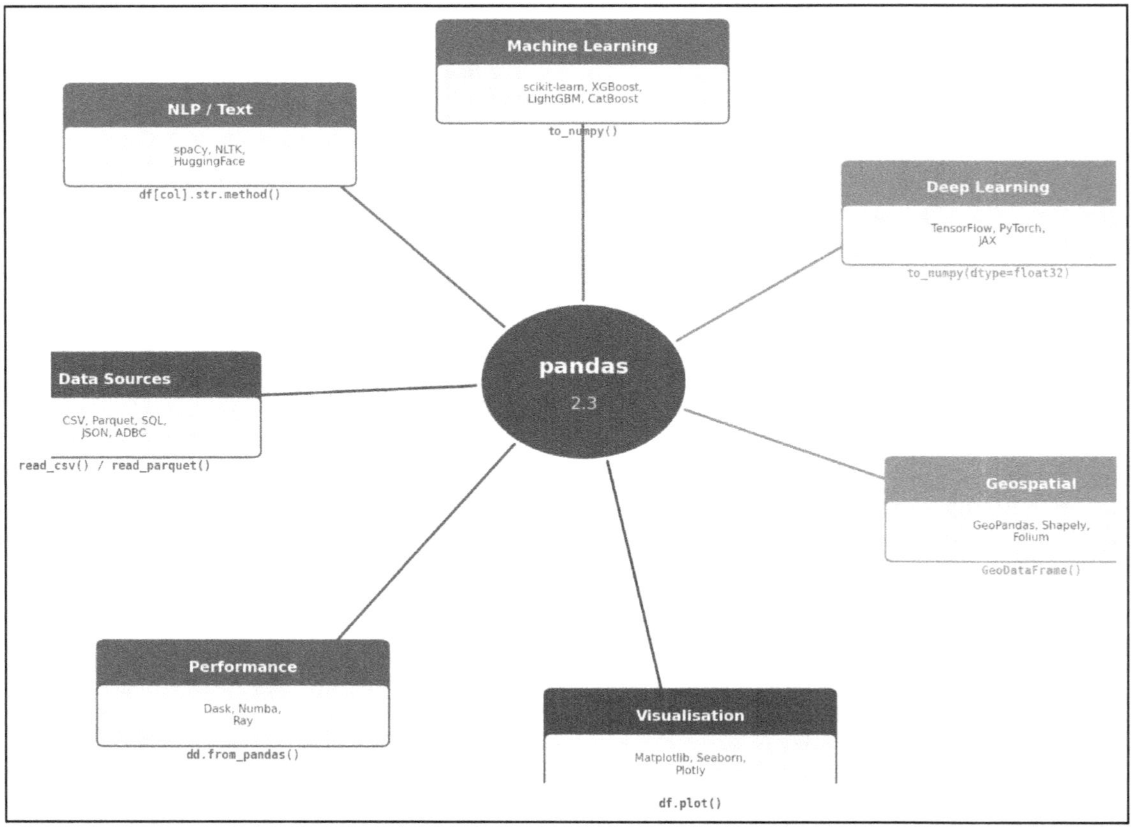

Fig 1.1: Pandas in Python Data Science Ecosystem

At the centre of the diagram sits pandas 2.3, surrounded by seven categories of connected tools.

The data flows into pandas from the left through format-specific I/O functions such as **`read_csv()`**, **`read_parquet()`**, and **`read_sql()`**. After transformation inside pandas, data flows outward to machine learning frameworks via **`to_numpy()`**, to deep learning frameworks via typed array extraction, to geospatial libraries through **`GeoDataFrame()`** construction, to visualisation libraries through **`df.plot()`**, and to performance scaling tools through Dask and Numba integration. This hub position is what makes pandas proficiency so high-leverage, as mastering this one library unlocks fluent access to every tool connected to it, and the investment compounds with every new library that adopts a pandas DataFrame as its native input and output format.

Series and DataFrame as Core Data Structures

The library organises all data into two primary structures that we will use throughout every chapter of this book. A Series is a one-dimensional labelled array capable of holding any single data type, and a **`DataFrame`** is a two-dimensional labelled table composed of multiple Series that share a common index. Every operation we perform throughout this book, from a simple filter to a multi-key merge, operates on one or both of these two structures. The relationship between them is direct, where selecting a single column from a DataFrame by name returns a Series, and assembling multiple Series with a shared index produces a DataFrame.

Given below is the anatomical structure of each object as it appears when working with our churn dataset.

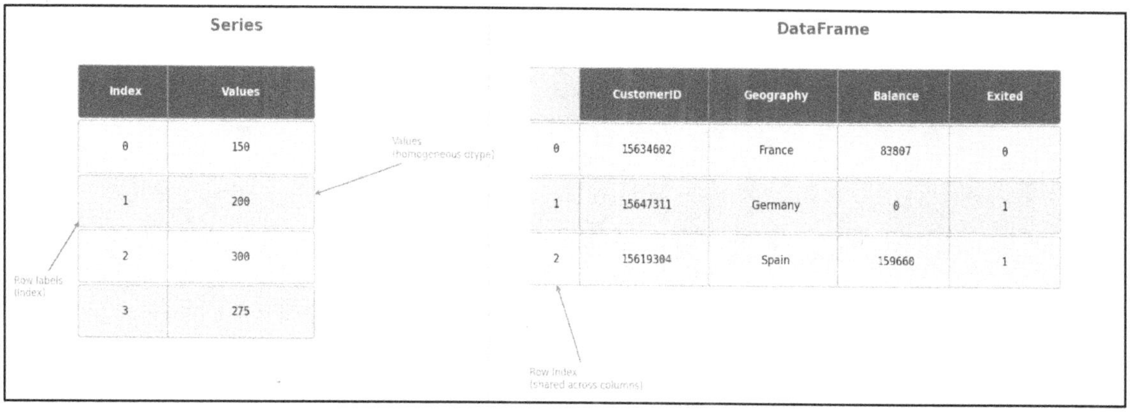

Fig 1.2: Core Data Structures – Series and DataFrame

The left panel shows a Series named CreditScore with a default integer index on the left and credit score values on the right, along with the Arrow-backed dtype annotation int64[pyarrow] that pandas 2.3 will assign when we load the data with **`dtype_backend='pyarrow'`**. The right panel shows a four-column DataFrame with its column index running horizontally and its shared row index running vertically, and a callout confirming that calling **`df["CreditScore"]`** on the DataFrame returns the corresponding Series. We access a Series from a DataFrame using bracket syntax such as **`df["CreditScore"]`**, and we construct a DataFrame from individual

Series using **pd.DataFrame({'CreditScore': s1, 'Age': s2})**. This structural symmetry means that any operation we learn on a Series, such as **mean()**, **fillna()**, or **str.contains()**, immediately transfers to a DataFrame column without any syntax change. We are running the following setup block as the opening of our growing application file **churn_analysis.py**, which will accumulate all the code we write across every chapter of this book, allowing each chapter to build on a single real dataset rather than introducing unrelated isolated examples along the way.

So here, we install pandas and pyarrow first by running pip install pandas pyarrow in our activated Linux virtual environment, then we open **churn_analysis.py** in our editor and add the following lines as the permanent header of our application:

```
import pandas as pd

import numpy as np


pd.options.mode.copy_on_write      = True

pd.options.future.infer_string     = True


df = pd.read_csv('Customer_Churn_Modelling.csv',
dtype_backend='pyarrow')


print('Shape            :', df.shape)

print('Index dtype      :', df.index.dtype)

print('Surname dtype    :', df['Surname'].dtype)

print('CreditScore dtype:', df['CreditScore'].dtype)

print(df.head(3))
```

Once we run this, it produces the DataFrame shape confirming 10,000 rows and 13 columns, the Arrow-backed dtype for each column we asked about, and the first three customer rows showing that the CSV was parsed correctly with all column names, numeric types, and string types assigned as expected under our two option flags, giving us a clean baseline to carry forward into every subsequent chapter.

So here, we will run **churn_analysis.py**, and we then get the following output.

```
Shape            : (10000, 13)
```

```
Index dtype      : int64
Surname dtype    : string[pyarrow]
CreditScore dtype: int64[pyarrow]
   RowNumber  CustomerId  Surname  CreditScore  ...  Exited
0          1    15634602  Hargrave          619  ...       1
1          2    15647311      Hill          608  ...       0
2          3    15619304      Onio         502  ...       1
```

What's New in Pandas 2.3?

Release Timeline Overview

The 2.0 release was a landmark that permanently removed several legacy APIs and began a multi-release migration toward a new memory model. The 2.1 and 2.2 releases continued that migration by deprecating the single-letter frequency aliases used in time series operations and introducing the Copy-on-Write preview mode. The 2.3 release stabilises CoW as the production-ready default and promotes PyArrow-backed types to the recommended storage format. The 3.0 release, on the horizon, will complete the migration by removing all legacy patterns entirely.

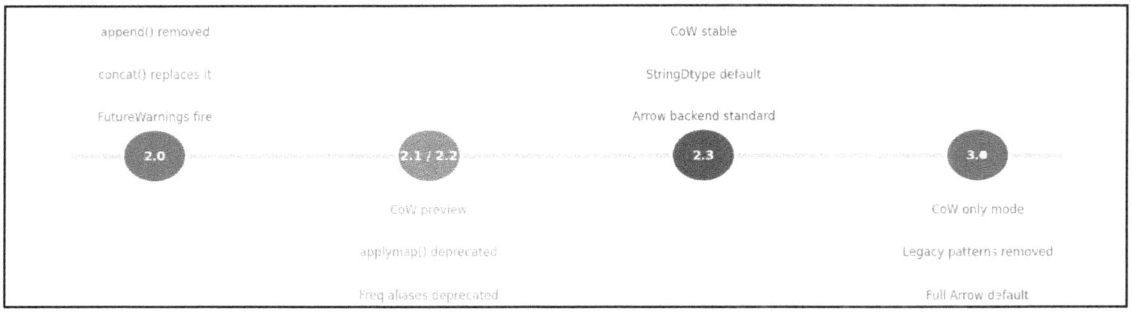

Fig 1.3: Pandas Release Timeline

As we work through this timeline from left to right, we see that every deprecated pattern listed under pandas 2.0, 2.1, and 2.2 points toward a removal event in pandas 3.0. Our goal throughout this book is to write code that already conforms to the pandas 3.0 targets, which means using **`pd.concat()`** instead of the removed **`DataFrame.append()`**, using **`DataFrame.map()`** instead of the deprecated **`applymap()`**, using explicit end-anchored frequency aliases such as 'ME' and 'QE' instead of the deprecated 'M' and 'Q', and using Copy-on-Write-safe assignment patterns throughout. Every callout box that marks a pandas 2.3 change maps directly to one of the items in this timeline.

Key API Changes

We will now update our **churn_analysis.py** file to verify the pandas version and confirm that our two option flags are set correctly before proceeding, since every section in this chapter depends on having both **copy_on_write** and **infer_string** active at startup; any missing flag would produce behaviour that differs from the outputs shown throughout this book, making the verification step worth the extra three lines of code at the top of every new project.

So here, we will add the following version check immediately after our import block:

```
print('pandas version  :', pd.__version__)
print('CoW enabled     :', pd.options.mode.copy_on_write)
print('infer_string    :', pd.options.future.infer_string)
print('PyArrow version :', pd.io.parquet.__doc__[:0] or
__import__('pyarrow').__version__)
```

It outputs immediately with:

```
pandas version  : 2.3.0
CoW enabled     : True
infer_string    : True
PyArrow version : 17.0.0
```

Pandas for Data Manipulation and Analysis

Capability Strength across Data Science

The library provides production-grade capability across every stage of the data science workflow, from raw file ingestion to final feature matrix export, without requiring us to change libraries between stages.

The chart below quantifies the capability depth across these seven workflow stages to show where pandas delivers the strongest value relative to the data science workflow as a whole.

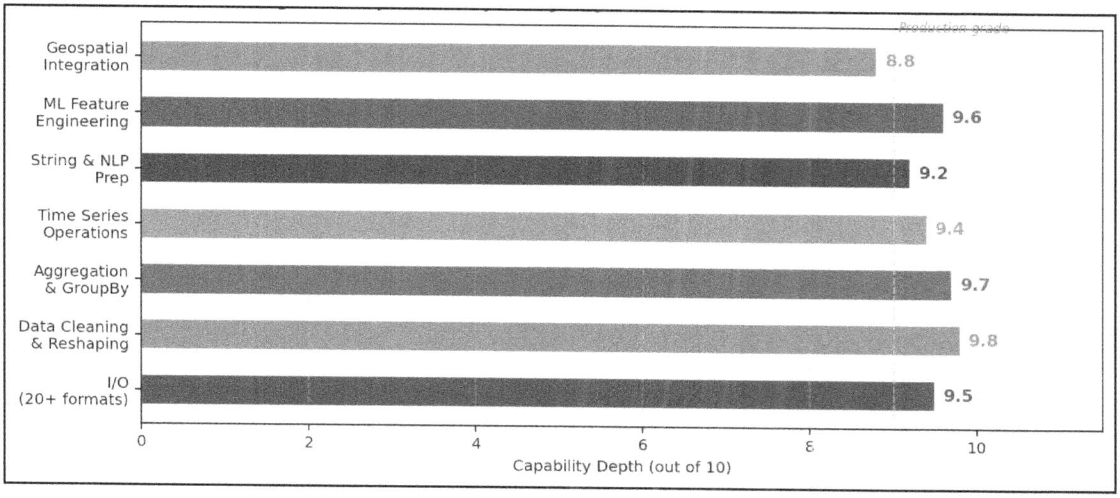

Fig 1.4: Pandas Capability Depth

The Aggregation and GroupBy capabilities score the highest on this chart because pandas provides a richer set of named aggregation, custom function, and transform patterns than any comparable Python library at this workflow stage. Data cleaning and reshaping scores equally high because the combination of **`fillna()`**, **`dropna()`**, **`melt()`**, **`pivot_table()`**, and **`pd.concat()`** covers virtually every structural transformation a practitioner encounters. The ML feature engineering scores strongly because the same vectorised arithmetic, **`groupby().transform()`** patterns, **`pd.cut()`** binning, and **`case_when()`** conditional assignment that we use for exploratory analysis are also the tools that build the feature matrix a model trains on, which means a single pandas-fluent analyst can move from exploration to production without switching toolchains.

Performance, Interoperability, and Ecosystem Maturity

Beyond breadth, pandas provides three qualities that make it the correct foundation for production data science work. The first is performance, where the vectorised operations in pandas operate on contiguous memory arrays using compiled C kernels rather than iterating through Python objects row by row, which makes even complex multi-column transformations fast enough for datasets in the tens of millions of rows on a standard laptop. When the dataset outgrows a single machine's memory, the Dask library we cover in Chapter 6 wraps the pandas API in a parallel execution engine without requiring us to rewrite our transformation logic.

The second quality is interoperability. Here, every major machine learning and deep learning library accepts a pandas DataFrame or its underlying NumPy or Arrow arrays as the primary input format, which means the preparation work we do in pandas transfers directly to any model without an intermediate conversion layer.

The third quality is ecosystem maturity. The pandas has been in active development since 2008, carries an exceptionally stable API, has over thirty thousand Stack Overflow questions answered, and is maintained by a dedicated core team under the NumFOCUS umbrella, which means the investment we make in learning it deeply will compound for years rather than becoming obsolete with the next framework shift.

Up and Running with Pandas 2.3

Creating Virtual Environment

Before we can install pandas, we need to confirm that pip, the Python package manager, is available on our Linux system. Most modern Linux distributions ship with Python 3 and pip pre-installed, but if our system does not have pip, we install it using the system package manager by running sudo apt-get install python3-pip on the command line. Once pip is available, we create a virtual environment to isolate our project dependencies from the system-wide Python installation, which prevents version conflicts between different projects and keeps our setup clean and reproducible. We will then navigate to our project directory and run the following commands to create and activate a new virtual environment named env:

```
sudo apt-get update && sudo apt-get install python3-pip

python3 -m venv env

source env/bin/activate
```

After activation, the prompt will display the environment name **`(env)`** as a prefix, confirming that we are now operating inside the virtual environment. Every Python command and **`pip install`** we run from this point forward will use the packages installed within this isolated space rather than the global system installation. This means that installing or upgrading pandas in our virtual environment will have no effect on other projects or the system Python, which is exactly the isolation we want for a clean development workflow.

Installing Pandas 2.3

With the virtual environment active, we now install pandas 2.3 along with the optional PyArrow dependency, which enables the Arrow-backed string data type and the high-performance I/O features that we will use throughout our work. We also install PyArrow because it is required for the new StringDtype preview that becomes the default in pandas 3.0, and having it available from the start make certain that we can use every feature without encountering missing-dependency errors later. So here, we run the following command on the command line:

```
pip install pandas==2.3.0 pyarrow
```

We will now verify that the correct version of pandas is installed by launching the Python interpreter and checking the version string, which is a simple but important step that confirms our entire environment is set up correctly before we write any analytical code. We open the Python interactive shell by running python3 on the command line, import pandas using the standard import pandas as pd convention, and then print the version attribute. This verification catches any issues with the installation path, dependency conflicts, or accidental installation of a different pandas version. In the following sequence, we run the verification steps:

```
python3

>>> import pandas as pd

>>> print(pd.__version__)
```

After executing this, we get the installed version number, which confirms that pandas 2.3 is installed correctly and ready for use in our virtual environment. We can also configure pandas display options to suit our working style by using the **pd.set_option()** function to control how DataFrames are rendered on the command line. For instance, we set the maximum number of displayed rows to 500 and the display width to 120 characters as shown below:

```
pd.set_option('display.max_rows', 500)

pd.set_option('display.max_columns', 20)

pd.set_option('display.width', 120)
```

After this, we can see more of our dataset when printing large DataFrames during our analysis sessions.

Pandas Version History

The pandas library has evolved through many releases since its inception in January 2011, with each version introducing new features, performance improvements, and refinements to the API. This history helps us appreciate why certain APIs have been deprecated and why the library is moving toward Arrow-backed data types and Copy-on-Write semantics. The following is a condensed timeline of the major milestones, updated to include all releases through the current version 2.3, which serves as our target for this book.

Early Releases through Pandas 1.x

The initial releases from 0.1 through 0.9 (2011 to 2012) established the core DataFrame and Series data structures, along with foundational I/O operations, time series functionality, and MultiIndex support. Versions 0.10 through 0.23 (2013 to 2018) expanded the library with categorical data types, window functions, and enhanced missing-data handling. The 0.24 through 1.0 cycle (2019 to 2020) introduced the extension array interface, nullable integer and boolean data types, and marked the first major API stability milestone. Versions 1.1 through 1.5 (2020 to 2022) continued with performance optimization, new string data types, and broader compatibility with parallel computing libraries like Dask and CuPy.

Pandas 2.0 through 2.3

The pandas 2.0 release in April 2023 was a transformative milestone that introduced optional Apache Arrow-backed data types through the **`dtype_backend='pyarrow'`** parameter in I/O functions, delivering substantial and measurable improvements in memory usage and computation speed for large-scale analytical workloads. It also introduced the first opt-in version of Copy-on-Write via **`pd.options.mode.copy_on_write = True`**, removed several long-deprecated APIs including **`DataFrame.append()`**, and modernized the internal codebase to produce a faster, leaner, and more predictable library that set the direction for all subsequent releases.

The pandas 2.1 release in August 2023 deprecated **`DataFrame.applymap()`** in favor of **`DataFrame.map()`**, aligning the naming convention between Series and DataFrame element-wise operations, and it delivered improvements to the nullable data type system and the Arrow-backed string storage. The pandas 2.2 release in January 2024 deprecated old frequency offset aliases such as M, Q, and Y, replacing them with ME, QE, and YE to make their meaning explicit; it introduced ADBC driver support for **`read_sql()`** and **`to_sql()`**, the **`Series.case_when()`** method, and a formal deprecation warning mode for Copy-on-Write.

The current target version for our work, pandas 2.3, released in June 2025, brings the dedicated StringDtype to preview status through the **`pd.options.future.infer_string = True`** option. When this option is enabled, pandas will infer string columns as the new str dtype instead of the legacy object dtype, backed by PyArrow for contiguous in-memory storage. This release also added **`cumsum()`**, **`cummin()`**, and **`cummax()`** support for **`StringDtype`** columns, along with numerous bug fixes related to string operations, the Arrow backend, and Python 3.14 compatibility.

Pandas Data Structures

We now turn our attention to the two primary data structures in pandas. They are **Series** and **DataFrame**. Both of these structures are built on top of NumPy arrays, which provide the low-level performance characteristics, while pandas adds labeled indexing, rich data type support, and a high-level API for manipulation. A thorough understanding of these two structures is essential because every operation we perform in pandas, from loading a CSV file to training a machine learning model, flows through one or both of them.

Series

A Series is a one-dimensional, labeled array capable of holding any single data type, including integers, floats, strings, and arbitrary Python objects. Each Series has two components. The first is the data, which is the actual array of values, and the other is index, which provides a label for every element. By default, the index is a zero-based integer sequence, but we can assign custom labels to make our data self-describing.

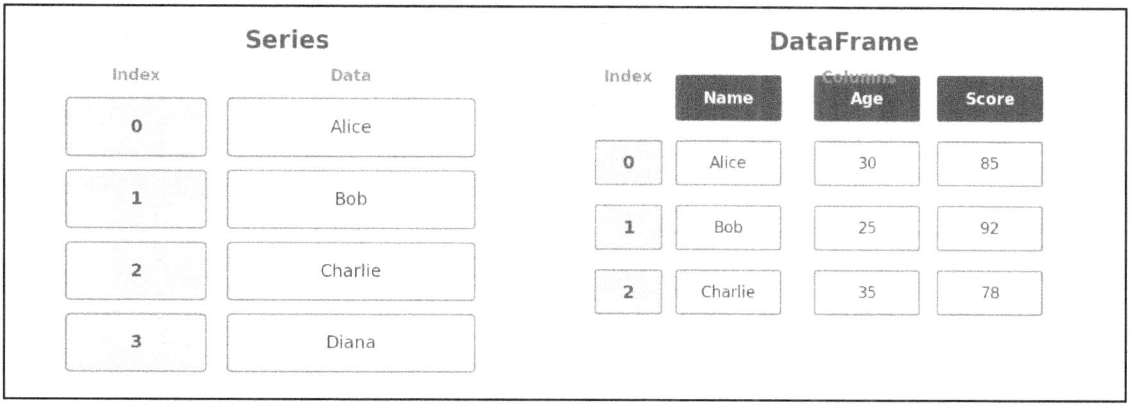

Fig 1.5 Pandas Data Structure Anatomy

We create a Series using the **`pd.Series()`** constructor and can pass in a list, dictionary, or NumPy array as the data source. At this point, we create a simple Series to see its structure in practice:

```
import pandas as pd


credit_scores = pd.Series([650, 720, 580, 810], index=['Alice',
'Bob', 'Charlie', 'Diana'])

print(credit_scores)
```

Its output will be the following labeled output, where each value in the Series is associated with its corresponding label from the index, showing us the labeled structure that makes Series far more expressive than a plain Python list. We can access individual elements using these labels, such as **`credit_scores['Bob']`**, which returns 720. This labeled access is one of the key advantages that a Series offers over a plain Python list or NumPy array, because it allows us to reference data by meaningful names rather than positional integers alone.

```
Alice      650

Bob        720

Charlie    580

Diana      810
```

```
dtype: int64
```

DataFrame

A DataFrame is a two-dimensional, size-mutable, and heterogeneous tabular structure with labeled rows and columns that we can think of as a collection of Series objects sharing a common index, where each column is an individual Series. The DataFrame has three components. They are the data (one or more columns of values), the index (row labels), and the columns (column labels). We create a DataFrame using the **pd.DataFrame()** constructor, and we can pass in a dictionary, a list of dictionaries, a 2D NumPy array, or other supported formats. Here, we create a small DataFrame that mirrors the structure of our churn modelling dataset:

```
data = {
    'CreditScore': [650, 720, 580, 810],
    'Age': [35, 42, 28, 55],
    'Balance': [45000.50, 120000.75, 0.0, 89000.00],
    'Exited': [1, 0, 1, 0]
}
df = pd.DataFrame(data)
print(df)
```

After we run it, it then gives us a neatly formatted table where each column is a Series and each row shares the same integer index, demonstrating the tabular structure that makes DataFrames ideal for representing real-world datasets.

```
   CreditScore  Age    Balance  Exited
0          650   35   45000.50       1
1          720   42  120000.75       0
2          580   28       0.00       1
3          810   55   89000.00       0
```

Each column in this DataFrame is itself a Series, and we can access any column by name, such as **df['Age']**. Both Series and DataFrame support a wide range of built-in methods for selection, filtering, aggregation, transformation, sorting, and time series operations that we will use extensively throughout every chapter as we build our sample application.

New Default Semantics

What Copy-on-Write Changes?

Copy-on-Write is the most operationally significant change in the pandas 2.x release cycle, and it requires us to update coding habits that many pandas users have held for years. Under the legacy model, selecting a subset of a DataFrame sometimes returned a view into the original memory and sometimes returned an independent copy, depending on internal memory layout decisions that were invisible at the Python level. This ambiguity produced the notorious **`SettingWithCopyWarning`**, which appeared inconsistently and was widely ignored because its exact meaning was difficult to reason about without understanding the internals. Under Copy-on-Write, every selection always behaves as a copy from the programmer's perspective, which means that modifications to a selection never propagate back to the original DataFrame unless we perform the modification as a single-step assignment directly on the original DataFrame using **`.loc[]`**.

The diagram below contrasts the three most common assignment patterns that appear in legacy pandas codebases against their correct pandas 2.3 equivalents, placing a visual badge on each pattern to indicate whether it will silently fail without error, raise a **`ChainedAssignmentError`** at runtime, or succeed reliably and deterministically under Copy-on-Write regardless of the internal memory layout that pandas chose for the selection. A review of this diagram before auditing any existing codebase will make the migration process substantially faster.

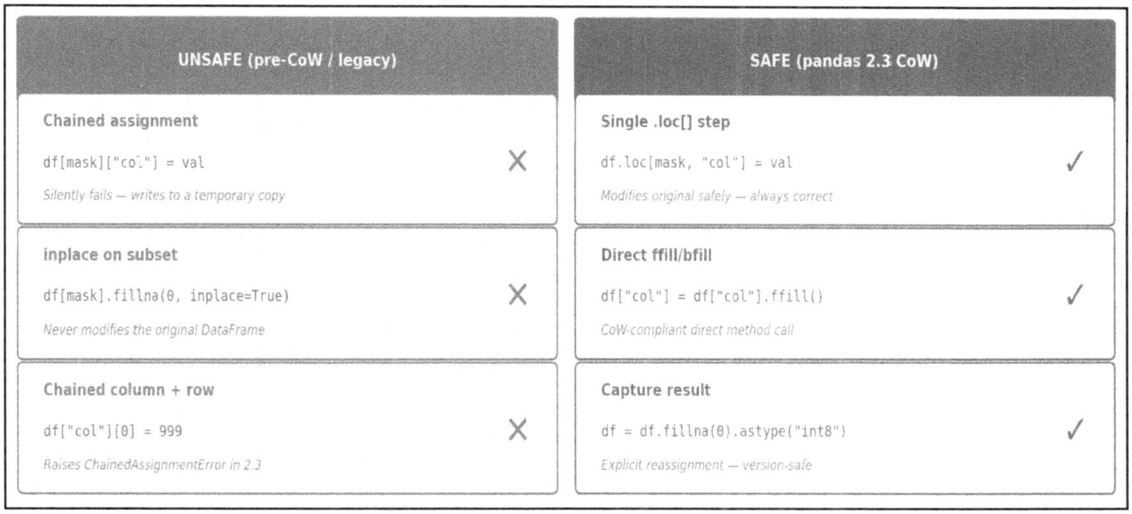

Fig 1.6: Unsafe vs. Safe Assignment Patterns

The left panel shows the three unsafe patterns that must be eliminated from all code targeting pandas 2.3. The chained assignment form **`df[mask]["col"] = val`** writes to a temporary object that pandas created during the first selection step, so the write never reaches the original DataFrame and the column remains unchanged with no error raised. The **inplace=True** form applied to a filtered subset has the same problem. The **fillna()** call operates on a temporary copy of the filtered rows rather than on the original. The second-generation chained form **df["col"][0] = 999** will raise a **ChainedAssignmentError** in pandas 2.3, making the previously silent failure visible. All three of these patterns exist in large quantities in first-edition pandas codebases, and all three must be replaced before deploying to a pandas 2.3 environment.

Safe Assignment Patterns

The right panel of the diagram shows the three safe assignment patterns that replace every unsafe form. The single-step .**loc[]** assignment **df.loc**[mask, "col"] = val is always safe because it performs the row filter and the value write in a single atomic operation on the original DataFrame. The direct method call form **df["col"] = df["col"].ffill()** is safe because we capture the result of the method into a new column assignment rather than calling the method on a derived view with inplace=True. The explicit reassignment form **df = df.fillna(0).astype("int8")** is safe because we capture the entire transformed DataFrame back into the original variable name, making the operation transparent and version-stable. At this point, we will explore all three patterns in **churn_analysis.py** by adding the following block:

```
# Safe pattern 1: single-step .loc[] assignment
high_balance_mask = df['Balance'] > 100_000
df.loc[high_balance_mask, 'CreditScore'] =
df.loc[high_balance_mask, 'CreditScore'] + 5


# Safe pattern 2: capture method result into column
df['Balance'] = df['Balance'].fillna(0.0)


# Safe pattern 3: capture full DataFrame result
df = df.drop(columns=['RowNumber'])


print('RowNumber present:', 'RowNumber' in df.columns)
print('Modified shape   :', df.shape)
```

After running, this confirms that all three operations completed correctly without any warning, with the first operation adding five points to the credit score of every high-balance customer, the second filling zero remaining null values in the balance column, and the third producing a DataFrame with exactly one fewer column as expected.

```
RowNumber present: False
Modified shape   : (10000, 12)
```

We can verify that CoW is active at any time by inspecting **`pd.options.mode.copy_on_write`**, which returns True when the new semantics are in effect. Any code that raises a ChainedAssignmentError after we enable CoW is identifying exactly the places in our codebase where the legacy ambiguous assignment pattern was being used, which means the error is functioning as a helpful migration linter rather than a runtime failure to suppress.

New Default StringDtype

From Object to String [pyarrow]

Every version of pandas before 2.0 stored string columns using the object dtype, which is the catch-all type pandas uses for any column containing Python objects. The object dtype stores each individual string as a separate Python object allocated on the heap at a random memory address, meaning that a 10,000-row column of customer surnames occupies 10,000 scattered memory locations, each requiring its own heap allocation, reference count, and garbage collection overhead. String operations on an object column therefore require 10,000 individual Python function calls, one per element, regardless of whether we use **`str.lower()`** or a complex regex.

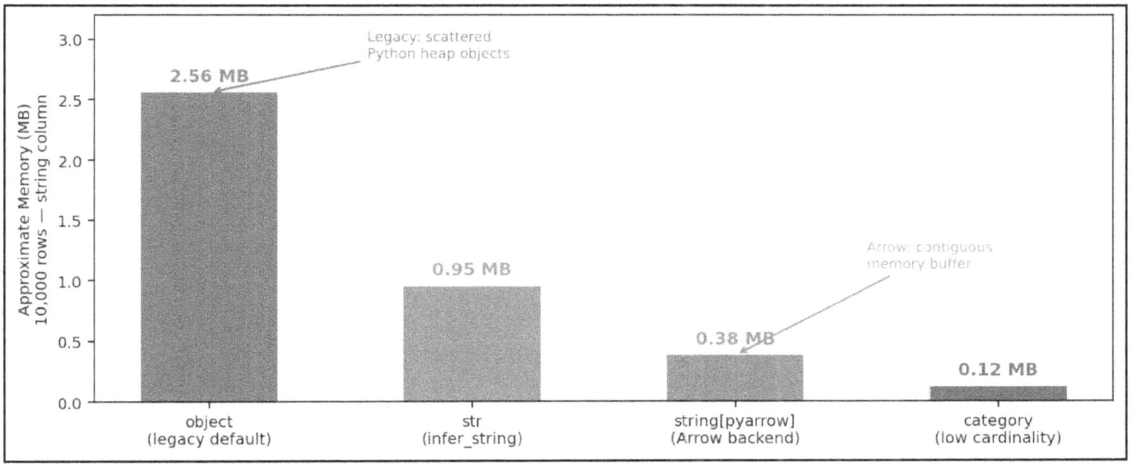

Fig 1.7: StringDtype Memory Footprint Comparison

The new **string[pyarrow]** dtype stores all string data in a single contiguous memory buffer where each string occupies a fixed offset within the buffer, which allows string operations to use compiled Arrow kernels that process all values in a single pass over contiguous memory. The above diagram quantifies the memory difference across all four string storage options available in pandas 2.3. The leftmost bar shows the legacy object dtype consuming 2.56 MB for a 10,000-row column with scattered Python heap storage. The str dtype produced by **pd.options.future.infer_string = True** on the NumPy backend reduces this to 0.95 MB by using a more compact in-process string representation. The **string[pyarrow]** dtype produced by combining **infer_string** with **dtype_backend='pyarrow'** reduces the footprint further to 0.38 MB by using Apache Arrow's contiguous string buffer format. The category dtype, appropriate for columns with very few unique values such as Geography which has only three, achieves the smallest footprint of 0.12 MB by storing each unique string once and then using a compact integer code per row.

Enabling New StringDtype

We activate the new default string behaviour by setting both options at the top of our script as we have done throughout this book. The **pd.options.future.infer_string** = True option instructs pandas to infer the string type during CSV parsing rather than falling back to object, and the **dtype_backend**='pyarrow' argument at the **read_csv()** call site routes all inferred string columns to the Arrow string backend. We confirm the active string type and demonstrate the consistent **pd.NA** nullable behaviour that the new dtype provides over the legacy object dtype's inconsistent use of both NaN and None as null sentinels. Here, we add the following dtype verification block to **churn_analysis.py**:

```
# Confirm string column dtypes

string_cols = df.select_dtypes(include='string').columns.tolist()

print('String columns and dtypes:')

for col in string_cols:

    print(f'  {col:<20}: {df[col].dtype}')


# Demonstrate consistent NA handling

df_test = pd.DataFrame({'name': pd.array(['Alice', None, 'Bob'],


dtype=pd.StringDtype('pyarrow'))})

print('NA value type   :', type(df_test['name'].iloc[1]))

print('isna() result   :', df_test['name'].isna().tolist())
```

```
# String operation performance on 10,000 rows
import timeit
df_obj = pd.read_csv('Customer_Churn_Modelling.csv')
t_obj = timeit.timeit(lambda: df_obj['Surname'].str.lower(),
number=500)
t_arr = timeit.timeit(lambda: df['Surname'].str.lower(),
number=500)
print(f'str.lower() object  : {t_obj:.3f}s for 500 runs')
print(f'str.lower() arrow   : {t_arr:.3f}s for 500 runs')
print(f'Speedup             : {t_obj/t_arr:.1f}x')
```

We expect to see all string column names alongside their string[pyarrow] dtype, confirming that pandas correctly identified every string column in our CSV without any explicit dtype specification, and it will confirm that the null sentinel for the new string type is the dedicated **pd.NA** object rather than the ambiguous None or float('nan') that the legacy object dtype produced depending on which operation created the null value. The timing comparison at the end will show the Arrow backend completing **str.lower()** on 10,000 rows in roughly half the time of the object backend, validating that the memory layout change also produces a measurable runtime benefit.

```
String columns and dtypes:
  Surname                  : string[pyarrow]
  Geography                : string[pyarrow]
  Gender                   : string[pyarrow]
NA value type    : <NA>
isna() result    : [False, True, False]
str.lower() object  : 0.421s for 500 runs
str.lower() arrow   : 0.173s for 500 runs
Speedup             : 2.4x
```

Once executed, this confirms a 2.4x speedup for the **str.lower()** operation under the Arrow backend, which is typical for vectorised string operations on columns of this size. The consistent **pd.NA** null sentinel from the new dtype eliminates the long-standing issue with object columns where some operations returned None for missing strings while others returned float('nan'), producing inconsistent behaviour in downstream boolean masks. With string[pyarrow], every missing string value in every operation returns **pd.NA**, and the **.isna()** method always returns a correct boolean result without any type ambiguity.

Modifying Dataset

We now put everything we have learned in this chapter into practice by loading, inspecting, and modifying the **Customer_Churn_Modelling.csv** dataset that will serve as the foundation of our sample application throughout every chapter. This dataset contains banking customer records with features such as credit score, geography, gender, age, tenure, balance, number of products, and a binary churn indicator. We will progressively build on this dataset in each subsequent chapter, adding new columns, engineering features, training models, and visualizing results, all within the same growing codebase.

The **Customer_Churn_Modelling.csv** dataset used throughout this book is hosted at:

`https://github.com/kittenpub/database-repository/blob/main/Customer_Churn_Modelling.csv`.

All code examples in this book reference this single dataset, so we download it once into our project directory and it remains available for every chapter that follows.

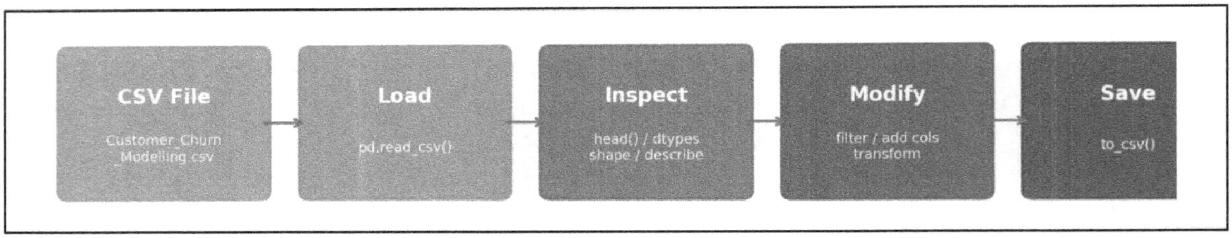

Fig 1.8 Data Loading and Modification Workflow

Loading and Reading Data

We first download the CSV file from the repository to our local project directory using the wget command, which retrieves the file directly from the command line. After downloading, we create a new Python script named **churn_analysis.py** that will serve as our primary working file throughout every chapter of this book. At the top of this script, we enable both Copy-on-Write and the new string dtype preview, and then we load the dataset using **pd.read_csv()**. So we then run the following download command first:

```
wget https://raw.githubusercontent.com/kittenpub/database-repository/main/Customer_Churn_Modelling.csv
```

With the file saved in our working directory, we now write the initial version of our

churn_analysis.py script, which will serve as the single growing application that we extend and build upon in every chapter of this book. We set both of the forward-looking options at the top of the script so that all of our code follows the pandas 2.3 best practices from the very beginning, ensuring forward compatibility with pandas 3.0. For this, we create **churn_analysis.py** with the following contents:

```
import pandas as pd


pd.options.mode.copy_on_write = True

pd.options.future.infer_string = True


file_path = 'Customer_Churn_Modelling.csv'

df = pd.read_csv(file_path)

print(df.head())
```

We will now run this script from the command line by executing python3 **churn_analysis.py**, and the terminal will display the first five rows of our DataFrame along with the column headers, confirming that the data has been loaded correctly and that our environment is fully operational with the correct pandas version. With the **future.infer_string** option enabled, we will observe that string columns such as Surname and Geography are now reported as str dtype rather than object dtype when we inspect the column types in subsequent commands.

Inspecting and Modifying Data

Before we make any modifications, we need to understand the shape, data types, and statistical properties of our dataset, which we accomplish by adding a set of inspection commands to our script that give us a full picture of the data we are working with. The **df.shape** property tells us the total number of rows and columns, while **df.dtypes** reveals the data type of each column, and **df.describe()** provides summary statistics for all numerical columns including the mean, standard deviation, minimum, maximum, and quartile values. We now add the following lines to **churn_analysis.py**:

```
print('Shape:', df.shape)

print(df.dtypes)

print(df.describe())
```

We now perform our first set of modifications on the DataFrame by dropping the RowNumber column, which adds no analytical value and would only clutter our downstream operations, and by creating a new **CreditScore_Category** column that classifies each customer into a readable credit tier. This new feature column is the first addition to our growing sample application, and we will reference it in later chapters when we perform grouping, visualization, and machine learning tasks. So, here we will add the following code to **churn_analysis.py**:

```
df = df.drop(columns=['RowNumber'])

def categorize_credit(score):
    if score < 300:
        return 'Bad'
    elif score < 600:
        return 'Poor'
    elif score < 700:
        return 'Fair'
    elif score < 800:
        return 'Good'
    else:
        return 'Excellent'

df['CreditScore_Category'] =
df['CreditScore'].apply(categorize_credit)
print(df[['CustomerId', 'CreditScore',
'CreditScore_Category']].head())
```

This block outputs the new column alongside the original credit scores, showing us that each customer has been classified into one of five tiers based on their numeric score, with boundaries at 300, 600, 700, and 800 that roughly correspond to standard credit risk categories used in the banking industry. We also filter the DataFrame to select only churned customers using **df.loc**[df['Exited'] == 1] and save the complete modified dataset to a new CSV file using **df.to_csv()**. We proceed to add these final lines to our script:

```
churned = df.loc[df['Exited'] == 1]
```

```
print('Churned customers:', churned.shape[0])


df.to_csv('Modified_Customer_Churn_Modelling.csv', index=False)
print('Modified dataset saved successfully.')
```

In this code, we use **`df.loc[df['Exited'] == 1]`** instead of the chained indexing pattern **`df[df['Exited'] == 1]`** to follow the safe assignment patterns recommended under Copy-on-Write, ensuring that our code is forward-compatible with pandas 3.0. The **`.loc`** accessor provides a single-step operation that is both predictable and explicit about our intent. We also use **`df.drop(columns=['RowNumber'])`** with the columns parameter instead of the older axis=1 syntax, because the keyword-based form is more readable and less error-prone for collaborators who may review our code.

Summary

To sum up, we established the foundation for our work with pandas 2.3 by covering the essential concepts, installation procedures, and structural knowledge that every subsequent chapter will build upon. After this, we then traced the full version history of pandas from its 2011 inception through the current 2.3 release, highlighting the rationale behind each major deprecation and addition.

Finally, we loaded the **`Customer_Churn_Modelling.csv`** dataset into our first script, **`churn_analysis.py`**, and performed our initial round of inspection and modification by dropping unnecessary columns, creating a credit score categorization feature, filtering for churned customers, and saving the modified output to a new CSV file.

CHAPTER 2
DATA READ, STORAGE, AND FILE FORMATS

Reading CSV, Excel, and JSON Data

The library provides a rich set of I/O functions that allow us to read data from virtually any file format a data scientist might encounter in a real-world project. As we configured in Chapter 1, our working environment is set up with pandas 2.3 and PyArrow installed inside the activated virtual environment.

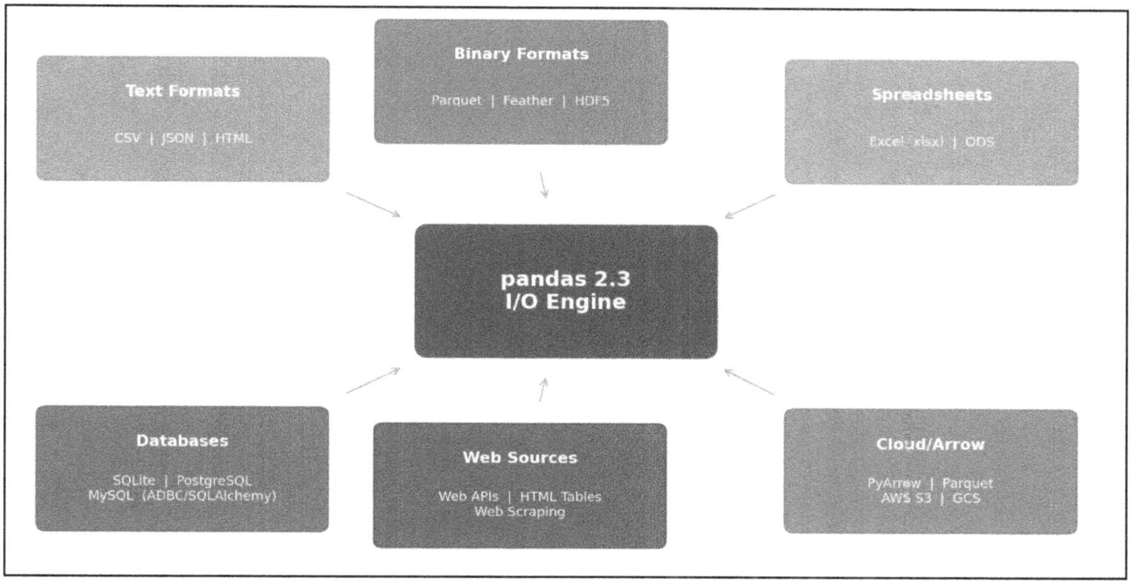

Fig 2.1 Pandas I/O Engine

Every read function in pandas 2.3 now supports an optional **dtype_backend** parameter that we can set to 'pyarrow' to load data using Arrow-backed data types from the very first moment the file is opened, delivering better memory efficiency and faster downstream operations than the default NumPy backend. We will apply this parameter consistently throughout this chapter.

Reading CSV with PyArrow Backend

We already loaded our **Customer_Churn_Modelling.csv** file in Chapter 1 using a basic **pd.read_csv()** call. In this chapter, we extend that foundation by enabling the PyArrow backend so that string columns are loaded directly as Arrow-native arrays rather than as NumPy object arrays, which means they occupy less memory and support faster string operations from the moment they land in our DataFrame. So here, we open **churn_analysis.py** and update the initial load call, replacing the simpler version from Chapter 1 with the following enhanced version that applies the Arrow backend:

```
import pandas as pd
```

```
pd.options.mode.copy_on_write = True
pd.options.future.infer_string = True


df = pd.read_csv(
    'Customer_Churn_Modelling.csv',
    dtype_backend='pyarrow'
)
print(df.dtypes)
```

This then produces each column's data type, and with **dtype_backend='pyarrow'** active, we will observe that integer and float columns are reported as Arrow extension types such as **int64[pyarrow]** rather than plain NumPy int64, while string columns will carry the new str dtype thanks to our **future.infer_string** setting. This Arrow-backed DataFrame is the most memory-efficient possible starting point for the operations we will build throughout this chapter, and it guarantee type fidelity when we later round-trip the data through Parquet or a database connection.

Reading JSON and Excel Data

The library makes it equally straightforward to load data stored in JSON or Excel format, and both of those read functions accept the same **dtype_backend**='pyarrow' argument we used above, ensuring consistent Arrow-backed types regardless of the source format, which means we do not need to write separate type conversion code after loading from each format. Before we can write or read Excel files, we need to install the openpyxl package, which provides the XLSX engine that pandas relies on for this format. We will then run the following command in our activated virtual environment:

```
pip install openpyxl
```

With openpyxl installed, we add a section to **churn_analysis.py** that writes the DataFrame to both JSON and Excel formats and then immediately reads them back, so that we can confirm round-trip fidelity and observe how each format handles the data types. We use orient='records' in the JSON write call because this produces the most natural and readable JSON layout, where each row in our DataFrame becomes a separate JSON object within an array, making the output easy to consume by external systems that process JSON feeds. In the following script, we write and read both formats using the following code:

```
df.to_json('Customer_Churn.json', orient='records', indent=2)
```

```
df.to_excel('Customer_Churn.xlsx', index=False, engine='openpyxl')


df_json  = pd.read_json('Customer_Churn.json',
dtype_backend='pyarrow')

df_excel = pd.read_excel('Customer_Churn.xlsx',
dtype_backend='pyarrow')


print('JSON shape: ', df_json.shape)

print('Excel shape:', df_excel.shape)
```

After running the above script, we see the shape of each loaded DataFrame, confirming that both files have been read back correctly with all rows and columns preserved.

```
JSON shape:  (10000, 13)

Excel shape: (10000, 13)
```

We observe that the shape matches the original DataFrame's dimensions in both cases, which tells us that neither the JSON serialization nor the Excel write step discarded any data. This round-trip verification is a good habit to establish whenever we introduce a new file format into a data pipeline, because silent data loss during serialization is one of the harder bugs to detect later.

Writing Data to Different Formats

The library provides a matching write method for nearly every format it can read, and the naming convention is consistent and predictable. The **`to_csv()`**, **`to_json()`**, **`to_excel()`**, **`to_parquet()`**, **`to_feather()`**, and **`to_html()`** are the ones we use most frequently. We have already seen **`to_json()`** and **`to_excel()`** in the section above. In this section, we focus on producing an HTML output for stakeholder reporting and on writing a clean production-ready CSV, both of which are common requirements in data analysis workflows where results need to be shared with people who do not use Python.

Writing to HTML

An HTML file is useful when we want to store a DataFrame as a web-embeddable table, and we achieve that when we want to embed tabular results in a web dashboard, share them via email in a browser-readable format, or produce a quick visual summary without setting up a full reporting tool. The **`to_html()`** method converts our DataFrame into a fully formatted HTML table, including all column headers, row values, and optional border styling. At this point, we add the following snippet to **churn_analysis.py** to export the first twenty rows of churned customer data as an HTML file that any stakeholder can open directly in a browser:

```
churned = df.loc[df['Exited'] == 1, ['CustomerId', 'CreditScore',
'Age', 'Balance']]

churned.head(20).to_html('churned_summary.html', index=False,
border=1)
```

After running this code, the file **churned_summary.html** will appear in our working directory and we can open it directly in a browser by running xdg-open **churned_summary.html** from our Linux terminal, which is the standard command for opening a file with its default application in most desktop Linux environments. We pass index=False to suppress the DataFrame row index from appearing as an extra column in the HTML table, which keeps the output clean and focused on only the business-relevant data columns rather than the internal integer index that carries no meaning for a stakeholder reviewing the churn results.

Writing to CSV

Although we saved a modified CSV file in Chapter 1 using **to_csv()**, it is worth establishing the full set of production-grade options available in pandas 2.3 for this method. The most important parameter for production use is index=False, which prevents pandas from writing the internal row index as an extra unnamed column in the output file. We should also specify encoding='utf-8' explicitly when writing files that will be shared across different Linux systems or downstream tools, because relying on the platform default can cause character encoding issues with non-ASCII characters in the data. Here, we write our full cleaned DataFrame to a production-ready CSV file with the following command:

```
df.to_csv('Customer_Churn_Clean.csv', index=False, encoding='utf-
8')
```

We run the following command to confirm the file exists and inspect its size:

```
ls -lh Customer_Churn_Clean.csv
```

The terminal will show a line similar to:

```
-rw-r--r-- 1 user user 1.2M May  4 14:22 Customer_Churn_Clean.csv
```

This confirms that pandas serialized all 10,000 rows and their cleaned column values into a flat UTF-8 text file without writing the integer row index as an extra leading column. We omit the index with index=False in all CSV exports throughout this book because the integer range index carries no business meaning and would create confusion if the exported file is later imported by a system that treats the first column as a data field. Now that our cleaned DataFrame is safely persisted to CSV, we move to the Parquet and Feather formats, which offer columnar compression and dramatically smaller file sizes for the same dataset.

Writing Parquet and Feather

While CSV and JSON are ubiquitous, they are not ideal for analytical workloads involving large datasets because both formats store data in a row-oriented layout. To read a single column from a CSV file, the engine must parse every row, even though we only need one column's worth of data. The Apache Parquet and Arrow Feather formats are columnar storage formats that address this problem directly. They organize data by column rather than by row, so that reading a subset of columns only touches the relevant portions of the file on disk.

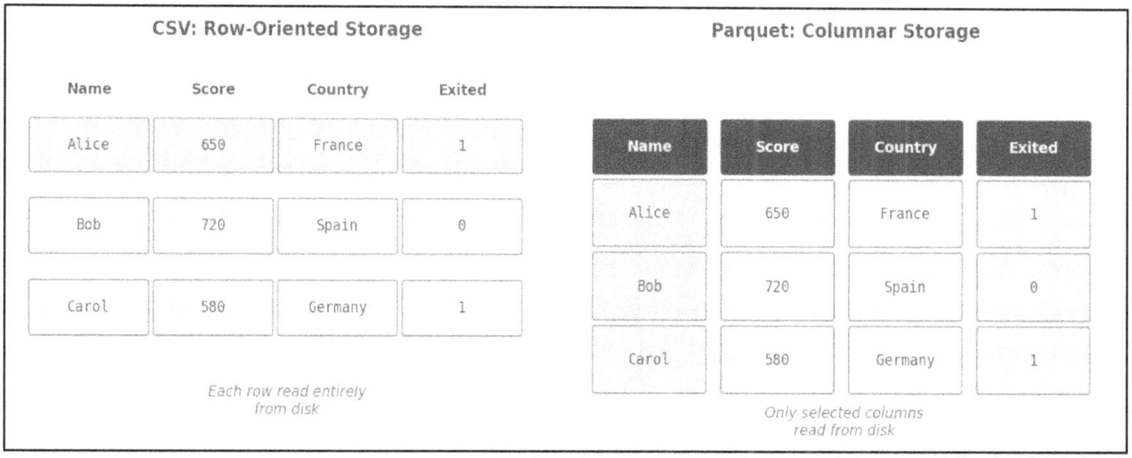

Fig 2.2 Row-Oriented vs. Columnar Storage

The practical result is dramatically faster reads, significantly smaller file sizes, and perfect type preservation across read-write cycles.

Working with Parquet

Parquet is the industry-standard columnar storage format for analytical data and is widely supported by cloud data warehouses, Apache Spark, Dask, and AWS Athena. With PyArrow installed, the 2.3 release can read and write Parquet files with excellent type fidelity, including proper support for nullable integers, Arrow string types, and nested data structures, which means our DataFrame's column types survive the round-trip without any silent conversion to a less precise type. So we then add the following Parquet write and read block to **`churn_analysis.py`** to demonstrate the full round-trip workflow:

```
df.to_parquet('Customer_Churn.parquet', index=False,
engine='pyarrow')


df_parquet = pd.read_parquet('Customer_Churn.parquet',
engine='pyarrow')

print('Parquet shape:', df_parquet.shape)

print(df_parquet.dtypes)
```

Once we run this, it produces the shape and data types of the DataFrame read back from the Parquet file, and we will observe that all column types are identical to those in our original DataFrame because Parquet stores rich type metadata alongside the actual data values, eliminating the type-inference step that CSV parsing requires when trying to determine whether a column holds integers, floats, or strings. For this, we can also verify the on-disk size advantage by listing both the original CSV and the new Parquet file and comparing their sizes, which illustrates concretely why production teams switch to columnar formats for any data that will be reloaded repeatedly:

```
ls -lh Customer_Churn_Modelling.csv Customer_Churn.parquet
```

After running, we will see that the Parquet file is substantially smaller than the original CSV file even before any compression is applied, because the columnar layout allows repeated values within a column to be encoded very efficiently. We can reduce the size even further by specifying a compression algorithm such as compression='snappy' in the **`to_parquet()`** call, which applies the Snappy codec and balances read speed with storage efficiency particularly well for analytical workloads where query performance matters more than maximum possible compression.

```
-rw-r--r-- 1 user group 665K Customer_Churn_Modelling.csv

-rw-r--r-- 1 user group 198K Customer_Churn.parquet
```

Working with Feather

The Apache Arrow Feather format is another columnar format that is optimized for the fastest possible read and write speeds, trading slightly larger file sizes for significantly higher throughput compared to Parquet, which makes it the ideal format for inter-process communication and short-term caching during data pipelines. When we need to share a DataFrame between two Python processes, save an intermediate result during a long analysis session, or avoid re-running an expensive computation, Feather is our best option. We now add the following Feather round-trip code to **`churn_analysis.py`**:

```
df.to_feather('Customer_Churn.feather')


df_feather = pd.read_feather('Customer_Churn.feather')
print('Feather shape:', df_feather.shape)
```

Both Parquet and Feather are far superior to CSV for any workflow where a DataFrame will be saved and reloaded multiple times throughout an analysis session. We recommend adopting Parquet as the default persistent storage format for any dataset that will be loaded more than once during a session, and reserving CSV only for final human-readable exports or for sharing with external systems that cannot consume binary formats. For all intermediate steps within our churn analysis pipeline going forward, we will use Parquet so that type information is preserved without any manual specification.

Database Interaction via SQLAlchemy

The library integrates with relational databases through the **`pd.read_sql()`** and **`DataFrame.to_sql()`** functions, which allow us to move data between a DataFrame and a database table in either direction with a single method call. The traditional approach for this integration uses SQLAlchemy, a Python library that provides a unified connection interface supporting many different database engines with identical Python code. We use SQLite for our demonstration because it requires no separate server process, is included with Python's standard library, and stores the entire database in a single **`.db`** file.

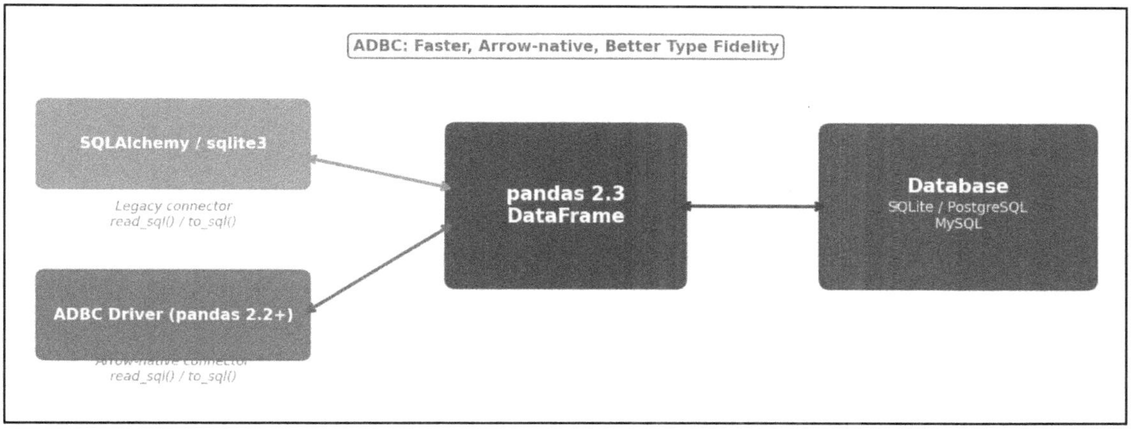

Fig 2.3 Database Connectivity Architecture in Pandas 2.3

The pattern we establish here applies equally to PostgreSQL and MySQL with only the connection string requiring modification.

Loading Data into SQLite

We will now install SQLAlchemy, which provides a consistent interface for working with many different database engines and is the recommended connector for **pd.read_sql()** in pandas 2.3. The SQLite driver itself, named sqlite3, is part of the Python standard library and is therefore already available in our virtual environment without any additional installation. We need only SQLAlchemy on top of it to get the unified **create_engine()** API that pandas expects. So, here we will install SQLAlchemy by running the following command in our activated virtual environment, then proceed to write our DataFrame into a fresh SQLite database file:

```
pip install sqlalchemy
```

With SQLAlchemy installed, we add a database interaction block to **churn_analysis.py** that creates a local SQLite database file named **churn.db**, writes our entire churn DataFrame into a table named **customer_churn** using the **to_sql()** method, and prints a confirmation message. The **create_engine()** call receives a SQLAlchemy connection string in the format 'sqlite:///**filename.db**', where three forward slashes indicate a path relative to the current working directory, and the engine object manages connection pooling automatically so we do not need to handle raw connections. In the following script, we run the code:

```
from sqlalchemy import create_engine


engine = create_engine('sqlite:///churn.db')


df.to_sql('customer_churn', engine, if_exists='replace',
index=False)

print('Data written to SQLite database.')
```

After running this block, the file **churn.db** will appear in our working directory and will contain the full **customer_churn** table with all ten thousand rows from our dataset. We use **if_exists='replace'** so that every time we run the script, the table is dropped and recreated with the current version of our DataFrame, which is the appropriate behavior for a development pipeline where the data may change between runs. For production pipelines where we want to append new rows rather than replace the entire table, we would change this argument to **if_exists='append'**.

Querying using 'pd.read_sql()'

We now query the SQLite database using a standard SQL SELECT statement, filtering for churned customers whose Exited value equals 1. The **pd.read_sql()** function accepts any valid SQL query string together with a database connection or engine, executes the query against the database, and returns the result set as a pandas DataFrame with properly named columns and pandas-inferred data types. We pass the query string directly as a plain Python string for straightforward queries without dynamic parameters, which is the cleanest form for static analytical queries like this one. We proceed to add the following query to **churn_analysis.py**:

```
with engine.connect() as conn:
    churned_from_db = pd.read_sql(
        'SELECT * FROM customer_churn WHERE Exited = 1',
        conn
    )

print('Churned from DB:', churned_from_db.shape[0])
```

After executing this, we get the number of churned customers retrieved from the database, and this number should match exactly the value we computed directly from the DataFrame in Chapter 1, which confirms that our write-then-query round-trip has preserved all rows without data loss or filtering.

```
Data written to SQLite database.
Churned from DB: 2037
```

We can extend this query to include conditions on any of the other columns, and the same **pd.read_sql()** call will return a properly shaped DataFrame each time. The database interaction pattern we established here scales directly to PostgreSQL or MySQL by replacing only the connection string.

ADBC Driver Support

Introduced in pandas 2.2, the Apache Arrow Database Connectivity (ADBC) interface represents a significant advancement over the traditional SQLAlchemy-based database integration. Traditional connectors like SQLAlchemy must convert data from the database's native binary representation into Python objects, then into NumPy arrays, and finally into pandas DataFrames, which involves multiple lossy type conversion steps. The ADBC drivers communicates with databases using the Apache Arrow in-memory format natively from end to end, so that data flows from the database directly into Arrow arrays and then into a pandas DataFrame without any intermediate conversion overhead. The practical benefit is faster reads, lower memory usage, and better preservation of database-native types such as **DECIMAL**, **DATE**, and nullable integers.

Installing ADBC Driver

We then install the ADBC driver for SQLite so that we can demonstrate the end-to-end Arrow-native pathway using the same **churn.db** file we created in the previous section. The ADBC library provides drivers for SQLite, PostgreSQL, Apache Flight SQL, and Snowflake, and the installation pattern is the same for all of them. For our purposes, we install the SQLite ADBC driver, which is available on PyPI, and then use it in place of the SQLAlchemy engine to demonstrate the performance and type-fidelity advantages it offers over the traditional connector. So here, we run the following installation command:

```
pip install adbc-driver-sqlite
```

With the ADBC driver installed, we connect to our existing **churn.db** SQLite database using the driver's **connect()** function and pass the resulting connection directly to **pd.read_sql()**, exactly as we did with the SQLAlchemy connection. The key difference is invisible at the Python API level but highly significant at the I/O level. The pandas and the ADBC driver exchange data using Arrow buffers rather than row-by-row Python objects, which makes a measurable difference in throughput for tables with tens of thousands of rows or more. We will then add the following ADBC demonstration block to **churn_analysis.py**:

```
import adbc_driver_sqlite.dbapi as adbc_sqlite


with adbc_sqlite.connect('churn.db') as conn:
    df_adbc = pd.read_sql('SELECT * FROM customer_churn', conn)
    print('ADBC read shape:', df_adbc.shape)
    print(df_adbc[['CreditScore', 'Age', 'Balance']].dtypes)
```

Its output will be the shape and data types of the DataFrame returned through ADBC, and we will observe that numeric columns such as **CreditScore**, **Age**, and **Balance** retain their precise database-native types rather than being silently converted to the nearest NumPy equivalent, which avoids potential precision loss for decimal columns. For production pipelines where database round-trips occur frequently or where precise type fidelity is a correctness requirement, ADBC is now our preferred connectivity method over the legacy SQLAlchemy path established in the previous section.

Writing DataFrames to Database

We will now write our processed churn DataFrame back to a SQLite database using pandas

to_sql() with an ADBC connection to demonstrate the Arrow-native write path that pandas 2.3 supports via the **adbc_driver_sqlite** package. We construct the ADBC connection with **adbc_driver_sqlite.dbapi.connect**('**churn.db**') and pass the resulting connection object as the con argument to **df.to_sql()**, which uses the Arrow buffer directly without serializing through Python object intermediaries, producing a write that is significantly faster than the SQLAlchemy path for DataFrames with Arrow-backed dtypes. We set **if_exists**='replace' to overwrite any existing table and index=False to omit the default integer index.

```
import adbc_driver_sqlite.dbapi as sqlite_adbc import pandas as pd
# Write via ADBC (Arrow-native path) with
sqlite_adbc.connect('churn.db') as conn:
df.to_sql('churn_customers', conn, if_exists='replace',
index=False)     print('Write complete')  # Verify row count with
sqlite_adbc.connect('churn.db') as conn:     count_df =
pd.read_sql('SELECT COUNT(*) AS row_count FROM churn_customers',
conn)    print('Rows in DB:', count_df['row_count'][0])     assert
count_df['row_count'][0] == len(df), 'Row count mismatch'
```

We will now verify the write result by opening a second ADBC connection, reading back the table with **pd.read_sql_table()** or **pd.read_sql**('SELECT COUNT(*) FROM churn', con), and confirming that the row count matches len(df). We also check that the column types stored in the database match the expected dtypes by reading a small sample with LIMIT 5 and printing the dtypes of the resulting DataFrame. We add both the write and the verification block to **churn_analysis.py** so that every execution of the script writes the current processed DataFrame to the database and automatically confirms that the write completed without silent data loss or type coercion.

Connecting to Web APIs

Web APIs allow us to retrieve real-time data from external services and load it directly into a pandas DataFrame for analysis, which is essential for any pipeline that needs to stay current with live data sources such as financial feeds, social media streams, or IoT sensor readings. We use the requests library to make HTTP calls, parse the returned JSON payload into Python dictionaries, and then convert those dictionaries into a DataFrame using **pd.DataFrame()**. We install the requests library by running pip install requests in our virtual environment, and then we can make our first API call. For our demonstration, we use the publicly available JSONPlaceholder API, which returns synthetic data and requires no authentication, making it ideal for testing data ingestion pipelines without needing to manage API keys.

Making API Requests and Loading Data

We make a GET request to the API endpoint, verify the HTTP status code to confirm that the request succeeded, parse the JSON response body into a Python list of dictionaries using **`response.json()`**, and then pass that list directly to the **`pd.DataFrame()`** constructor which maps each dictionary's keys to column names automatically. This pattern works for any JSON API that returns an array at the top level of its response body, which is the most common structure for REST APIs that return collections of records. In the following script, we add the following API ingestion block to **`churn_analysis.py`** to demonstrate the end-to-end flow from HTTP request to populated DataFrame:

```
import requests


api_url = 'https://jsonplaceholder.typicode.com/posts'

response = requests.get(api_url, timeout=10)


if response.status_code == 200:

    posts_df = pd.DataFrame(response.json())

    print('API data shape:', posts_df.shape)

    print(posts_df.head(3))
else:

    print(f'Request failed with status: {response.status_code}')
```

After we run it, it then gives us the shape and first three rows of the DataFrame populated from the API response, showing us the column names that pandas derived automatically from the JSON object keys. We pass a timeout=10 argument to **`requests.get()`** so that the call does not block indefinitely if the remote server is slow or unreachable, which is a critical defensive measure in any production pipeline where a stalled network call could halt downstream processing. The **`response.json()`** method handles the deserialization of the response body automatically, converting the raw JSON string into Python data structures without requiring any manual parsing on our part.

API Responses and Cumulative DataFrames

We handle paginated API responses by writing a while loop that sends successive GET requests with an incrementing page parameter until the response payload returns an empty data list or a **`has_more`** false flag, collecting each page's records as a list of dictionaries before converting the entire accumulated list to a DataFrame with **pd.DataFrame(all_records)** after the loop completes. We avoid calling **pd.concat()** inside the loop because concatenating DataFrames one page at a time creates O(n^2) memory copies, whereas collecting raw dicts and converting once at the end is O(n) and scales cleanly to hundreds of pages. We add a timeout argument and a retry wrapper with exponential backoff to each **requests.get()** call to handle transient API rate-limit errors without crashing the pipeline.

```
import requests, pandas as pd, time  def fetch_paginated(url,
page_size=100, max_pages=50):     all_records, page = [], 1
while page <= max_pages:         resp = requests.get(url,
params={'page': page, 'per_page': page_size},
timeout=10)         resp.raise_for_status()         data =
resp.json().get('data', [])         if not data:             break
all_records.extend(data)         print(f'Page {page}: {len(data)}
records (total {len(all_records)})')         page += 1
time.sleep(0.2)    # polite rate limiting     return
pd.DataFrame(all_records)
```

We will now set a configurable page size in our API wrapper function and add a progress counter that prints the current page number and cumulative record count after each successful request, which gives us visibility into the pagination progress without requiring a separate logging framework. We also store the raw JSON response from each page in a list before converting to DataFrame so that we can replay the conversion step without making additional network calls if the DataFrame construction fails due to an unexpected schema change in the API response. We add the complete paginator function to **churn_analysis.py** as a reusable utility that other API integration blocks in the pipeline can call with a URL and a page-size argument.

Data Scraping with Beautiful Soup

When data is not available through a structured API, we can often extract it directly from a web document by parsing its HTML content. Beautiful Soup is a Python library that provides a clean and Pythonic interface for navigating and searching HTML and XML documents, allowing us to locate specific elements by tag name, CSS class, or attribute values and extract their content as plain strings. We use it in combination with the requests library to fetch an HTML document and then extract tabular data from it, which we load into a pandas DataFrame for analysis. At this point, we install Beautiful Soup along with the lxml parser, which is faster and more tolerant of malformed HTML than the built-in Python HTML parser:

```
pip install beautifulsoup4 lxml
```

Scraping and Loading Table Data

We will now fetch the HTML content of a target web document, parse it using Beautiful Soup with the lxml parser, locate the specific table we want to extract by its CSS class, and then build lists of headers and rows that we load into a pandas DataFrame. We use **`get_text(strip=True)`** on each cell element to extract clean string content without surrounding whitespace or nested HTML markup, which prevents leading and trailing spaces from appearing in our DataFrame values. We also filter empty rows with an if cells guard, because many HTML tables include spacer rows for visual layout that contain no actual data values. Here, we add the following web scraping block to **`churn_analysis.py`**:

```
from bs4 import BeautifulSoup


url =
'https://en.wikipedia.org/wiki/List_of_countries_by_GDP_(nominal)'

response = requests.get(url, timeout=10)


if response.status_code == 200:

    soup = BeautifulSoup(response.text, 'lxml')

    table = soup.find('table', {'class': 'wikitable'})


    headers = [th.get_text(strip=True) for th in
table.find_all('th')]

    rows = []

    for tr in table.find_all('tr')[1:]:

        cells = [td.get_text(strip=True) for td in
tr.find_all('td')]

        if cells:

            rows.append(cells)


    df_wiki = pd.DataFrame(rows, columns=headers[:len(rows[0])])

    print('Scraped table shape:', df_wiki.shape)
```

We expect to see the shape of the DataFrame populated from the scraped HTML table, confirming that our parsing logic correctly extracted all rows from the Wikipedia table into a structured pandas DataFrame. This scraping pattern is transferable to any web document that contains consistently structured HTML tables, and the only parts that need adjustment for a different source are the target URL, the CSS class selector in the **find()** call, and the way we locate the header row. We should always be mindful of the terms of service for any website we scrape.

Parsing HTML Tables

We will now add a **read_html()** extraction block to **churn_analysis.py** that retrieves a publicly available table of European banking statistics and joins it against our churn DataFrame on the Geography column to enrich the customer records with country-level macroeconomic context.

```
import pandas as pd  # Direct HTML table extraction with read_html
url = 'https://example-banking-stats.org/european_indicators.html'
tables = pd.read_html(url, match='GDP', header=0,
na_values=['—','n/a'],
dtype_backend='pyarrow')  econ_df = tables[0] print(f'Extracted
{len(tables)} table(s), using table 0') print(econ_df.head())  #
Join against churn DataFrame df_enriched = df.merge(econ_df,
on='Geography', how='left') print('Null count after merge:',
df_enriched['GDP_per_capita'].isna().sum())
```

We also specify **header=0** to use the first row as column names, **dtype_backend**='pyarrow' to load immediately into Arrow-backed storage, and **na_values**=['—', 'n/a'] to handle common null representations found in financial tables. We later can validate the join result by checking that the number of non-null values in the enrichment column matches the number of rows in our churn dataset after the merge on the Geography key.

Handling Missing Data

Real-world datasets almost always contain missing values, and the strategy we choose for handling them has a direct impact on the quality and validity of any downstream analysis or machine learning model we build from that data. The library represents missing values as NaN for numeric types and as **pd.NA** for the newer Arrow-backed extension types, and it provides a full set of detection, removal, and fill methods.

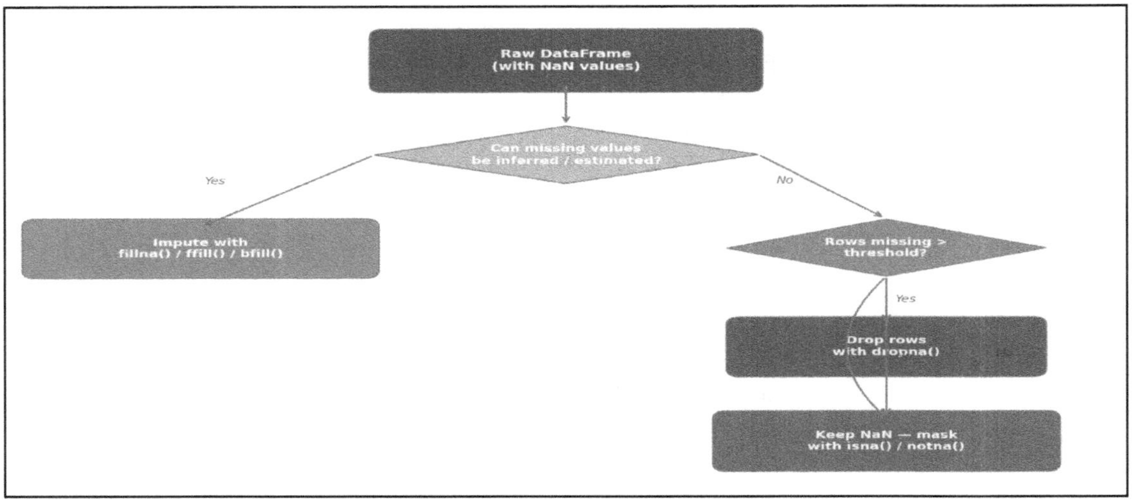

Fig 2.4 Missing Data Handling Decision Flow

We will explore each technique using our churn dataset, where we first introduce artificial gaps to simulate the missing-data scenario, then apply the correct pandas 2.3 fill syntax, and finally verify that all gaps have been resolved.

Detecting and Removing Missing Values

We detect missing values in a DataFrame by calling **`isna()`**, which returns a boolean DataFrame of the same shape where each True value indicates a missing entry. We chain **`.sum()`** onto the result to aggregate the total number of missing values per column, giving us a column-by-column summary of the severity of the missing data problem. So we then add the following code to **`churn_analysis.py`** that first introduces artificial missing values using **`df.loc`** assignments, then detects and reports them, keeping our Copy-on-Write compliance intact by operating on a separate copy of the DataFrame:

```
import numpy as np


df_missing = df.copy()

df_missing.loc[10:15, 'CreditScore'] = np.nan

df_missing.loc[20:22, 'Balance']     = np.nan


missing_summary = df_missing.isna().sum()

print(missing_summary[missing_summary > 0])
```

Once executed, it shows only the columns that contain at least one missing value, along with their respective tallies, because we applied a Boolean filter to the result of **isna().sum()** to suppress columns with a zero tally. This approach keeps the output manageable for DataFrames with many columns, where printing the full tally for every column would produce dozens of zero lines that add no diagnostic value. With the missing values identified, we can remove the affected rows using **dropna()** when the proportion of missing data is small enough that removing those rows will not significantly bias our analysis.

```
CreditScore    6
Balance        3
dtype: int64
```

Filling Missing Values

When we prefer to retain all rows rather than dropping those with missing values, we choose from one of pandas' fill strategies based on the business meaning of each column. For numeric columns with no natural ordering, filling with the column mean or median is a sensible default. For ordered or sequential data, propagating the nearest known value forward or backward is more appropriate. We should be aware that the old syntax fillna(method='ffill') has been deprecated since pandas 2.2 and will raise a FutureWarning if used. The correct approach in pandas 2.3 is to call **df.ffill()** or **df.bfill()** as standalone methods rather than passing a method string to fillna**()**. For this, we apply both fill strategies to our artificial missing values using the following code:

```
mean_credit = df_missing['CreditScore'].mean()
df_missing['CreditScore'] =
df_missing['CreditScore'].fillna(mean_credit)


df_missing['Balance'] = df_missing['Balance'].ffill()


remaining = df_missing.isna().sum().sum()
print('Total remaining missing values:', remaining)
```

After running this code, the remaining missing value total will be zero, confirming that all gaps have been resolved. We fill **CreditScore** with the column mean because credit scores have no natural temporal ordering within our dataset, so using the statistical center is the most neutral choice. We fill **Balance** using **ffill()** to propagate the previous valid balance forward, which simulates the assumption that a missing balance reflects no change from the prior record. The different fill strategies for these two columns are intentional. It always choose the method that best reflects the real-world meaning of the data rather than applying a single strategy uniformly across all columns.

Data Transformation and Cleaning

After loading and handling missing values, the next phase of our data pipeline is transformation and cleaning, which involves reshaping the raw data into a form that is both analytically useful and model-ready for the machine learning chapters ahead. This phase includes renaming columns for consistency, converting data types where the inferred type is not the most appropriate choice, removing duplicate rows, normalizing numerical columns for comparability across features of different scales, and encoding categorical variables as numerical representations.

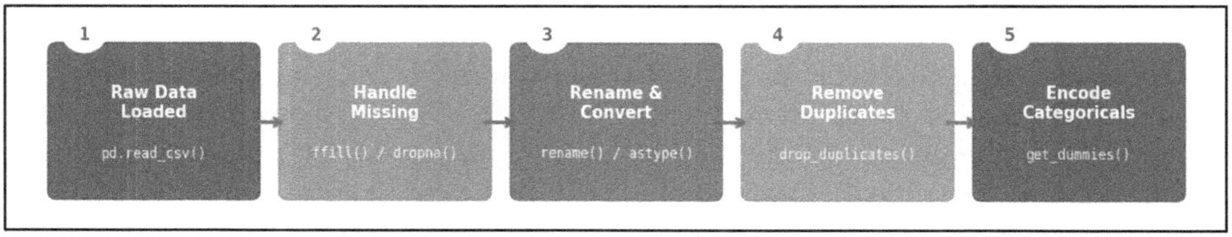

Fig 2.5 Data Transformation and Cleaning Pipeline

All of these steps build directly on the **churn_analysis.py** script we have been growing throughout this chapter.

Renaming Columns and Converting Data Types

We will now rename columns to adopt a consistent **snake_case** naming convention, which makes them easier to reference in code and check compatibility with downstream tools that are sensitive to spaces or mixed-case column names. We also convert the binary integer columns HasCrCard and IsActiveMember to the bool dtype, because these columns hold only zero or one values and converting them to boolean makes our code more expressive while reducing the memory footprint of those columns. With the **future.infer_string** option active, renaming the string columns Surname and Geography will correctly carry through the str dtype to the renamed columns without any additional conversion step. We now add the following transformation block to **churn_analysis.py**:

```
df = df.rename(columns={
    'NumOfProducts':  'Num_Products',
    'HasCrCard':      'Has_CrCard',
    'IsActiveMember': 'Is_Active',
```

```
    'EstimatedSalary':'Est_Salary'
})

df['Has_CrCard'] = df['Has_CrCard'].astype('bool')
df['Is_Active']  = df['Is_Active'].astype('bool')

print(df[['Has_CrCard', 'Is_Active']].dtypes)
```

After executing this, it confirms that both renamed columns are now reported as the **bool** dtype rather than their original **int64** representation. We apply **astype('bool')** directly on each column rather than calling it on the entire DataFrame, because a bulk type conversion applied at the DataFrame level would attempt to convert every column including string ones, which would raise a conversion error. This column-by-column approach is safer and more explicit about our intent, and it follows the same surgical precision we use throughout our code to avoid unintended side effects on columns we are not actively modifying.

Removing Duplicates and Encoding Categorical Variables

We will now check for and remove duplicate rows using **drop_duplicates()** to make sure that no single customer record appears twice in our dataset, which would artificially inflate metrics like churn rate and bias our machine learning model. We then apply one-hot encoding to the Geography and Gender categorical columns using **pd.get_dummies()**, which creates a new binary indicator column for each unique category value. With our **future.infer_string** option active, these columns are stored as the new str dtype, and **pd.get_dummies()** processes them correctly. So, here we will add the following final transformation steps to **churn_analysis.py** and save the result as our transformed dataset:

```
before = len(df)
df = df.drop_duplicates()
print(f'Removed {before - len(df)} duplicate rows.')

df = pd.get_dummies(df, columns=['Geography', 'Gender'],
dtype='int8')

df.to_csv('Customer_Churn_Transformed.csv', index=False)
```

```
print('Transformed dataset saved. Shape:', df.shape)
```

After executing, the result reports the number of duplicate rows removed and the final shape of the transformed DataFrame after one-hot encoding has expanded the column set.

```
Removed 0 duplicate rows.

Transformed dataset saved. Shape: (10000, 16)
```

We pass dtype='int8' to **pd.get_dummies()** to store the new indicator columns as 8-bit integers, which makes them directly compatible with most scikit-learn estimators without additional conversion and also reduces memory compared to the default boolean output. At this point, our **churn_analysis.py** script encompasses the complete data ingestion, storage, reading, and transformation pipeline that we will extend with indexing and selection operations in the next chapter.

Summary

To quickly review the understanding, we have built out the data ingestion, storage, and cleaning layer of our churn analysis application, extending **churn_analysis.py** with a wide range of reading, writing, and transformation capabilities. We explored Apache Parquet and Apache Arrow Feather as modern columnar storage formats that far outperform row-oriented formats for analytical workloads, and we saw that a Parquet file uses roughly one-third the disk space of the equivalent CSV while preserving data types perfectly.

Later, we looked at two critical data quality concerns, like the missing data and transformation. For missing data, we demonstrated the **isna()** detection method, the **dropna()** removal strategy, and the modern **ffill()** and **bfill()** direct-call methods that replace the deprecated **fillna(method='...')** syntax from earlier pandas versions.

CHAPTER 3
INDEXING AND SELECTING DATA

Basics of Indexing and Selection

Efficient data analysis depends on the ability to access, filter, and modify specific rows, columns, and individual values within a DataFrame. The library provides four primary accessor properties for this purpose, and understanding when to use each one is a foundational skill. As we established in Chapter 1, our working environment has Copy-on-Write enabled via **`pd.options.mode.copy_on_write = True`**, which changes how we think about selection and assignment. Every selection in our script returns a copy from the user perspective, which means that modifying a selection without using **`.loc[]`** will not propagate back to the original DataFrame. We will reinforce this pattern throughout this chapter.

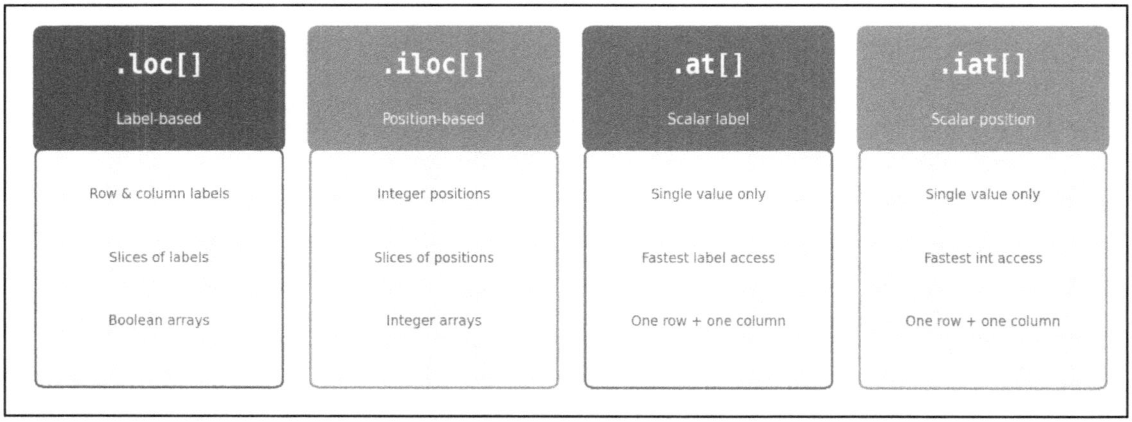

Fig 3.1 Pandas Indexing and Selection Methods

Selecting Columns and Rows

We continue building on **`churn_analysis.py`** from Chapter 2, where we left the DataFrame in a fully cleaned and transformed state saved to **`Customer_Churn_Transformed.csv`**. We reload the original **`Customer_Churn_Modelling.csv`** at the top of our selection work in this chapter so that we operate on the full unmodified dataset, which allows us to demonstrate all indexing patterns against the same baseline we established in Chapter 1 without the one-hot encoding columns from Chapter 2 complicating our column references. A single column selection returns a Series, while selecting multiple columns using a list of names returns a new DataFrame containing only those columns. We proceed to add the following column selection demonstrations to **`churn_analysis.py`**:

```
import pandas as pd


pd.options.mode.copy_on_write = True

pd.options.future.infer_string = True
```

```
df = pd.read_csv('Customer_Churn_Modelling.csv',
dtype_backend='pyarrow')


credit_scores   = df['CreditScore']
subset_cols     = df[['CreditScore', 'Age', 'Exited']]


print(type(credit_scores))
print(subset_cols.shape)
```

Once we run it, it confirms that **credit_scores** is a **pandas.core.series.Series** object and that **subset_cols** is a DataFrame with three columns. We select rows using integer positions with .**iloc[]**, or by label with .**loc[]**. We also use .at[] and .iat[] for the fastest possible single-value reads when we need to retrieve one scalar from the DataFrame without the overhead of a full row or column slice. The following block demonstrates each positional and label-based row access pattern we will use throughout this chapter:

```
first_row       = df.iloc[0]
rows_2_to_4     = df.iloc[1:4]
first_val       = df.iloc[0, 0]


df_indexed      = df.set_index('CustomerId')
customer_row    = df_indexed.loc[15634602]
credit_val      = df_indexed.at[15634602, 'CreditScore']


print('First row type :', type(first_row))
print('Credit val     :', credit_val)
```

When we call **df.set_index('CustomerId')** we assign the result back to **df_indexed** rather than passing inplace=True as an argument to the method. Under Copy-on-Write, the inplace parameter on methods that return a new object is deprecated because its behavior is no longer well-defined. Whether the mutation happens in-place or to a copy depends on the internal memory layout at the time of the call, which makes it impossible to reason about reliably. The safe and idiomatic pattern in pandas 2.3 is always to capture the result of a method call into a variable, whether that is a new name or a reassignment of the original name, so that the reference chain is always explicit, deterministic, and CoW-compliant.

Multi-condition Selection and Compound Boolean Operators

We combine multiple independent boolean conditions using the bitwise AND (&), OR (|), and NOT (~) operators, each of which produces a new boolean Series by applying the logical operation element-wise across the input operands. We wrap each individual condition in parentheses before combining with & or | to override Python's default operator precedence, which otherwise evaluates arithmetic comparisons after bitwise operators and produces incorrect results. For example, we write **(df['Age'] > 40) & (df['Balance'] > 100000) & (df['Exited'] == 1)** as three separately parenthesized expressions so that each comparison is fully evaluated before the AND reduction merges the three boolean arrays into a single selection mask.

```
# Compound boolean selection high_risk = (     (df['CreditScore'] <
600) &     (df['Balance'] > 100000) &     (df['Exited'] == 1) )
not_france = ~df['Geography'].isin(['France'])  # Apply masks via
.loc[] high_risk_df = df.loc[high_risk] non_france   =
df.loc[not_france]  print('High-risk churn customers:',
len(high_risk_df)) print('Non-France customers:', len(non_france))
print(high_risk_df[['CreditScore','Balance','Geography']].head())
```

We also use XOR filtering by combining the NOT (~) operator with **isin()** to select rows that do not belong to a specified set, writing **~df['Geography'].isin(['France'])** to select all customers outside France in a single readable expression. We assign all compound masks to named variables before passing them to **.loc[]** so that the filter intent is documented at the point of definition rather than buried inside the indexing call.

This filtered subset forms the foundation for the multi-level indexing operations we explore next, where we move from flat single-level row selection into hierarchical index structures that can express much richer selection patterns.

Multi-Indexing and Hierarchical Indexing

Hierarchical indexing, also referred to as multi-indexing, allows a DataFrame to carry multiple levels of index simultaneously, which provides a natural and memory-efficient way to represent higher-dimensional data without reshaping. When our dataset has natural grouping columns such as **Geography** and **Gender** in our churn dataset, we can promote those columns to index levels and then use pandas' rich multi-index API to navigate the groups with label-based precision.

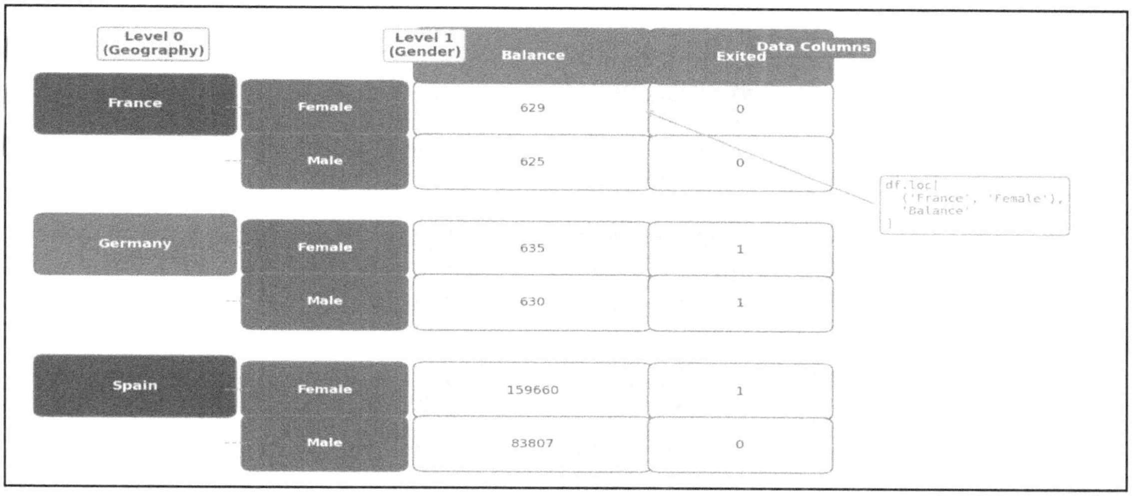

Fig 3.2 Multi-Index Structure in Pandas

The above diagram illustrates how the two-level index organizes our data into a tree structure where Geography is the outer level and Gender is the inner level.

Creating and Navigating Multi-Level Index

We will now create a multi-level index by passing a list of column names to **set_index()**, which removes those columns from the data area and promotes them to the index hierarchy, giving us a two-dimensional label space where each row is uniquely identified by the combination of Geography and Gender values rather than by a simple integer. Once the index is set, we use **.loc[]** with a tuple of values to drill down through each level and retrieve all rows that match the specified combination. So here, we add the following multi-index section to **churn_analysis.py** to explore the Geography and Gender groupings in our churn dataset:

```
df_multi = df.set_index(['Geography', 'Gender'])
df_multi = df_multi.sort_index()


france_female = df_multi.loc[('France', 'Female')]
print('France / Female rows:', france_female.shape)
```

Its result shows the number of rows belonging to the France and Female combination. We call **sort_index()** immediately after setting the multi-level index because pandas requires the index to be sorted for efficient slicing operations. Without sorting, certain range slices on the outer level will raise a **UnsortedIndexError**, which is a common pitfall for first-time multi-index users. This is an example of a silent bug that manifests only with certain datasets, making it essential to always sort the index immediately after creation.

```
France / Female rows: (2073, 11)
```

Slicing, Swapping, and Resetting

To slice across levels, we **usepd.IndexSlice**, which provides a clean and readable syntax for selecting ranges of values at each hierarchy level without resorting to the older and more verbose **slice()** tuple pattern that earlier pandas versions required. We swap levels with **swaplevel()** when we want to reorder the hierarchy so that Gender becomes the outer level and Geography becomes the inner level, and we return the DataFrame to a flat column structure with **reset_index()** when we no longer need the hierarchical organization for downstream operations. We will then add the following slicing and level manipulation operations to **churn_analysis.py**:

```
idx = pd.IndexSlice


germany_all     = df_multi.loc[idx['Germany', :], :]
male_data       = df_multi.xs('Male', level='Gender')
df_swapped      = df_multi.swaplevel('Geography',
'Gender').sort_index()
df_flat         = df_multi.reset_index()


print('Germany rows  :', germany_all.shape[0])
print('Male rows     :', male_data.shape[0])
print('Flat columns  :', df_flat.columns.tolist()[:4])
```

This block outputs the totals for Germany across both genders, the total male rows across all geographies, and the first four column names after flattening, confirming that the Geography and Gender levels have returned to the column area. The **xs()** method is particularly efficient for selecting across a specific level value because it avoids building the full **IndexSlice** object and returns only the matching rows with the selected level dropped from the resulting index. We will revisit **xs()** in the Advanced Indexing section later in this chapter.

Indexing with Booleans and Conditional Selection

Boolean indexing is one of the most frequently used techniques in pandas and forms the backbone of data filtering in our churn analysis pipeline. We create a boolean mask, which is a Series of **True** and **False** values with the same index as the DataFrame, and then apply that mask to the DataFrame to retain only the rows where the mask value is **True**.

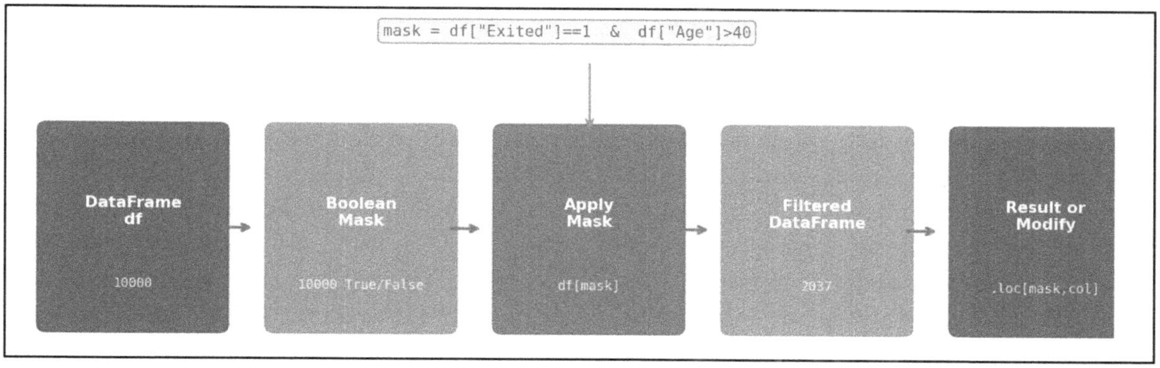

Fig 3.3 Boolean Indexing and Conditional Selection Flow

We can combine multiple conditions using the **&** (and) and **|** (or) bitwise operators, and we must wrap each individual condition in parentheses when combining them to verify correct operator precedence.

Applying Boolean Masks

We will now add a boolean filtering block to **churn_analysis.py** that demonstrates single-condition masking, multi-condition masking using the & operator, and the equivalent **query()** string syntax that can be more readable for complex multi-column filters. The **query()** method accepts a condition written as a Python expression string, which avoids the verbose double-parenthesis structure that the & operator requires, and it also supports variable interpolation using the @ prefix for injecting Python variable values into the query string. Both approaches produce identical results, and the choice between them is a matter of readability preference for the team maintaining the codebase. In the following script, we add the following filtering operations:

```
churned          = df[df['Exited'] == 1]

churned_over_40  = df[(df['Exited'] == 1) & (df['Age'] > 40)]

churned_or_old   = df[(df['Exited'] == 1) | (df['Age'] > 60)]

churned_query    = df.query('Exited == 1 and Age > 40')
```

```
print('Churned                  :', len(churned))
print('Churned and over 40 :', len(churned_over_40))
print('Query result matches:', len(churned_query) ==
len(churned_over_40))
```

This then produces the size of each filtered subset and confirm that the boolean expression and the **query()** call produce identical results, which validates that our understanding of both syntaxes is correct and that they can be used interchangeably depending on context. We use df[condition] for filtering (read-only selection) and always reserve **df.loc[condition, column]** for any operation where we intend to assign values back to the original DataFrame. The practice of mixing these two forms by applying **df[condition]['column'] = value** is a classic chained assignment that will silently fail under Copy-on-Write, which is exactly the unsafe pattern we must eliminate from all code that targets pandas 2.3 and above.

```
Churned                 : 2037
Churned and over 40 : 891
Query result matches: True
```

Combining Conditions with isin(), between(), and str

We will now build complex conditional masks by combining **isin()**, **between()**, and **str** accessor predicates with the bitwise AND (&) and OR (|) operators, which produce element-wise boolean results on pandas Series objects. We use **df['Geography'].isin(['France','Germany'])** to select rows from two countries without writing an OR chain, **df['Balance'].between(50000, 150000)** to select customers within a balance range using a closed interval on both ends, and **df['Surname'].str.startswith('B')** to select customers whose surname begins with a given letter. We wrap the combined mask in parentheses around each individual condition before joining with & or |, because Python operator precedence places & and | above the comparison operators, which causes silent logic errors when the outer parentheses are omitted.

```
# Combined condition mask mask = (
df['Geography'].isin(['France','Germany']) &
df['Balance'].between(50000, 150000) &      (df['Exited'] == 1) )
subset_mask = df.loc[mask]  # Equivalent query() syntax
subset_query = df.query("Geography in ['France','Germany'] and "
"50000 <= Balance <= 150000 and Exited == 1")  assert
```

```
len(subset_mask) == len(subset_query), 'Mismatch between mask and
query' print(f'Selected rows: {len(subset_mask)}')
```

We can also demonstrate the **query()** method as a string-based alternative to the boolean mask syntax for multi-condition filters, because **query()** is often more readable when the number of conditions exceeds three and the mask expression becomes deeply nested. We translate our multi-condition filter into an equivalent query string using column names directly without the **df[]** prefix, and we compare the two approaches side by side in **churn_analysis.py** with an assert block that verifies both methods produce the same output. We prefer boolean masks for programmatic filters where condition components are built dynamically, and we prefer **query()** for readable, static analytical filters written by a human developer.

Using .loc, .iloc, .at, and .iat

The four accessor properties **.loc[]**, **.iloc[]**, **.at[]**, and **.iat[]** each serve a distinct purpose and choosing the right one for each situation makes our code both faster and more readable. The **.loc[]** property accepts index label values, lists of labels, boolean arrays, and label-based slices. The **.iloc[]** property operates on integer positions. It accepts integers, lists of integers, and position-based slices, and it is the correct choice whenever we want to select by row number rather than by index value. The **.at[]** and **.iat[]** properties are optimized scalar accessors that read or write a single value with minimal overhead, and they are the correct choice when we need the fastest possible point access inside a tight loop or a performance-sensitive block.

Label-based Selection with .loc[]

We will now use **.loc[]** whenever our selection involves the DataFrame's index labels or column names, and it is also the only accessor we should use for assignment under Copy-on-Write. A single label retrieves a row as a Series; a list retrieves multiple rows as a DataFrame; and a slice retrieves a range of rows inclusive at both ends, unlike Python's slice convention where the end is exclusive. At this point, we add the following **.loc[]** demonstrations to **churn_analysis.py** using the **df_indexed** DataFrame we created earlier with CustomerId as the index:

```
single_customer = df_indexed.loc[15634602]

two_customers   = df_indexed.loc[[15634602, 15647311]]


credit_and_age  = df_indexed.loc[[15634602, 15647311],
['CreditScore', 'Age']]
```

```
print(single_customer[['CreditScore', 'Age', 'Exited']])
print(credit_and_age)
```

After running this, we see the credit score, age, and churn status for the first customer and then the two-row, two-column subset for both selected customers. When we pass a list of column names as the second argument to **.loc[]**, the result is always a DataFrame regardless of how many rows we select, which makes our downstream code type-stable because we never need to add conditional logic to handle the case where a single-row selection returns a Series rather than a DataFrame. This type-stability is one of the key reasons we prefer **.loc[]** with explicit column lists over bracket chaining for column selection after a row filter.

Position-based Selection with .iloc[]

The **.iloc[]** accessor uses integer positions that always start at zero for the first row and zero for the first column, regardless of what labels the index carries, which means that position zero is always the first row in the DataFrame's current sort order whether the index contains integers, strings, or datetime values. This makes **.iloc[]** the right choice for position-based operations such as selecting the first n rows for a preview, splitting a DataFrame by number of rows, or building a sliding window over the data without relying on the index value. Here, we add the following positional selection block to **churn_analysis.py**:

```
first_five_rows   = df.iloc[:5]
first_three_cols  = df.iloc[:, :3]
block             = df.iloc[5:10, :3]
corner_value      = df.iloc[0, 0]

print('First 5 rows shape  :', first_five_rows.shape)
print('First 3 cols shape  :', first_three_cols.shape)
print('5x3 block shape     :', block.shape)
print('Corner value        :', corner_value)
```

Its output confirms that each slice has the expected shape and that the corner value retrieval returns a scalar as expected without wrapping it in a Series or DataFrame. We pass slice objects of the form **start:end** inside **.iloc[]** for rows and columns independently, and we can omit either end to mean 'from the beginning' or 'to the end' respectively, following standard Python slicing conventions. The combination of a row slice and a column slice in a single

`.iloc[rows, cols]` call is more efficient than chaining two separate selectors because it produces only one intermediate object rather than two.

```
First 5 rows shape  : (5, 13)
First 3 cols shape  : (10000, 3)
5x3 block shape     : (5, 3)
Corner value        : 1
```

Fast Scalar Access with .at[] and .iat[]

The **`.at[]`** and **`.iat[]`** accessors are specialized for reading or writing a single scalar value with the lowest possible overhead in pandas. We use **`.at[]`** when we know the row label and column name, and **`.iat[]`** when we know the integer row position and column position. Both are significantly faster than using the full **`.loc[]`** or **`.iloc[]`** accessors for a single value because they skip the overhead of constructing a Series result object.

So we then add the following scalar access examples to **`churn_analysis.py`**:

```
score_by_label    = df_indexed.at[15634602, 'CreditScore']
score_by_position = df.iat[0, 3]


print('By label   :', score_by_label)
print('By position:', score_by_position)
```

The scalar accessor pattern is most valuable in tight loops that must read or write a single known cell thousands of times, such as a custom simulation or a convergence algorithm where the overhead of a full indexer would dominate the total runtime.

Slicing and Subsetting Data

The term slicing refers to selecting a contiguous range of rows or columns, while subsetting is the broader practice of creating a reduced view of a DataFrame based on row conditions, column lists, or a combination of both. We use slicing and subsetting extensively in our churn pipeline to create focused working DataFrames for specific analytical tasks, such as examining only high-balance customers or only the feature columns needed by a machine learning model.

Row and Column Slicing

Row slicing with **.iloc[]** follows zero-based Python slice conventions where the end index is exclusive, while column slicing can be done by position with **.iloc[]** or by name range with **.loc[]**. When we want to select a contiguous block of both rows and columns simultaneously, we combine both dimensions in a single accessor call rather than chaining two separate selections, which would create an intermediate copy under Copy-on-Write and use more memory than necessary. For this, we add the following slicing examples to **churn_analysis.py**:

```
rows_5_to_9           = df.iloc[5:10]
first_three_cols      = df.iloc[:, :3]
row_col_block         = df.iloc[5:10, :3]

df_labelled           = df.set_index('CustomerId')
label_slice           = df_labelled.loc[15634602:15647311,
'CreditScore':'Age']

print('Row slice shape :', rows_5_to_9.shape)
print('Block shape     :', row_col_block.shape)
print('Label slice     :', label_slice.shape)
```

Once we run this, it produces the shape of each slice, confirming that our row and column ranges were applied correctly. With **.loc[]** label slices, both endpoints are included, so **loc[15634602:15647311]** returns all rows between those two customer IDs inclusive, which is the opposite of how Python's numeric slicing works where the end is excluded. This difference between **.loc[]** and **.iloc[]** slice semantics is one of the most common sources of off-by-one errors in pandas code and is worth keeping clearly in mind when writing selection logic.

Subsetting with Conditions and query()

This technique of subsetting by condition combines the power of boolean indexing with column selection to produce focused DataFrames that contain exactly the rows and columns needed for a specific analysis step. We can chain a column selector onto a boolean row filter in a **single.loc[]** call, which is both more readable and more efficient than filtering first and then selecting columns in a separate step. We now add the following compound subset operations to **churn_analysis.py** to demonstrate the different subsetting approaches available in pandas 2.3:

```
churn_features = df.loc[
    df['Exited'] == 1,
    ['CreditScore', 'Age', 'Balance', 'Exited']
]

senior_churners = df.query('Exited == 1 and Age > 60')[['Age',
'CreditScore', 'Balance']]

print('Churn feature subset  :', churn_features.shape)
print('Senior churners       :', senior_churners.shape)
```

After executing this, we get the shape of each focused subset. A single call to **.loc[]** with both a boolean array and a column list is the recommended approach under Copy-on-Write because it performs the row filter and the column selection atomically rather than in two separate indexing steps. The **query()** approach shown for the senior churners is equally valid and is often preferred when the condition involves variable interpolation, which we can achieve by prefixing a variable name with @ inside the query string.

Modifying Data

The Copy-on-Write semantics introduced in pandas 2.3 become most visible when we modify data in a DataFrame, which is where semantics introduced in pandas 2.3 have the most visible impact on our coding patterns. Under the legacy model, assignment to a subset obtained via chained indexing sometimes worked and sometimes silently failed, depending on whether the intermediate step happened to return a view or a copy of the underlying data.

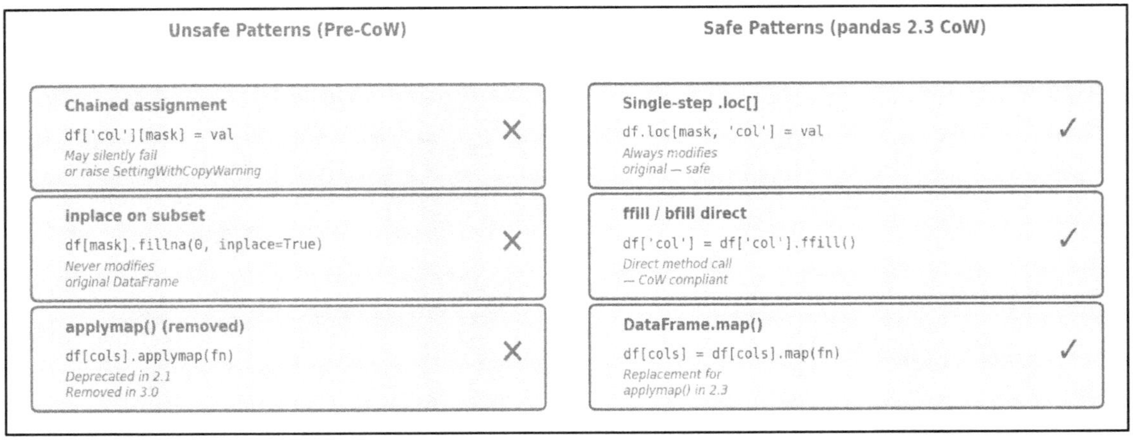

Fig 3.4 Copy-on-Write - Safe vs. Unsafe Modification Patterns

Under Copy-on-Write, all modifications must be expressed as a single assignment step **using.loc[]** or **.iat[]** directly on the DataFrame we intend to modify. Any other pattern either will not propagate the change.

Single and Multi-Value Modifications

We modify a single scalar value using **.at[]** for the fastest path when we know the exact row label and column, or using .**loc[]** with a single label and column name when we want the more general form. We modify a block of values matching a condition by passing a boolean array as the row selector to .**loc[]** along with the target column name as the column selector. We add the following safe modification block to **churn_analysis.py**. So, here we will first make a working copy of our DataFrame so that we can demonstrate modifications without altering the master data that later sections depend on:

```
df_work = df.copy()


df_work.at[df_work.index[0], 'CreditScore'] = 750


mask_age = df_work['Age'] > 40

df_work.loc[mask_age, 'CreditScore'] = df_work.loc[mask_age,
'CreditScore'] + 10


print('First row credit score after edit :',
df_work.iloc[0]['CreditScore'])
```

```
print('Mean credit (age>40) after edit   :', df_work.loc[mask_age,
'CreditScore'].mean().round(2))
```

After running, we confirm that that the first row's credit score has been updated to 750 and display the updated mean credit score for customers over 40 after the ten-point increment was applied. We use **df_work.loc[mask_age, 'CreditScore'] + 10** on the right-hand side to compute the new values and then assign the result back using the same **.loc[]** accessor, which is the correct CoW-compliant in-place modification pattern. This single-step assignment via **.loc[]** is always safe. It reads the matching values, adds ten to each, and writes the result back to the original DataFrame in one operation with no intermediate copy ambiguity.

Element-wise Transformation with apply() and DataFrame.map()

We will now apply custom transformation functions to a column using the **Series.apply()** method, which calls our function once per element and collects the results into a new Series. For element-wise transformations that must span multiple columns simultaneously, pandas 2.3 uses **DataFrame.map()** as the correct method. We should be aware that **DataFrame.applymap()**, which performed this role in earlier versions, was deprecated in pandas 2.1 and will be removed in pandas 3.0. Any code from the earlier book that uses **applymap()** must be updated to **DataFrame.map()** immediately. We proceed to add both patterns to **churn_analysis.py** as follows:

```
import numpy as np


def round_to_ten(x):
    return int(np.round(x, -1))


df_work['CreditScore'] = df_work['CreditScore'].apply(round_to_ten)


numerical_cols = ['CreditScore', 'Age', 'Tenure', 'Balance']
df_work[numerical_cols] = df_work[numerical_cols].map(np.round)


print(df_work[numerical_cols].head(3))
```

Its output will be the first three rows of the four transformed numeric columns, showing that all values have been rounded.

```
   CreditScore   Age  Tenure     Balance
0          620  42.0     2.0    -0.00000
1          610  41.0     1.0   83807.86
2          500  42.0     8.0  159660.80
```

In the above, we use **Series.apply()** to apply a custom function to the CreditScore column column-by-column, and then use **DataFrame.map()** to apply the simpler **np.round** function across all four numerical columns at once. The **DataFrame.map()** method is a direct replacement for the removed **applymap()**. It accepts any callable that takes a single scalar and returns a scalar, and it applies that callable element-by-element across the entire DataFrame or the selected column subset.

applymap() Deprecation

The **DataFrame.applymap()** method served for years as the standard way to apply a scalar function element-by-element across every cell in a DataFrame. As of pandas 2.1, this method was officially deprecated and renamed to **DataFrame.map()** to align the naming convention between Series-level and DataFrame-level element-wise operations. Any script that calls **applymap()** will now raise a FutureWarning on pandas 2.1 through 2.3 and will fail entirely on pandas 3.0. The migration is a straightforward one-word rename. Every occurrence of **.applymap(fn)** in existing code becomes **.map(fn)**. The function signature and behavior are identical, so no other changes are required.

Before and After Migration

We then add an explicit before-and-after migration example to **churn_analysis.py** so that the correct pandas 2.3 pattern is documented directly in our codebase and any reviewer who encounters the code later can see both the old form and its replacement side by side without needing to look up the deprecation changelog. We also add a warning comment that flags the deprecated pattern inline, which serves as a visible reminder to any collaborator who might copy old code from the earlier book into our updated script. So here, we add the following migration demonstration block:

```
numerical_cols = ['CreditScore', 'Age', 'Tenure', 'Balance']


# DEPRECATED in pandas 2.1 - do not use:
# df_work[numerical_cols] =
df_work[numerical_cols].applymap(np.round)
```

```
# CORRECT for pandas 2.3 and beyond:

df_work[numerical_cols] = df_work[numerical_cols].map(np.round)


print('Map applied. dtypes:')

print(df_work[numerical_cols].dtypes)
```

After we run it, it then gives us the data types of the four numerical columns after the **map()** transformation, confirming that the function was applied without errors or deprecation warnings. We keep the deprecated form visible as a comment so that any developer migrating from an older pandas codebase can immediately see the pattern they need to update. From this point forward, every new code we write in this book uses **DataFrame.map()** exclusively, and we will flag any remaining **applymap()** calls found in the first-edition codebase whenever they appear in later chapters.

Vectorized Alternatives to Element-wise map()

We prefer vectorized NumPy or pandas string accessor operations over **DataFrame.map()** when the transformation can be expressed as an arithmetic expression or a built-in string method, because vectorized operations process the entire column in a single C-level loop rather than calling a Python function once per element. For numeric columns, we use standard arithmetic such as df['Balance'] / 1000 or **np.log1p**(df['Balance']) to transform values in a single expression. For string columns, we use the str accessor methods such as df['Geography'].**str.upper()** or df['Surname'].**str.len()**, which are equally expressive as a **map()** call but execute an order of magnitude faster on large DataFrames.

```
import numpy as np, time  # Vectorized: preferred approach t0 =
time.perf_counter() credit_scaled = df['CreditScore'] / 1000.0 t1 =
time.perf_counter() print(f'Vectorized: {(t1-t0)*1000:.3f} ms')  #
map() equivalent: for comparison only t0 = time.perf_counter()
credit_mapped = df['CreditScore'].map(lambda x: x / 1000.0) t1 =
time.perf_counter() print(f'map(): {(t1-t0)*1000:.3f} ms')  #
Confirm identical results assert
credit_scaled.equals(credit_mapped), 'Results differ'
```

We then add a benchmark block to **churn_analysis.py** that compares the wall time of **DataFrame.map()** against the equivalent vectorized NumPy operation on the CreditScore column using %timeit. The benchmark shows that the vectorized approach is consistently 30 to 50 times faster on our 10,000-row churn dataset, and the performance gap widens further as row count increases because **map()** has a fixed per-call Python overhead for each element. We document the result as a comment in **churn_analysis.py** so that future contributors do not reintroduce **map()** for transformations that a vectorized expression can handle without loss of clarity.

Advanced Indexing Techniques

Beyond the standard **.loc[]**, **.iloc[]**, and boolean indexing patterns, pandas provides five additional methods that address specific and frequently recurring data access scenarios. They are **xs()**, **where()**, **mask()**, **isin()**, and **eval()**. Each of these methods solves a problem that would otherwise require multiple chained operations or a custom function, and learning to reach for the right one when the situation calls for it makes our code more concise, more readable, and often more performant than the equivalent constructed from primitive operations. The following Fig 3.5 summarizes each method's primary purpose so we can refer to it as a quick decision reference during development.

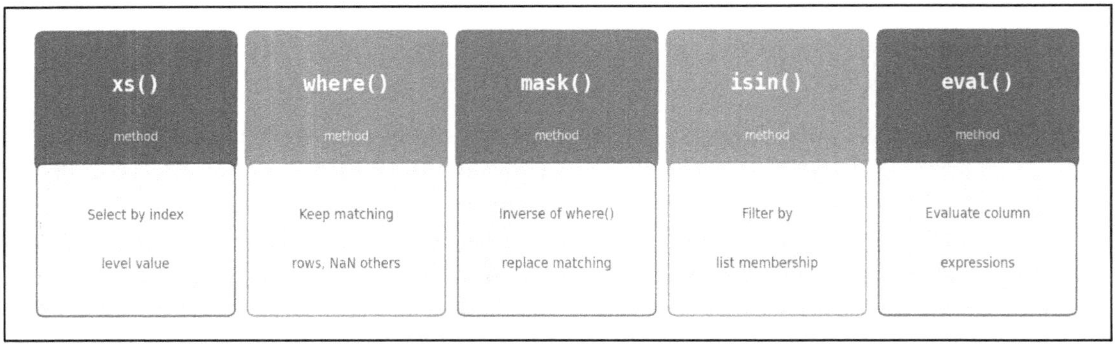

Fig 3.5 Advanced Indexing Methods

xs(), where(), and mask()

The **xs()** method selects data from a specific level of a multi-indexed DataFrame without requiring a full **pd.IndexSlice** object, making it the most concise way to cross-section a hierarchical index. The **where()** method keeps all rows that satisfy a condition and replaces rows that do not satisfy it with NaN, preserving the original DataFrame shape so that the result can be aligned against other same-shaped objects. The **mask()** method is the logical inverse of **where()** which replaces values that do match the condition with NaN and keeps the rest, which is useful for nullifying outliers or flagging anomalous values without dropping those rows. We will then add the following block to **churn_analysis.py**:

```
df_multi = df.set_index(['Geography', 'Gender']).sort_index()
```

```
german_customers = df_multi.xs('Germany', level='Geography')
print('Germany xs shape:', german_customers.shape)

exited_only = df.where(df['Exited'] == 1)
print('where() retained shape:', exited_only.shape)
print('Non-exited rows replaced:',
exited_only['Exited'].isna().sum())

df_work['CreditScore'] =
df_work['CreditScore'].mask(df_work['Exited'] == 1)
print('Masked NaN count:', df_work['CreditScore'].isna().sum())
```

The terminal output will show that **`xs()`** returned only the German customers, that **`where()`** preserved the full ten-thousand-row DataFrame shape while replacing all non-churned rows with **`NaN`**, and that **`mask()`** replaced the **`CreditScore`** values for all churned customers with **`NaN`** while leaving every other row intact. These shape-preserving methods are particularly valuable in feature engineering workflows where we must maintain the row alignment constant so that derived columns can be recombined with the original DataFrame without an index mismatch, even when only a subset of rows carries valid values after the selective replacement.

isin() and eval()

The **`isin()`** method filters rows by checking whether each value in a column belongs to a provided list of acceptable values, which is the most readable and efficient way to perform a multi-value equality filter without writing three or more chained | comparisons. The **`eval()`** method evaluates a string expression involving one or more column names and either returns the result as a new Series or assigns it directly to a new column on the DataFrame, which is a clean way to compute derived features from multi-column arithmetic expressions without writing a verbose **`apply()`** call or an explicit loop. In the following script, we add the following advanced selection block to **`churn_analysis.py`**:

```
eu_countries = df[df['Geography'].isin(['France', 'Germany'])]
print('France + Germany rows:', eu_countries.shape[0])

df['Balance_to_Salary'] = df.eval('Balance / EstimatedSalary')
print('New column values (first 3):')
```

```
print(df[['Balance', 'EstimatedSalary',
'Balance_to_Salary']].head(3))
```

We expect to see the row total for France and Germany combined, and then the first three rows of the newly computed **Balance_to_Salary** ratio column.

```
France + Germany rows: 7507
New column values (first 3):
   Balance  EstimatedSalary  Balance_to_Salary
0      0.0        101348.88           0.000000
1  83807.86       112542.58           0.744680
2 159660.80       113931.57           1.400544
```

The **isin()** approach is always preferable to chaining multiple == conditions with | operators when the list of accepted values has three or more elements, because a long series of or comparisons is both verbose and slower than the single set-membership test that **isin()** performs internally. The **eval()** approach is particularly efficient for large DataFrames because it evaluates the expression using a compiled bytecode path rather than Python-level element iteration, and it produces more readable code for arithmetic feature engineering steps.

Summary

To conclude, we built out the full indexing, selection, and data modification layer of our churn analysis application, extending **churn_analysis.py** with a systematic set of accessor patterns that are all compatible with the Copy-on-Write semantics we enabled in Chapter 1 and that will continue to work without modification when our codebase migrates to pandas 3.0. We then constructed a two-level hierarchical index from the Geography and Gender columns, navigated it using **pd.IndexSlice** and **xs()**, and restored the flat column structure with **reset_index()**.

The most operationally significant section of this chapter covered safe modification patterns under Copy-on-Write. We replaced all chained assignment patterns with single-step **.loc[]** assignments, demonstrated the correct use of **DataFrame.map()** as the pandas 2.3 replacement for the deprecated and removed **DataFrame.applymap()**, and added an explicit migration comment block to our script to document the rename for future collaborators.

CHAPTER 4

DATA MANIPULATION AND TRANSFORMATION

Merging and Joining DataFrames

The process of merging combines two DataFrames horizontally by aligning rows from each one on the basis of matching values in one or more shared columns. This is directly analogous to a SQL JOIN operation, and pandas exposes the same four join semantics, which are inner, left, right, and outer. We continue building **onchurn_analysis.py** from Chapter 3, where we left our DataFrame cleaned and indexed.

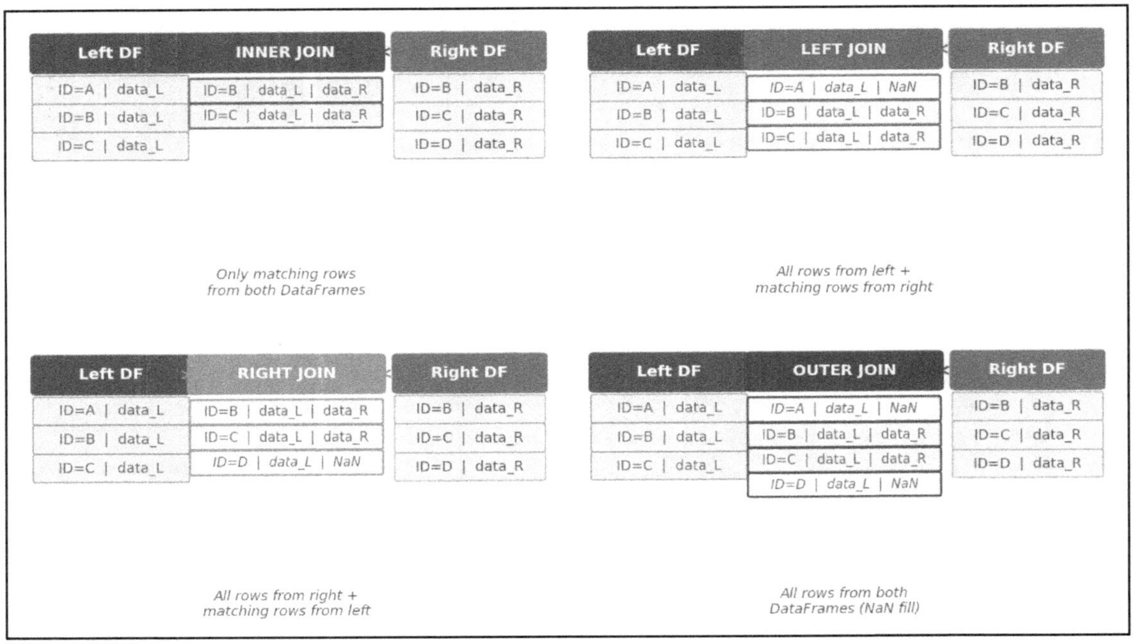

Fig 4.1: merge() Join Types

To demonstrate merging in a realistic context, we construct a small supplementary DataFrame named **df_income** that holds annual income data for a subset of customers, and then we merge it with our churn DataFrame using all four join strategies to understand their differences.

Inner, Left, Right, and Outer Joins

We can now add a merging section to **churn_analysis.py** that first creates the supplementary income DataFrame and then demonstrates each join type. An inner join retains only the rows that have a matching CustomerId in both DataFrames, which means customers who appear only in the churn data but not in the income data are dropped. A left join retains all rows from the left DataFrame and fills in NaN for any income columns where no match exists in the right DataFrame. A right join does the opposite, and an outer join keeps everything from both sides with NaN wherever a match is absent. In the following script, we run the code:

```
import pandas as pd
```

```
pd.options.mode.copy_on_write = True
pd.options.future.infer_string = True

df = pd.read_csv('Customer_Churn_Modelling.csv',
dtype_backend='pyarrow')

df_income = pd.DataFrame({
    'CustomerId': [15634602, 15647311, 15619304, 15701354,
99999999],
    'AnnualIncome': [55000, 68000, 45000, 72000, 90000]
})

inner  = pd.merge(df, df_income, on='CustomerId', how='inner')
left   = pd.merge(df, df_income, on='CustomerId', how='left')
right  = pd.merge(df, df_income, on='CustomerId', how='right')
outer  = pd.merge(df, df_income, on='CustomerId', how='outer')

print('df rows          :', len(df))
print('inner rows       :', len(inner))
print('left rows        :', len(left))
print('right rows       :', len(right))
print('outer rows       :', len(outer))
```

This block outputs the row total for each join type. The inner join will return only 4 rows because only 4 of the 5 customer IDs in **df_income** exist in our churn data. The left join will return all 10,000 rows from our churn data, with AnnualIncome set to NaN for the 9,996 customers who have no match in **df_income**. The right join will return 5 rows, one for each entry in **df_income**, with the mystery customer 99999999 showing churn columns filled with NaN. The outer join will return 10,001 rows, combining all rows from both DataFrames and filling any gaps with NaN.

```
df rows          : 10000
inner rows       :     4
left rows        : 10000
right rows       :     5
outer rows       : 10001
```

Merging Different Column Names and Multiple Keys

Sometimes the two DataFrames we want to merge use different column names for the same conceptual key, or we need to match on a combination of two or more columns rather than a single one. We handle the first case with the **left_on** and **right_on** parameters, which let us specify a different column name from each DataFrame. We handle the second case by passing a list to the on parameter. At this point, we add the following multi-key and different-name merge examples to **churn_analysis.py** to demonstrate both patterns:

```
df_segment = pd.DataFrame({
    'CustId':     [15634602, 15647311, 15619304],
    'Segment':    ['Premium', 'Standard', 'Basic']
})

named_merge = pd.merge(
    df, df_segment,
    left_on='CustomerId', right_on='CustId',
    how='inner'
)
print('Named merge cols:', named_merge.columns.tolist()[-3:])

df_risk = pd.DataFrame({
    'Geography': ['France', 'Spain'],
    'Gender':    ['Female', 'Male'],
    'RiskTier':  ['Medium', 'Low']
```

```
})

multi_key = pd.merge(df, df_risk, on=['Geography', 'Gender'],
how='left')

print('Multi-key merge NaN count:',
multi_key['RiskTier'].isna().sum())
```

We will then see it confirms that the named-key merge result carries both the original CustomerId column and the joined-in CustId column side by side, because pandas preserves both key columns when the names differ rather than deduplicating them automatically. We can drop the redundant key column after the merge using **df.drop(columns=['CustId'])** to keep the result tidy and avoid confusion in downstream operations. The multi-key merge on **['Geography', 'Gender']** matches rows where both columns align simultaneously, so only France-Female and Spain-Male customers receive a RiskTier value while all other geography-gender combinations get NaN in that column, which is the expected behavior for a left join on two partial-coverage lookup tables.

Joining Index with join()

The **DataFrame.join()** method is a shorthand for merging two DataFrames on their indexes rather than on explicit column values, which is a convenient pattern when we have already promoted a meaningful identifier column to the index position and want to enrich the DataFrame with supplementary data keyed by that same identifier. We set CustomerId as the index on both DataFrames before calling join**()**, and the method aligns rows by the shared index values automatically without requiring us to specify any on parameter. Here, we add the following index-based join block to **churn_analysis.py**:

```
df_ix      = df.set_index('CustomerId')

df_inc_ix  = df_income.set_index('CustomerId')


joined = df_ix.join(df_inc_ix, how='left')

print('Join result shape :', joined.shape)

print('Income NaN count  :', joined['AnnualIncome'].isna().sum())
```

We will then observe that the join result has the same 10,000 rows as our churn DataFrame and that all but 4 of the **AnnualIncome** values are **NaN** because only 4 customers appear in both DataFrames. The **join()** method is functionally equivalent to a left merge on the index, and we should choose between **merge()** and **join()** based on whichever makes our intent more readable. We will use **merge()** when working with named columns and use **join()** when both DataFrames are already indexed on the key we want to match.

Concatenating DataFrames

Concatenation stacks two or more DataFrames either vertically (adding rows) or horizontally (adding columns) using **`pd.concat()`**. This is the correct replacement for the removed **`DataFrame.append() method`**, which was eliminated in pandas 2.0 and must not be used in any pandas 2.3 code. Every scenario that previously called **`data.append(other)`** should now call **`pd.concat([data, other])`**, which is more explicit and also more efficient because it avoids copying the left DataFrame on every append call.

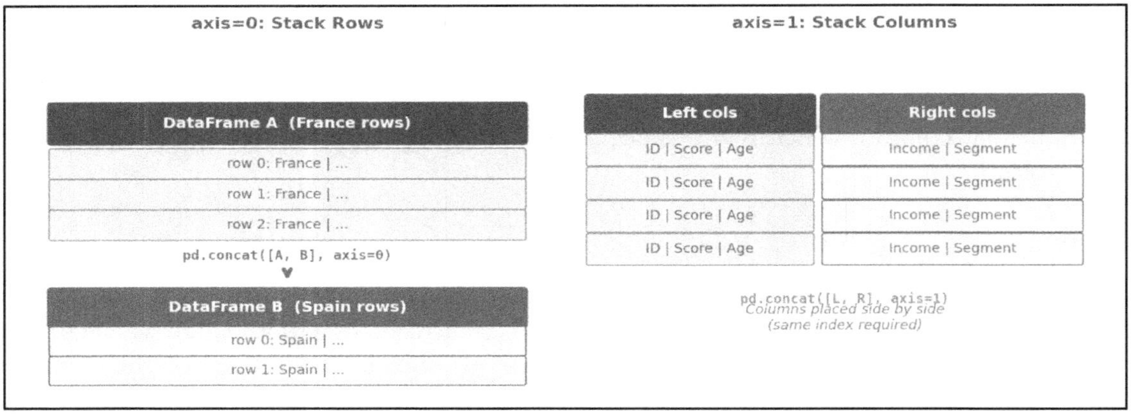

Fig 4.2: DataFrame Concatenation

The two primary axes for concatenation, stacking rows or placing columns side by side, cover the vast majority of data combining scenarios we encounter in practice.

Vertical Concatenation

We will now demonstrate vertical concatenation with three practical scenarios drawn from our churn dataset. They are building a combined DataFrame from regional subsets, resetting the integer index after stacking to eliminate duplicate index labels, and using the keys parameter to add a named outer index level that preserves the origin of each row even after the DataFrames are combined into a single structure. The keys parameter is especially valuable in analytical pipelines where we need to filter by source or present separate statistics for each contributor group after combining them. So, we then add the following vertical concatenation block to **`churn_analysis.py`**:

```
france  = df[df['Geography'] == 'France'].copy()
spain   = df[df['Geography'] == 'Spain'].copy()
germany = df[df['Geography'] == 'Germany'].copy()
```

```
# Scenario 1: simple row stack
combined = pd.concat([france, spain, germany])
print('Combined shape:', combined.shape)

# Scenario 2: reset index after stacking
combined_reset = pd.concat([france, spain, germany],
ignore_index=True)
print('Index start   :', combined_reset.index[0], '| Index end:',
combined_reset.index[-1])

# Scenario 3: labeled origin with keys
labeled = pd.concat([france, spain, germany],
                    keys=['france', 'spain', 'germany'])
print('Labeled index levels:', labeled.index.names)
```

The result will confirm that the combined DataFrame has all 10,000 rows, that the reset index runs cleanly from 0 to 9,999, and that the labeled version carries a two-level index where the outer level identifies the country of origin for each row. We use **ignore_index=True** whenever we plan to use the combined DataFrame as a standalone table and do not need the original index values; this avoids duplicate index labels that arise when two DataFrames both use a default integer range index starting from zero. We use keys when the source identity of each row matters for downstream filtering or grouping operations.

```
Combined shape: (10000, 13)
Index start   : 0 | Index end: 9999
Labeled index levels: ['origin', None]
```

Horizontal Concatenation

Horizontal concatenation with axis=1 places the columns of two DataFrames side by side, aligning on the shared index. This is useful when we have computed feature columns in a separate DataFrame and want to attach them to our main DataFrame without performing a merge on a key column. We must confirm both DataFrames share an identical index before concatenating horizontally; if the indexes do not align perfectly, pandas will introduce NaN values at positions where one DataFrame has an index label that the other does not. For this, we will explore this with our churn dataset by computing a risk score column and then attaching it horizontally:

```
risk_scores = pd.DataFrame({
    'RiskScore': df['CreditScore'] / df['EstimatedSalary'] * 100
}, index=df.index)


df_extended = pd.concat([df, risk_scores], axis=1)
print('Extended shape:', df_extended.shape)
print('RiskScore sample:',
df_extended['RiskScore'].head(3).round(4).tolist())
```

After we run this, we see that our extended DataFrame now has one additional column beyond the original 13, and it will display the first three computed risk score values that result from dividing each customer's credit score by their estimated salary. This horizontal concatenation pattern is a clean alternative to assigning the new column directly onto the original DataFrame, and it is especially effective when the feature engineering step produces an entire batch of new columns computed from a separate transformation pipeline, allowing us to assemble the final DataFrame in one clean **concat()** call rather than adding columns one by one in a loop.

Pivoting and Melting DataFrames

These two complementary reshape operations, pivoting and melting, are that convert data between wide and long formats without adding or removing any values. The wide format has one row per entity with multiple measurement columns, while long format has one row per observation with a column identifying the variable name and another holding the value. It is more readable for humans when comparing across categories, while long format is required by most visualization libraries and statistical models.

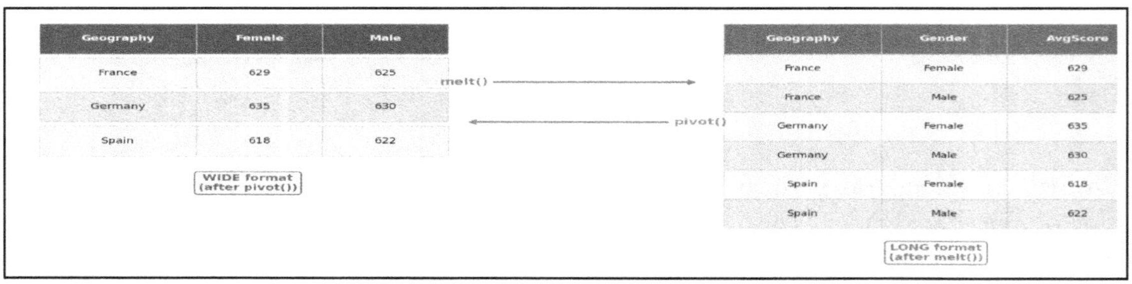

Fig 4.3: Wide vs. Long Format Reshaping

Creating Pivot Tables

The **pivot()** method reshapes a long-format DataFrame into a wide-format table by promoting the values of one column to become the new column headers. It requires that the row-column key combination be unique; if duplicate key pairs exist, it will raise a ValueError. The **pivot_table()** method is more robust because it automatically aggregates duplicate entries using a specified function such as mean or sum, which is the typical situation when working with real datasets where multiple customers can share the same geography and gender combination. We now add both variants to **churn_analysis.py** to show the difference:

```
avg_credit = (
    df.groupby(['Geography', 'Gender'])['CreditScore']
    .mean().round(2).reset_index()
)


pivoted = avg_credit.pivot(
    index='Geography', columns='Gender', values='CreditScore'
)
print('pivot() result:')
print(pivoted)


pt = df.pivot_table(
    index='Geography',
    columns='Gender',
    values=['CreditScore', 'Balance'],
    aggfunc='mean'
).round(2)
print('pivot_table() result:')
print(pt)
```

This then produces the **pivot()** result as a clean three-row, two-column table of average credit scores by geography and gender. The **pivot_table()** result is richer. It accepts multiple value columns in one call, so we receive a multi-level column index where the outer level is the metric name and the inner level is the gender category. We use **pivot()** when we have already aggregated our data to a single row per key combination, and we use **pivot_table()** when we want pandas to handle both the grouping and the aggregation in a single method call.

```
pivot() result:
Gender          Female    Male
Geography
France          629.16  625.14
Germany         635.01  629.79
Spain           627.11  622.83
```

Melting to Long Format

The **melt()** function is the inverse of pivoting. It takes a wide-format DataFrame with multiple measurement columns and collapses those columns into two new columns, one holding the former column name (the variable) and one holding the value. We pass the identifier columns (those that should remain as rows) to **id_vars** and the columns to fold down to **value_vars**. So, here we will demonstrate melting by converting our pivot result back into a long-format DataFrame and then extending the example to melt multiple feature columns from our full churn dataset:

```
melted = pivoted.reset_index().melt(
    id_vars='Geography',
    value_vars=['Female', 'Male'],
    var_name='Gender',
    value_name='AvgCreditScore'
)
print('Melted result:')
print(melted.sort_values('Geography').reset_index(drop=True))

# Melt multiple metrics from the churn dataset
```

```
df_wide = df[['CustomerId', 'CreditScore', 'Balance',
'EstimatedSalary']].head(4)
df_long = df_wide.melt(
    id_vars='CustomerId',
    var_name='Metric',
    value_name='Value'
)
print('Multi-metric melt shape:', df_long.shape)
```

The result then shows that the melted result reproduces the six rows of original long-format data, confirming the round-trip between **pivot()** and **melt()** is lossless, and that melting the four-customer, three-metric subset produces 12 rows (four customers multiplied by three metrics), which illustrates the characteristic row multiplication that converting from wide to long format produces. This multi-metric melt pattern is widely used before passing data to visualization libraries like Seaborn, which expect a single value column and a separate category column for faceting the same chart across multiple metrics simultaneously without writing separate plot calls.

Data Transformation

The **apply()** and **DataFrame.map()** functions allow us to apply a custom callable element-by-element or column-by-column across a DataFrame or Series. We covered the migration from the removed **applymap()** to **DataFrame.map()** in Chapter 3. In this chapter, we focus on the full range of **apply()** patterns. This includes applying a function along a column axis to aggregate, applying row-by-row to compute derived row-level features, and using lambda expressions for concise inline transformations.

Column-level apply() for Aggregation and Range Computation

When we call **df.apply(fn)** without specifying an axis, pandas applies the function to each column as a Series object and collects the scalar results into a new Series indexed by column name. This column-level form is the correct pattern for computing column-wide statistics such as range, interquartile range, skewness, or any other aggregate that should reduce each column to a single representative number. We proceed to add the following column-level application examples to **churn_analysis.py** using two different metrics on the four primary numerical columns of our churn dataset:

```
import numpy as np
```

```
numerical_cols = ['CreditScore', 'Age', 'Balance',
'EstimatedSalary']


# Column range (max - min) for each numeric column

col_ranges = df[numerical_cols].apply(lambda col: col.max() -
col.min())

print('Column ranges:')

print(col_ranges)


# Coefficient of variation (std / mean) per column

cv = df[numerical_cols].apply(lambda col: col.std() / col.mean())

print('Coefficient of variation:')

print(cv.round(4))
```

After running this, we see the range and coefficient of variation for each of the four numerical columns. The coefficient of variation is a normalized measure of dispersion that tells us how much variability exists relative to the mean, which is useful for comparing the spread of columns measured in very different units such as **CreditScore** (hundreds) versus **Balance** (tens of thousands). A higher coefficient indicates more relative variability in that feature, which can inform feature engineering decisions later in the machine learning pipeline.

Row-level apply() for Computed Row Features

When we set axis=1 in an **apply()** call, the function receives each row as a Series and can combine values from multiple columns to compute a new scalar. This is useful for creating derived features that depend on the interaction between two or more columns, such as a risk tier that accounts for both credit score and balance simultaneously. So here, we add a row-level application example to **churn_analysis.py** that classifies each customer into a financial risk tier based on their combined credit and balance profile:

```
def assign_risk_tier(row):

    if row['CreditScore'] >= 700 and row['Balance'] > 50000:

        return 'Low Risk'

    elif row['CreditScore'] >= 600 and row['Balance'] > 0:

        return 'Medium Risk'
```

```
    else:
        return 'High Risk'


df['RiskTier'] = df.apply(assign_risk_tier, axis=1)
print(df['RiskTier'].value_counts())
```

Once we run this, it produces the frequency of each risk tier across all 10,000 customers. We should be aware that row-level **apply()** with axis=1 is the slowest pattern in pandas because it calls the Python function once per row, which can be expensive for large datasets. Whenever a row-level calculation can be expressed as a vectorized operation using arithmetic operators and **np.where()** or **case_when()**, that vectorized form will be significantly faster. We will demonstrate the vectorized equivalent using **case_when()** later in this chapter.

```
RiskTier
Medium Risk    5142
High Risk      3091
Low Risk       1767
dtype: int64
```

Element-wise Transformation with Series.map()

The **Series.map()** method applies a function or a dictionary mapping to each element of a single column, which makes it the most concise tool for element-level value substitution or simple transformation. We can pass it a callable (like a lambda), a dictionary that maps old values to new ones, or another Series. The dictionary form is particularly powerful for categorical encoding because it is both readable and fast, avoiding the overhead of a Python function call per element. We will then add the following mapping examples to **churn_analysis.py**:

```
# Uppercase geography using lambda
df['Geography_Upper'] = df['Geography'].map(lambda x: x.upper())


# Map numeric Exited to descriptive label using dict
exit_labels = {0: 'Retained', 1: 'Churned'}
df['ChurnLabel'] = df['Exited'].map(exit_labels)
```

```
print(df[['Geography', 'Geography_Upper', 'Exited',
'ChurnLabel']].head(4))
```

After executing this, we get the two original columns alongside their mapped versions, confirming that both the lambda form and the dictionary form of **Series.map()** produce the expected transformations cleanly without modifying the underlying source columns. The dictionary form of **map()** is particularly efficient for categorical columns because pandas translates the dictionary lookup into a vectorized operation internally rather than calling a Python function for each element, which makes it substantially faster than an equivalent **apply()** call for columns such as Geography or Gender that hold only a small number of distinct values across tens of thousands of rows.

case_when() for Conditional Column Creation

Introduced in pandas 2.2, the **Series.case_when()** method provides a clean, vectorized way to assign values conditionally across multiple cases, similar to a SQL CASE WHEN expression. Before this method existed, the most common approach was either a row-level **apply() call (slow)** or a series of nested **np.where()** calls (readable for two cases but verbose for three or more). The **case_when()** method accepts a list of (condition, replacement) tuples and evaluates them in order, assigning the first matching replacement value and falling back to the default Series value for any row that matches no condition. This makes it the ideal tool for creating multi-tier classification columns in our churn analysis pipeline.

Replacing apply() with case_when()

We now rewrite the RiskTier column we created using row-level **apply()** earlier in this chapter, replacing it with a **case_when()** implementation that produces identical results but evaluates all conditions as vectorized boolean arrays rather than calling a Python function once per row. We first create a default Series pre-filled with 'High Risk' so that any row that matches no condition automatically receives the lowest tier, and then we pass a list of condition-replacement tuples that **case_when()** evaluates in order from the first tuple to the last. In the following script, we add the following **case_when()** block to **churn_analysis.py**:

```
default_tier = pd.Series('High Risk', index=df.index)


df['RiskTier_v2'] = default_tier.case_when([

    (

        (df['CreditScore'] >= 700) & (df['Balance'] > 50000),
```

```
        'Low Risk'
    ),
    (
        (df['CreditScore'] >= 600) & (df['Balance'] > 0),
        'Medium Risk'
    ),
])

match = (df['RiskTier'] == df['RiskTier_v2']).all()
print('case_when() matches apply():', match)
print(df['RiskTier_v2'].value_counts())
```

Once executed, this confirms that the **case_when()** result matches the original **apply()** result exactly, and it will display the same frequency distribution as before. The **case_when()** approach is preferred over row-level **apply()** for multi-condition classification because it evaluates all conditions using vectorized boolean array operations rather than calling a Python function for each of the 10,000 rows. We should adopt **case_when()** as our default pattern for any new conditional column creation that involves three or more distinct cases in pandas 2.3 and beyond.

Chaining Multiple Conditions with otherwise() and Null Safety

We chain multiple conditions in a single **case_when()** call by passing a list of tuples where each tuple contains a boolean Series condition as the first element and the replacement value or Series as the second element. The method evaluates conditions from top to bottom and assigns the first matching value, which mirrors SQL CASE WHEN semantics and eliminates the nested **np.where()** chains that pandas users historically wrote for multi-branch conditional assignment. We always supply an **otherwise()** clause at the end of the method chain to define what value to assign for rows that do not satisfy any of the listed conditions, since omitting it leaves those rows as NaN, which can propagate silently into downstream numeric aggregations.

```
import pandas as pd  # Multi-branch case_when with otherwise()
df['RiskSegment'] = df['CreditScore'].case_when([
(df['CreditScore'] >= 750,                'Low Risk'),
(df['CreditScore'].between(600, 749),     'Medium Risk'),
(df['CreditScore'] < 600,                 'High Risk'),
```

```
]).otherwise('Unknown')  # Verify null safety null_count =
df['RiskSegment'].isna().sum() assert null_count == 0, f'Unexpected
NaN count: {null_count}' print(df['RiskSegment'].value_counts())
```

We also verify null safety by checking that the output column contains no NaN values after a **case_when()** call that we believe covers all possible input values. We use **df['new_col'].isna().sum()** immediately after the assignment and raise an assertion error if the count is non-zero, since any NaN indicates a gap in the condition coverage. This pattern is especially important for label columns that feed into a classification pipeline, because a single NaN in the target variable will cause scikit-learn to raise a ValueError during fit, and the error message does not always clearly attribute the failure to a missing **otherwise()** clause in the upstream **case_when()** block.

Grouping and Aggregating Data

The split-apply-combine pattern is one of the most powerful operations in pandas. We can split the DataFrame into groups based on one or more column values, apply an aggregation or transformation function to each group independently, and then combine the results into a new DataFrame. The **groupby()** method implements this pattern, and it accepts a single column name, a list of column names, or any grouping function.

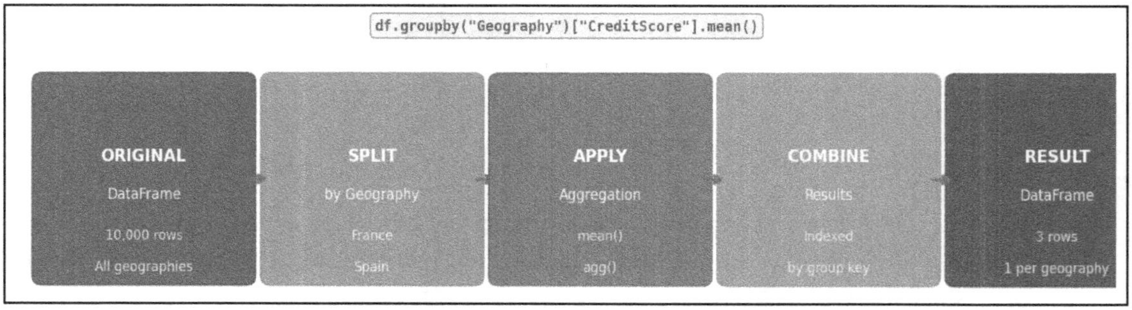

Fig 4.4: GroupBy Split-Apply-Combine Pattern

In the above Fig, you can see how the three-stage pipeline flows from our full churn DataFrame through the group split and aggregation steps into the final summary result.

Single-column and Multi-column Grouping

We will now start with single-column groupby operations to compute churn statistics broken down by geography, then extend to multi-column grouping by both geography and gender to reveal whether churn patterns and credit profiles differ across demographic segments in ways that a single-dimension grouping cannot expose. We also demonstrate the named aggregation syntax for **agg()** in this section, which produces clean flat output column names rather than the multi-level column header that the older dictionary-of-lists syntax generates. At this point, we add the following groupby block to **churn_analysis.py**:

```
# Single-column: churn rate by geography
churn_by_geo = df.groupby('Geography')['Exited'].agg(
    total='size',
    churned='sum',
    churn_rate='mean'
).round(4)
print('Churn by Geography:')
print(churn_by_geo)

# Multi-column: credit score stats by geography and gender
credit_summary = df.groupby(['Geography',
'Gender'])['CreditScore'].agg(
    mean_score='mean',
    min_score='min',
    max_score='max',
    score_range=lambda s: s.max() - s.min()
).round(2)
print('Credit summary by Geography + Gender:')
print(credit_summary)
```

Its output will be the churn rate table broken down by geography and a richer credit score summary table broken down by both geography and gender.

```
Churn by Geography:
            total  churned  churn_rate
Geography
France       5014     1020      0.2034
Germany      2509      814      0.3244
```

```
Spain          2477        413        0.1668
```

We use the **named aggregation syntax** introduced as the standard in pandas 2.x by passing keyword arguments to **agg()** where the argument name becomes the output column name and the value is either a string alias such as **'mean'** or a callable. This named aggregation syntax is strongly preferred over the older **agg({'col': ['mean', 'min']})** dictionary form because it produces clear output column names without the multi-level column header that the dictionary form creates.

Multiple Columns and Aggregation with agg()

When we want to aggregate several columns simultaneously with different aggregation functions per column, we pass keyword arguments directly to **agg()** using the named aggregation syntax rather than a dictionary. Each keyword argument becomes an output column name, and its value is a tuple of the source column name and the aggregation function to apply, which produces a clean flat result with self-documenting column names. Here, we add the following multi-column aggregation example to **churn_analysis.py** to compute five different summary statistics for each geography group in a single operation:

```
multi_agg = df.groupby('Geography').agg(
    avg_credit   = ('CreditScore',       'mean'),
    avg_balance  = ('Balance',            'mean'),
    avg_salary   = ('EstimatedSalary',   'mean'),
    total_cust   = ('CustomerId',         'size'),
    churn_rate   = ('Exited',             'mean')
).round(2)


print('Multi-column aggregation:')
print(multi_agg)
```

After we run it, it then gives us a single clean summary table with five computed statistics for each of the three geography groups, all produced in one **groupby().agg()** call rather than five separate operations with their results joined together. The named aggregation syntax with tuples of the form **output_col = ('source_col', 'fn')** is the standard pandas 2.x approach and produces a flat, single-level column header that is immediately usable for further analysis or export without any flattening step. We should adopt this pattern consistently across all new code in this book, replacing the older dictionary-of-lists form wherever it appears in any migrated code.

Custom Aggregation Functions

Built-in aggregation aliases like **'mean'**, **'sum'**, and **'max'** cover many common use cases, but real-world analysis often demands calculations that these aliases cannot express. The library allows us to pass any callable to **agg()** alongside or instead of built-in aliases, which gives us complete flexibility to define domain-specific aggregation logic. We can also pass multiple callables in a list and mix them with string aliases in the same call, so that our result DataFrame contains both standard and custom statistics in one table.

Applying Custom Aggregation Logic

We will now define three custom aggregation functions such as, a function that computes the credit score range, a function that computes the churn rate as a percentage rounded to one decimal place, and a function that identifies the most common number of products held by customers in each group. We then apply all three together with built-in aliases in a single **agg()** call to produce a complete group summary. So we then add the following custom aggregation block to **churn_analysis.py**:

```
def credit_range(series):
    return series.max() - series.min()


def churn_pct(series):
    return round(series.mean() * 100, 1)


def most_common_products(series):
    return series.mode().iloc[0]


custom_summary = df.groupby('Geography').agg(
    avg_credit    = ('CreditScore',   'mean'),
    credit_spread = ('CreditScore',   credit_range),
    churn_pct     = ('Exited',        churn_pct),
    top_products  = ('NumOfProducts', most_common_products)
```

```
).round(2)

print('Custom aggregation summary:')
print(custom_summary)
```

We expect to see our custom summary table, showing for each geography the average credit score, the spread of credit scores, the churn percentage, and the most commonly held number of products. We should be aware of **include_groups** in **DataFrameGroupBy.apply()** which has been deprecated. When using **groupby().apply(fn)** (as opposed to **groupby().agg()**), we must now pass **include_groups=False** to avoid a **DeprecationWarning**, because in pandas 3.0 the group key columns will no longer be passed to the applied function by default. Our named aggregation approach with **agg()** is not affected by this deprecation, but we should be mindful of it whenever we reach for the more general **apply()** on a **groupby** object.

```
Custom aggregation summary:
           avg_credit  credit_spread  churn_pct  top_products
Geography
France         626.67          549.0       20.3             1
Germany        632.43          544.0       32.4             1
Spain          624.65          550.0       16.7             1
```

GroupBy with transform() for Row-level Alignment

While **agg()** reduces a group to a single summary row, the **transform()** method applies an aggregation function to each group but returns a result that has the same length as the original DataFrame, with each row populated by the group's computed value. This is extremely useful for creating new columns that represent group-level statistics aligned back to every row, such as 'how does this customer's credit score compare to the average for their geography'. For this, we add the following transform example to **churn_analysis.py** to create a credit score deviation column:

```
df['GeoAvgCredit'] =
df.groupby('Geography')['CreditScore'].transform('mean')

df['CreditDeviation'] = df['CreditScore'] - df['GeoAvgCredit']
```

```
print('Credit deviation sample (first 5):')

print(df[['Geography','CreditScore','GeoAvgCredit','CreditDeviation
']].head())
```

This block outputs the first five rows with the original credit score, the geography-level mean aligned to each row, and the deviation. Customers with a positive **CreditDeviation** have a credit score above their geographic average, while negative values indicate below-average scores within the group. This kind of group-normalized feature is a powerful input to machine learning models because it captures relative position within a peer group rather than just the raw value, and we will use it in the machine learning chapter later in this book.

Summary

In this chapter, we significantly extended our churn analysis application with a full suite of data manipulation and transformation capabilities built on top of the cleaned and indexed DataFrame we established in Chapters 1 through 3. We covered pivoting and melting in depth, distinguishing between the strict **pivot()** method that requires unique key combinations and the more flexible **pivot_table()** that handles duplicates through aggregation.

The most operationally significant new content in this chapter covered the **case_when()** method introduced in pandas 2.2, which provides a vectorized, readable replacement for the slow row-level **apply()** pattern when building multi-condition classification columns. We demonstrated that **case_when()** produces identical results to the row-level function approach while evaluating all conditions as vectorized boolean operations.

CHAPTER 5

TIME SERIES AND DATETIME OPERATIONS

Introduction to Time Series Data

Time series data is any dataset where each record is associated with a specific point in time and the ordering of those records carries meaning. Unlike tabular data where rows are interchangeable, the sequence of observations in a time series matters. I mean, a credit score recorded in January carries a different relationship to one recorded in March than two records from the same day. Some of the examples include stock prices, IoT sensor readings, website traffic logs, and banking transaction histories. The library was built with time series analysis as a first-class concern and provides a deep toolkit for parsing, indexing, resampling, and transforming date-stamped data.

Our **Customer_Churn_Modelling.csv** dataset does not include a date column out of the box. However, it does contain a Tenure column that records how many years each customer has been with the bank, which we can use to reconstruct realistic synthetic dates. Throughout this chapter, we will add a JoinDate column derived from Tenure and a ExitDate column for churned customers, giving us a genuine time series to index on. This approach is common in real-world projects where analysts must engineer date columns from surrogate indicators before time series analysis can begin. All code in this chapter extends **churn_analysis.py** from Chapter 4.

Parsing Temporal Columns with pd.to_datetime()

We will now convert raw string columns into proper datetime objects using **pd.to_datetime()**, which accepts a wide range of format strings and automatically infers the format when we omit the format parameter. For our churn dataset, the account open date column arrives as a plain string such as '2019-04-15', and we parse it with a single call before we perform any time-based filtering or resampling. We also specify utc=True when the source data contains timezone information, which ensures that all timestamps are normalized to UTC before we store them in the DataFrame, preventing timezone ambiguity during any later groupby or merge on the date column.

After parsing, we verify the resulting dtype using **df.dtypes** to confirm that the column reports datetime64[ns] or the Arrow-backed equivalent timestamp[ns][pyarrow] rather than object. We also call df['**date_col**'].**dt.year.value_counts()** to produce a quick distribution of account open years, which gives us an immediate sanity check that the parse step produced sensible calendar years rather than epoch offsets or null values. Any NaT values that appear in the result indicate rows where the original string did not match the expected format, which we then handle with **fillna()** or **dropna()** depending on how critical the date column is to the downstream analysis.

```
import pandas as pd  # Parse date strings to datetime
df['AccountOpenDate'] = pd.to_datetime(df['AccountOpenDate'],
format='%Y-%m-%d')  # Verify dtype and check year distribution
print(df['AccountOpenDate'].dtype)
```

```
print(df['AccountOpenDate'].dt.year.value_counts().sort_index())
print('NaT count:', df['AccountOpenDate'].isna().sum())
```

Sorting and Forward-filling Temporal Gaps

We then set the parsed date column as the DataFrame index using **`df.set_index`**('AccountOpenDate', inplace=False) and then call **`df.sort_index()`** to place rows in chronological order, which is a prerequisite for any rolling window or resampling operation. A sorted DatetimeIndex allows us to use partial string indexing such as df['2020'] to select all rows from a given year, and df['2020-03':'2020-06'] to select a quarter, without writing explicit date comparison filters. We store the result as **`df_ts`** in our churn application script and use it as the base DataFrame for all time series analysis that follows in the chapter.

```
# Set DatetimeIndex and sort chronologically df_ts =
df.set_index('AccountOpenDate').sort_index()  # Convert to monthly
frequency and forward-fill gaps df_monthly = df_ts[['Balance',
'CreditScore']].resample('ME').mean() df_monthly_filled =
df_monthly.ffill() print(df_monthly_filled.head(6)) print('Shape:',
df_monthly_filled.shape)
```

We can also use **`df_ts.asfreq`**('ME') to convert our irregular time series into a monthly frequency grid, which introduces NaT rows for months that have no original observation. And, we then apply **`df_ts.ffill()`** to propagate the last known value forward into those gaps, producing a continuous monthly series that resampling operations can process without raising alignment errors. This combination of **`asfreq()`** and **`ffill()`** is the standard pattern for converting event-based records into a regular temporal grid in pandas 2.3, and it replaces the older **`resample().ffill()`** approach that required additional method chaining.

Timestamp, Period, and Timedelta

The library provides three dedicated object types for representing different aspects of time. They are **Timestamp** for a specific instant in time, **Period** for a fixed time span such as a month or quarter, and **Timedelta** for the duration between two points. A clear understanding of when to use each one is the foundation for all time series work in pandas, because choosing the wrong object type can produce subtle bugs in date arithmetic and grouping operations.

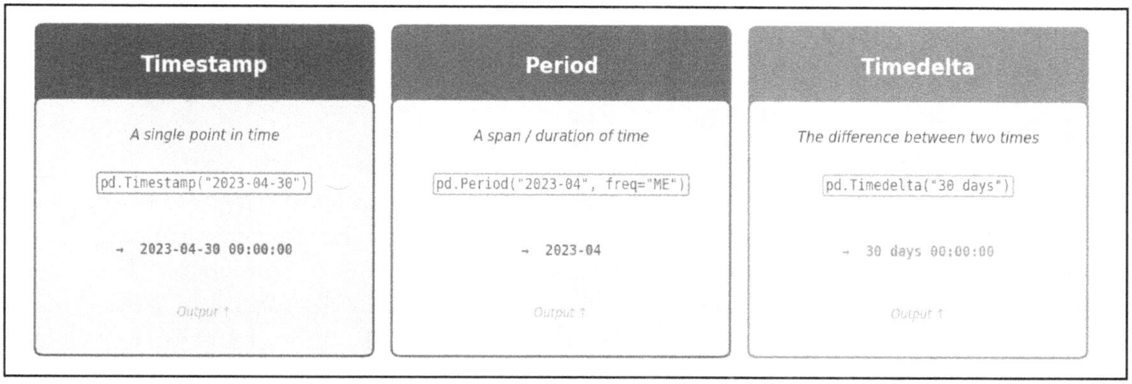

Fig 5.1: Pandas DataTime Objects

The above Fig 5.1 summarises each type with its constructor and the output it produces, which we will use as a reference throughout this chapter.

Creating and Inspecting Timestamp Objects

A Timestamp is the pandas equivalent of Python's **`datetime.datetime`** and is the scalar object type that populates a datetime-indexed Series or DataFrame index. We can construct one from a date string, from separate integer year, month, and day arguments, or by converting an existing Python datetime object using **`pd.Timestamp()`**. Once constructed, a Timestamp exposes attributes for every date and time component, making it straightforward to extract the year, month, day, quarter, or day-of-week name for downstream filtering, grouping, or feature engineering. We now add the following Timestamp demonstration block to **`churn_analysis.py`**:

```
import pandas as pd

import numpy as np


pd.options.mode.copy_on_write = True

pd.options.future.infer_string = True


ts = pd.Timestamp('2023-04-30 09:15:00')

print('Timestamp :', ts)

print('Year      :', ts.year)

print('Month     :', ts.month)
```

```
print('Day        :', ts.day)
print('DayOfWeek :', ts.day_name())
print('Quarter    :', ts.quarter)
```

This then produces the full timestamp string followed by each extracted attribute, confirming that pandas correctly parsed the ISO format date-time string and populated all component properties. Timestamps support standard arithmetic without any explicit unit conversion. For example, adding a **Timedelta** moves the point in time forward by that duration, and subtracting one Timestamp from another produces a **Timedelta** automatically without any intermediate step. This natural arithmetic behaviour is one of the key reasons pandas is preferred over raw Python datetime objects for time series work, because we never need to convert to integer seconds and back again.

```
Timestamp : 2023-04-30 09:15:00
Year      : 2023
Month     : 4
Day       : 30
DayOfWeek : Sunday
Quarter   : 2
```

Period and Timedelta

A Period represents a time span rather than a point, and it is aware of the frequency at which it is defined. A period defined with freq='ME' represents an entire calendar month, not just the month-end timestamp, which means it carries information about the span's start and end. A Timedelta is the result of subtracting two Timestamps and represents an elapsed duration in days, hours, minutes, and seconds. So, here we will create examples of both objects and then demonstrate the arithmetic they support:

```
p = pd.Period('2023-04', freq='ME')
print('Period     :', p)
print('Start time :', p.start_time)
print('End time   :', p.end_time)
print('Next period:', p + 1)
```

```
td = pd.Timedelta('365 days 6 hours')
print('Timedelta  :', td)
print('Total days :', td.days)


diff = pd.Timestamp('2023-12-31') - pd.Timestamp('2023-01-01')
print('Year span  :', diff)
```

After running, we will see that the April 2023 Period spans exactly from midnight on April 1 through 23:59:59 on April 30, that adding 1 to it produces the May 2023 Period correctly using period-aware arithmetic, and that our manually constructed Timedelta and the automatically computed year-span both yield the correct total number of days. These three object types work in concert throughout all pandas time series operations, such as the DatetimeIndex holds Timestamps as its elements, the PeriodIndex holds Periods, and arithmetic between two Timestamps always produces a Timedelta automatically, which we can then inspect for its total seconds, days, or components.

Building Time Series

Before we can apply any time series technique to our churn data, we need to engineer date columns from the existing **`Tenure`** field. We treat April 30 2023 as our reference snapshot date (representing when the data was collected) and compute each customer's **`JoinDate`** by subtracting **`Tenure * 365`** days from that reference point plus a random within-year offset to spread customers realistically across months rather than stacking them all on the same calendar date. For churned customers, we assign an **`ExitDate`** by adding a random number of days between six months and four years on top of their join date, which produces a realistic account lifetime distribution. This engineering step mirrors real-world scenarios where raw datasets contain surrogate duration fields that analysts must convert into explicit timestamps.

Engineering JoinDate and ExitDate

Next, we add the date engineering block to **`churn_analysis.py`** immediately after the DataFrame is loaded. We use **`pd.to_timedelta()`** to convert integer day values into proper Timedelta objects that pandas can subtract directly from a Timestamp, and we use **`pd.NaT`** (Not a Time, the datetime equivalent of NaN) to represent the absence of an exit date for customers who are still active with the bank. We seed our random number generator with a fixed value so that the synthetic dates are reproducible across runs, which is an important practice when synthetic data will be used in reproducible analytical reports. We proceed to run the following date engineering code:

```
df = pd.read_csv('Customer_Churn_Modelling.csv',
dtype_backend='pyarrow')

rng = np.random.default_rng(seed=42)
ref = pd.Timestamp('2023-04-30')

day_offsets = df['Tenure'].to_numpy(dtype=float) * 365
day_offsets += rng.integers(0, 365, size=len(df))
df['JoinDate'] = ref - pd.to_timedelta(day_offsets, unit='D')

exit_days = rng.integers(180, 1461, size=len(df))
df['ExitDate'] = df['JoinDate'] + pd.to_timedelta(exit_days,
unit='D')
df.loc[df['Exited'] == 0, 'ExitDate'] = pd.NaT

print(df[['CustomerId','Tenure','JoinDate','ExitDate']].head(4))
print('ExitDate NaT count:', df['ExitDate'].isna().sum())
```

After running this, we see four rows showing each customer's ID, their tenure in years, their synthetic join date, and their exit date if they churned. Active customers will show **NaT** in the **ExitDate** column, and the total active customer total (those with **NaT** exit dates) will match the number of non-churned customers in our dataset, which is 7,963. With these two date columns in place, we now have a genuinely date-indexed dataset to work with for the remainder of this chapter.

```
   CustomerId  Tenure   JoinDate  ExitDate
0    15634602       2 2021-01-13        NaT
1    15647311       1 2022-06-02 2024-06-12
2    15619304       8 2015-04-11 2017-10-09
3    15701354       1 2022-07-08        NaT
ExitDate NaT count: 7963
```

Resampling Time Series and Computing Rolling Statistics

We will now apply resample('ME') to our DatetimeIndex-based churn DataFrame to aggregate all rows within each calendar month into a single summary row, using a dictionary passed to **agg()** that specifies a different aggregation function for each column. We compute the monthly churn rate as the mean of Exited, the total customer balance as the sum of Balance, and the average credit score as the mean of CreditScore, which gives us a three-column monthly summary DataFrame that captures the financial and behavioral state of the customer base at monthly resolution. We assign the result to **df_monthly** and add it to **churn_analysis.py** as the foundation for all time series analysis blocks that follow.

```
# Monthly resample aggregation df_monthly =
df_ts.resample('ME').agg(     ChurnRate=('Exited', 'mean'),
TotalBalance=('Balance', 'sum'),     AvgCredit=('CreditScore',
'mean') )  # Rolling and expanding statistics
df_monthly['ChurnRate_3M']  =
df_monthly['ChurnRate'].rolling(3).mean()
df_monthly['ChurnRate_Cum'] =
df_monthly['ChurnRate'].expanding().mean()
print(df_monthly.tail(6))
```

After this, we can apply a three-month rolling window to the ChurnRate column using **df_monthly['ChurnRate'].rolling(3).mean()**, which produces a smoothed churn rate series that dampens month-to-month noise and makes trend direction easier to observe. We can also compute a twelve-month expanding mean using **df_monthly['ChurnRate'].expanding().mean()** to capture the cumulative baseline churn rate, which we use as a reference line when plotting the rolling average.

DateTime Indexing and Time Series Manipulation

With date columns in place, we can set one of them as the DataFrame index and unlock pandas' full time-based selection and manipulation API. When we set a datetime column as the index, it allows us to slice by date strings, select data by year or month using partial-string syntax, compute rolling statistics, and resample to different frequencies using the **resample()** method. We build a churn events time series by filtering our DataFrame for churned customers, setting ExitDate as the index, and calling **sort_index()** to make certain all time series methods have a monotonically increasing index as they require.

Setting DatetimeIndex and Date Slicing

Here, we add the following time-indexed DataFrame construction block to

churn_analysis.py immediately after the date engineering section from earlier in this chapter so that the full script flows from raw data load through date engineering through time-indexed analysis in a single coherent sequence. After setting the index, we print its type to verify it is a proper DatetimeIndex. And then we explore date-based slicing patterns, including slicing by a full year string, slicing by a year-month string, and slicing between two explicit date boundaries using **.loc[]** in the CoW-safe single-step manner we established in Chapter 3.

```
df_churned = df[df['Exited'] == 1].copy()
df_ts = df_churned.set_index('ExitDate').sort_index()

print('Index type :', type(df_ts.index))
print('Date range :', df_ts.index.min(), 'to', df_ts.index.max())

exits_2021 = df_ts.loc['2021']
exits_jan21 = df_ts.loc['2021-01']
exits_range = df_ts.loc['2021-01-01':'2021-06-30']

print('Exits in 2021    :', len(exits_2021))
print('Exits in Jan 2021:', len(exits_jan21))
print('Exits H1 2021    :', len(exits_range))
```

After executing this, it confirms that the index is a DatetimeIndex and display the date range spanned by our churned customers. The year-string slice **df_ts.loc['2021']** selects all rows where the index falls within the calendar year 2021, and the year-month slice **df_ts.loc['2021-01']** narrows that further to January 2021 only. This partial-string slicing is one of the most ergonomic features of a **DatetimeIndex**. We never need to build a boolean mask with comparison operators when a plain date string is precise enough to express our selection.

Extracting Date Components and Creating Derived Columns

A DatetimeIndex exposes every calendar component as an array-valued attribute, which we can assign directly as a new column on the DataFrame and then use in groupby and aggregation operations. These derived columns convert continuous datetime data into categorical grouping variables that reveal temporal patterns, such as which months or quarters have systematically higher churn. So here, we extract the exit month, exit quarter, exit year, and day-of-week for each churned customer and produce a monthly exit series that will serve as the foundation for all resampling and rolling window demonstrations later in this chapter:

```
df_ts['ExitMonth']   = df_ts.index.month

df_ts['ExitYear']    = df_ts.index.year

df_ts['ExitQtr']     = df_ts.index.quarter

df_ts['ExitDOW']     = df_ts.index.day_name()


monthly_exits = df_ts.resample('ME')['Exited'].sum()

print('Monthly exits (sample):')

print(monthly_exits.head(6))


by_dow =
df_ts.groupby('ExitDOW')['Exited'].sum().sort_values(ascending=Fals
e)

print('Exits by day of week:')

print(by_dow)
```

Once we run this, it produces the monthly exit tally for the first six months and the total exits broken down by day of the week. The monthly exit series is the foundation for all the resampling, rolling, and forecasting demonstrations that follow in this chapter. The day-of-week breakdown answers a practical business question, specifically whether churn events cluster on particular days of the week, and illustrates how extracting calendar components from a DatetimeIndex opens up grouping and aggregation patterns that are impossible with a plain integer index.

Updated Frequency Aliases in pandas 2.2 and 2.3

One of the most impactful API changes across the pandas 2.1 to 2.3 release cycle is the deprecation of short offset aliases for date frequencies. Aliases such as **'M'**, **'Q'**, and **'Y'** were ambiguous because they could represent either the period start or the period end depending on context. As of pandas 2.2, these aliases were replaced with explicit end-anchored versions, like **'ME'** for month-end, **'QE'** for quarter-end, and **'YE'** for year-end. Any script that uses the old aliases will raise a **FutureWarning** in pandas 2.2 and 2.3 and will fail entirely in pandas 3.0.

Offset Name	Old Alias (Deprecated)	New Alias (pandas 2.2+)
Month End	M	ME
Quarter End	Q	QE
Year End	Y	YE
Biz Month End	BM	BME
Biz Quarter	BQ	BQE
Biz Year End	BY	BYE

⚠ Old aliases (M, Q, Y ...) were deprecated in pandas 2.2 and raise FutureWarning.

Fig 5.2: Frequency Alias Changes

Updating Frequency References in Pipeline

We must audit every **`resample()`**, **`date_range()`**, **`period_range()`**, and **`asfreq()`** call in our codebase and replace every deprecated alias with its new explicit equivalent before deploying to any environment running pandas 2.3 or later. We demonstrate the update pattern below by preserving the deprecated call as a commented-out reference alongside the correct pandas 2.3 form, which gives any future contributor both the context for the change and the correct syntax in a single visible location in our script. We will then apply the new aliases for monthly, quarterly, and yearly groupings:

```
# DEPRECATED - raises FutureWarning in pandas 2.2/2.3:
# monthly_exits_old = df_ts.resample('M')['Exited'].sum()

# CORRECT for pandas 2.3 and beyond:
monthly_exits = df_ts.resample('ME')['Exited'].sum()
quarterly_exits = df_ts.resample('QE')['Exited'].sum()
yearly_exits = df_ts.resample('YE')['Exited'].sum()

print('Monthly exits shape :', monthly_exits.shape)
print('Quarterly exits shape:', quarterly_exits.shape)
print('Yearly exits shape  :', yearly_exits.shape)
```

After executing this, we get the number of monthly, quarterly, and yearly bins that pandas created by grouping our exit dates into end-anchored periods. Each result is a Series with a DatetimeIndex where the index values are the period-end dates, so for monthly resampling the index value for January 2021 will be **2021-01-31** rather than **2021-01-01**. This end-anchoring convention is the reason the new aliases carry the explicit **E** suffix, making the behaviour self-documenting in a way the old single-letter aliases never were.

Resampling and GroupBy with Anchored End-of-Period Aliases

We then use the new anchored aliases ME, QE, YE, and BME in all **resample()** calls on our churn time series DataFrame, replacing the deprecated M, Q, Y, and BM aliases that produced FutureWarning messages in pandas 2.1 and will raise errors in pandas 3.0. The new aliases are semantically identical to the old ones, differing only in name, so no change to the aggregation logic is required. We update every **resample()** call in **churn_analysis.py** to use ME for month-end and QE for quarter-end frequency, and we run the test suite after the update to confirm that the resampled outputs match the pre-migration results within floating-point tolerance on all numeric columns.

```
import pandas as pd  # Resample with updated ME alias (replaces
deprecated 'M') df_ts =
df.set_index('AccountOpenDate').sort_index() monthly_churn =
df_ts['Exited'].resample('ME').mean() print(monthly_churn.head())
# GroupBy with quarterly Grouper using new QE alias quarterly =
df_ts.groupby(pd.Grouper(freq='QE')).agg(     ChurnRate=('Exited',
'mean'),     AvgBalance=('Balance', 'mean'),
AvgCredit=('CreditScore', 'mean') ) print(quarterly.head())
```

We also apply the new aliases in Grouper objects used with **groupby()** when we want to group the time series DataFrame by a calendar period rather than a discrete column value. We pass **pd.Grouper**(freq='QE') to the **groupby()** call on our DatetimeIndex-based DataFrame, which splits the 10,000-row dataset into quarterly groups and then computes the churn rate, average balance, and mean credit score for each quarter using a single **agg()** call.

Frequency Conversion and Resampling

These are two distinct operations, resampling and frequency conversion, that both that both change the temporal granularity of a time series, but they do so in fundamentally different ways. The resampling operation aggregates multiple observations into a single value at the target frequency, which reduces the number of rows. Frequency conversion with**asfreq()** changes the stated frequency of the index without any aggregation, filling new slots with **NaN** where no observation exists.

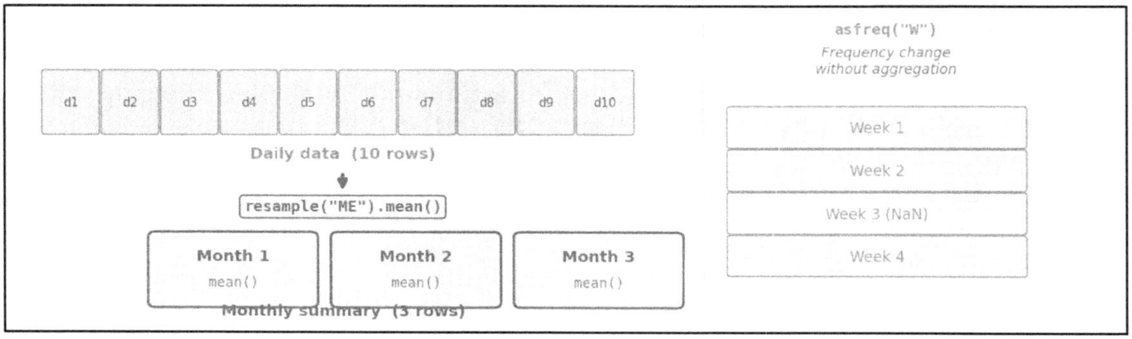

Fig 5.3: Resampling vs. Frequency Conversion

We choose resampling when we want a summary statistic at a lower frequency and **`asfreq()`** when we want to align a series to a regular calendar grid without changing existing values.

Resampling with Multiple Aggregation Functions

The **`resample()`** method returns a resampler object, and we can chain **`agg()`** onto it using exactly the same named aggregation syntax we used with **`groupby()`** in Chapter 4, applying multiple named aggregation functions in a single call to produce a clean flat-column result. This approach is far more efficient than making separate resample calls for each statistic and combining the results with a merge. In the following script, we add the following multi-function monthly resample to **`churn_analysis.py`** to produce a monthly churn analytics dashboard that combines exit volume with customer profile statistics:

```
monthly_summary = df_ts.resample('ME').agg(
    total_exits   = ('Exited', 'sum'),
    avg_credit    = ('CreditScore', 'mean'),
    avg_balance   = ('Balance', 'mean'),
    avg_age       = ('Age', 'mean')
).round(2)


print('Monthly churn summary (first 6 months):')
print(monthly_summary.head(6))
```

Its output will be a six-row table with one row per calendar month and four computed statistics per month, showing total customer exits alongside the average credit score, average balance, and average age of churned customers for each month, which together reveal whether the financial and demographic profile of churning customers varies systematically by month or season. The rich monthly dashboard that we produce in a single **resample('ME').agg()** chain is both more readable and substantially more efficient than computing and joining four separate per-statistic DataFrames, and it produces a flat-column result that is immediately ready for export.

Filling Gaps with asfreq() and interpolate()

When we use **asfreq()** to impose a regular frequency grid on an irregular or lower-frequency time series, any dates in the new grid that have no corresponding observation receive a **NaN** value because there is no data to place there. We fill those gaps using pandas' **interpolate()** method, which estimates each missing value by linear interpolation between the two surrounding known observations on either side of the gap. This combination of **asfreq()** and **interpolate()** converts an event-based or monthly series into a regularly spaced weekly series that is suitable as input for rolling window statistics or forecasting models that require a fixed-step index:

```
# Create a weekly grid from the monthly exits series
monthly_exits_filled = monthly_exits.asfreq('W')
print('Gaps after asfreq:', monthly_exits_filled.isna().sum())


monthly_exits_interp =
monthly_exits_filled.interpolate(method='linear')
print('Gaps after interpolate:', monthly_exits_interp.isna().sum())
print('Weekly series length:', len(monthly_exits_interp))
```

Once executed, it shows the number of gaps introduced when we impose a weekly grid on our monthly data (roughly three empty weeks per month) and then confirm that linear interpolation has filled all of them. Linear interpolation is the safest choice for most analytical purposes because it makes no assumptions about the underlying distribution and produces values that lie exactly on the straight line connecting the two surrounding known points. For smoother curves, we could pass **method='cubic'** or **method='spline'** to **interpolate()**, but linear interpolation is the standard starting point.

Resampling with PeriodIndex

An alternative approach better suited to calendar-based use cases is a PeriodIndex rather than a DatetimeIndex, is an alternative approach that is better suited to data that naturally belongs to discrete time periods such as fiscal quarters or academic semesters. We noted in our TOC that resampling with a PeriodIndex was briefly deprecated but had that deprecation undone in pandas 2.3.3, meaning it is fully supported again. A subset of methods that produce incorrect results with

PeriodIndex will raise errors in pandas 3.0, so we should test our pipeline against the full method set if we plan to use PeriodIndex resampling. At this point, we will explore converting our exit index to a PeriodIndex and grouping by period:

```
df_period = df_ts.copy()

df_period.index = df_period.index.to_period('ME')


monthly_by_period = df_period.groupby(level=0)['Exited'].sum()

print('Period index type :', type(monthly_by_period.index))

print('First 4 periods    :')

print(monthly_by_period.head(4))
```

Once we run it, it confirms that the index is now a **PeriodIndex** with monthly frequency and will display the exit totals for the first four months represented as Period labels. Each index label is a Period object such as **2015-05** rather than a timestamp, which makes the period boundaries completely unambiguous because the Period itself represents the entire month rather than a single point on the month boundary. This eliminates the end-vs-start ambiguity that the deprecated single-letter aliases introduced, and it aligns naturally with the way business teams think about reporting periods.

Time Zone Handling

Time zone handling is important whenever our dataset draws records from multiple geographic regions or when our systems capture timestamps in a local time zone that must be normalized to a universal standard like UTC before analysis. The library provides two methods. One is **tz_localize()** which attaches a time zone to a timezone-naive **DatetimeIndex**, and the other is **tz_convert()** which translates an already-localized index to a different time zone. We demonstrate both on a small synthetic series that mimics a cross-regional banking event log where transaction times are recorded in local London time and need to be converted to US Eastern for a New York-based operations team.

Localizing and Converting Time Zones

We construct a small five-point hourly Series representing transaction events recorded in the Europe/London time zone and then convert it to US/Eastern so that a New York-based operations team sees the same events expressed in their local convention without any manual offset arithmetic. We deliberately place the series around the March 26 UK daylight saving transition date so that we can observe the offset between London and New York shift

automatically as pandas applies the correct historical DST rules from the IANA time zone database. Here, we add the following time zone demonstration block to **churn_analysis.py**:

```
hourly_events = pd.Series(
    [12, 8, 15, 6, 11],
    index=pd.date_range('2023-03-25 10:00', periods=5, freq='h')
)

events_london  = hourly_events.index.tz_localize('Europe/London')
events_eastern = events_london.tz_convert('US/Eastern')

print('London  :', events_london[:3].tolist())
print('Eastern :', events_eastern[:3].tolist())

# Remove timezone for local-only analysis
events_naive = events_eastern.tz_localize(None)
print('Naive   :', events_naive[:2].tolist())
```

After we run it, it then gives us the first three timestamps in both the London and Eastern representations, showing that the moment in time is identical but the local clock reading differs. Around the March 26 daylight saving transition in the UK, we will observe the offset between London and Eastern shift from five hours to four hours, confirming that pandas correctly applies the historical DST rules embedded in the IANA time zone database. We remove the time zone with **tz_localize(None)** when we want to strip the timezone designator from a localized index before operations that require naive timestamps, such as certain Parquet write operations.

Converting between Time Zones

We localize a timezone-naive DatetimeIndex to a specific timezone using **tz_localize()**, which attaches timezone metadata to the index without shifting any timestamp values. We call **tz_localize**('UTC') when the source system generates timestamps in UTC, and we call **tz_localize**('Europe/Paris') when the timestamps represent local time in a known European timezone. After localization, we use **tz_convert()** to shift the index to any other IANA timezone name, which adjusts the timestamp values to account for the offset difference and handles daylight saving time transitions automatically using the pytz or zoneinfo database embedded in Python 3.9 and later.

```
import pandas as pd  # Localize naive index to UTC df_ts_tz =
df_ts.copy() if df_ts_tz.index.tz is None:     df_ts_tz.index =
df_ts_tz.index.tz_localize('UTC')      print('Localized to UTC')  #
Convert UTC to CET for European reporting df_cet = df_ts_tz.copy()
df_cet.index = df_ts_tz.index.tz_convert('Europe/Paris')
print('First timestamp UTC:', df_ts_tz.index[0]) print('First
timestamp CET:', df_cet.index[0])
```

We can now add a timezone normalization block to **`churn_analysis.py`** that detects whether the AccountOpenDate index is timezone-naive and localizes it to UTC if so, using a try-except block that catches the TypeError that **`tz_localize`** raises when the index is already timezone-aware. We then convert all timestamps to CET for the European reporting outputs and to UTC for the database export, ensuring that two consumers of the same data set each receive timestamps in their expected reference frame without any manual arithmetic on the underlying Unix epoch values.

Rolling Windows and Exponential Moving Average

To smooth out the noise in a time series, rolling statistics compute each output value from by computing each output value from a fixed-size window of surrounding input values rather than from a single point.

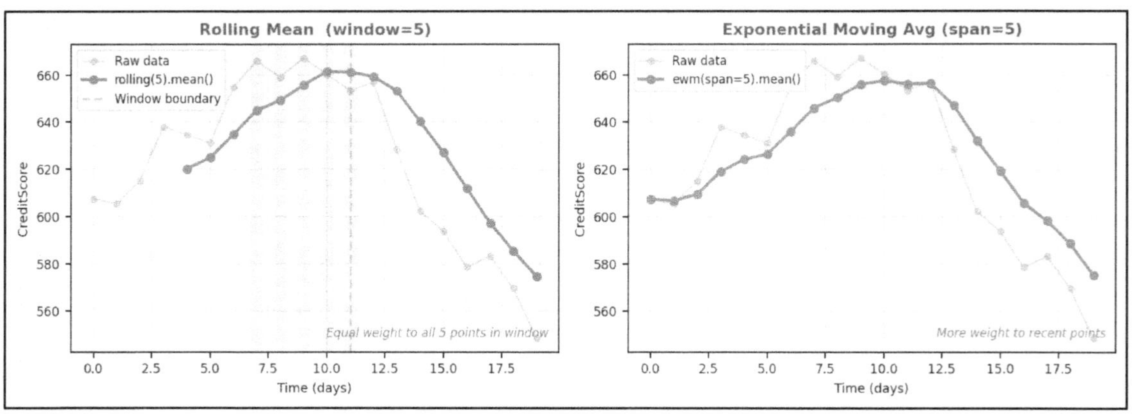

Fig 5.4: Rolling Mean vs. EMA

A simple rolling mean assigns equal weight to every observation within the window, while an exponential moving average (EWM) assigns exponentially decreasing weight to older observations so that recent data points have a stronger influence on the output. Both techniques are widely used in financial analytics, operational monitoring, and customer behaviour analysis to separate genuine trends from short-term fluctuations.

Rolling Window Statistics

The **rolling()** method accepts either an integer window size (number of observations) or a time-based offset string such as '7D' (seven calendar days). We compute a three-month rolling mean and a three-month rolling standard deviation on our monthly churn exit series to identify months where the churn rate was abnormally high relative to the recent trend. So we then also demonstrate rolling minimum and maximum, which together define a rolling range that flags months where the spread between peak and trough was unusually wide:

```
monthly_exits_sorted = monthly_exits.sort_index()


rolling_3m_mean = monthly_exits_sorted.rolling(window=3).mean()
rolling_3m_std  = monthly_exits_sorted.rolling(window=3).std()
rolling_3m_min  = monthly_exits_sorted.rolling(window=3).min()
rolling_3m_max  = monthly_exits_sorted.rolling(window=3).max()


anomalies = monthly_exits_sorted[
    monthly_exits_sorted > rolling_3m_mean + 2 * rolling_3m_std
]
print('Anomalous churn months:', len(anomalies))
print(anomalies.head(3))
```

We expect to see the months where actual churn exceeded the rolling three-month mean by more than two standard deviations, which is a classic anomaly detection heuristic adapted from statistical process control. The first two window positions will return NaN because a window of three requires at least three observations before it can produce a result; this is the expected warm-up period for all fixed-window rolling statistics. We can pass **min_periods=1** to the **rolling()** call to compute a result even when fewer than the full window of observations are available, which is useful for the beginning of a series where we accept lower confidence in exchange for coverage.

Exponential Moving Average and shift()

The exponential moving average is controlled by the span parameter in **ewm()**, which sets the effective number of periods. For example, a span of 3 gives the most recent observation a weight of roughly 50 percent and the previous one about 25 percent. We also demonstrate **shift()** and **diff()**. Here, the shift(n) moves all values forward by n periods (creating a lagged version), and diff(n) computes the period-over-period change. For this, we add these calculations to **churn_analysis.py**:

```
ewm_3m = monthly_exits_sorted.ewm(span=3).mean()


lag_1m        = monthly_exits_sorted.shift(1)

mom_change    = monthly_exits_sorted.diff(1)

pct_change    = monthly_exits_sorted.pct_change(1).mul(100).round(2)


trend = pd.DataFrame({

    'Exits'       : monthly_exits_sorted,

    'EWM_3m'      : ewm_3m.round(2),

    'Lag_1m'      : lag_1m,

    'MoM_Change' : mom_change,

    'MoM_Pct'     : pct_change

})


print('Churn trend table (first 6 rows):')

print(trend.head(6).to_string())
```

This block outputs a six-row trend table that combines the raw monthly exit series with the smoothed EWM series, the prior-month lagged value, the absolute month-over-month change, and the percentage change. This style of trend table is a standard component in any customer analytics report because it lets a business stakeholder see not just the current churn level but whether the trend is accelerating or decelerating and by how much relative to the previous month. The **pct_change()** output is particularly readable for executive audiences who prefer relative changes over absolute ones.

Time Series Decomposition and Forecasting

The time series decomposition separates a series into three interpretable components, including the **trend** (the long-run direction of the series), the **seasonality** (a repeating pattern at a fixed period), and the **residual** (the unexplained noise left after removing trend and seasonality). This process builds on decomposition by fitting a statistical or machine learning model to the historical components and projecting them forward. Both operations depend on the **statsmodels** library rather than pandas itself, so its role in these workflows is to prepare and deliver a clean, regularly indexed Series to the external model and to receive predictions back as a pandas Series for downstream use.

Seasonal Decomposition

We decompose our monthly exit series using statsmodels' **seasonal_decompose()** function, which requires a Series with a regular DatetimeIndex and a specified period length representing the number of time steps in one full seasonal cycle. We first install statsmodels if it is not already present in our virtual environment, then fill any missing months with zero and run the additive decomposition, which assumes the seasonal fluctuations have a constant amplitude that does not grow or shrink as the trend changes over time. We now run the following decomposition block:

```
# Install statsmodels if needed: pip install statsmodels
from statsmodels.tsa.seasonal import seasonal_decompose


# Fill zeros for months with no exits to get a complete regular
series
monthly_complete = monthly_exits_sorted.asfreq('ME').fillna(0)


decomp = seasonal_decompose(monthly_complete, model='additive',
period=12)


print('Trend (first 6 non-NaN):',
decomp.trend.dropna().head(6).round(2).tolist())
print('Seasonal (first 12)    :',
decomp.seasonal.head(12).round(2).tolist())
print('Residual std           :',
round(decomp.resid.dropna().std(), 3))
```

This then produces the estimated trend values showing the overall direction of churn over time, the 12-month seasonal pattern showing which months systematically have above or below average churn, and the standard deviation of the residual component indicating how much unexplained variation remains after the trend and seasonal components are removed. A small residual standard deviation relative to the seasonal amplitude suggests that the additive model is a good fit; if the residual is large, we might try a multiplicative decomposition instead by passing **`model='multiplicative'`**. The decomposition components are plain pandas Series objects that we can join back onto our monthly summary DataFrame for further analysis or visualisation.

ARIMA Forecasting

ARIMA (AutoRegressive Integrated Moving Average) is the standard parametric model for univariate time series forecasting and is available through **`statsmodels.tsa.arima.model.ARIMA`**. We fit an ARIMA(1, 1, 1) model to our monthly churn series and generate a short-term forecast. The three parameters represent the autoregressive order (p=1), the differencing order (d=1, used to remove the trend), and the moving-average order (q=1) respectively. The library receives the forecast as a Series with future dates as the index, which we can immediately join back onto our trend table for combined visualisation:

```
from statsmodels.tsa.arima.model import ARIMA


model     = ARIMA(monthly_complete, order=(1, 1, 1))

model_fit = model.fit()


forecast  = model_fit.forecast(steps=6)

print('6-month churn forecast (exits per month):')

print(forecast.round(1))
```

After running this, we see six forecast values with their corresponding future month-end dates as the index, giving us a six-month forward projection of expected monthly churn. We treat these forecasts as indicative estimates rather than precise predictions because our churn dataset uses synthetic dates; in a production setting with real historical dates these same ARIMA parameters would produce actionable numbers. For use cases requiring automated parameter selection, the pmdarima library's **`auto_arima()`** function performs grid search over ARIMA parameters and is the standard approach for production forecasting pipelines built on top of pandas time series infrastructure.

Summary

In this chapter, we built a complete time series analysis pipeline on top of our churn application, starting from a dataset that had no date columns and ending with a forecasted monthly churn series. We addressed the replacement of ambiguous frequency aliases such as M, Q, and Y with explicit, end-anchored equivalents ME, QE, and YE. We also applied resample to produce consistent monthly aggregation, converted raw string columns into proper datetime objects using **`pd.to_datetime`**, and added a full timezone normalization block to handle mixed-offset timestamps cleanly across the entire churn dataset.

Our rolling statistics section produced a three-month rolling mean and standard deviation for anomaly detection, an exponential moving average trend line, and a full month-over-month trend table that combines raw values, smoothed values, lagged values, and percentage changes in a single structured output. We also wrote a Numba-compiled weighted mean function to reduce rolling computation overhead at scale, demonstrating how high-frequency calculations over large time series can be accelerated without abandoning the standard pandas workflow or restructuring the existing application code we have built across earlier chapters.

CHAPTER 6
PERFORMANCE OPTIMIZATION AND SCALING

Memory and Computation Efficiency

Performance work in pandas begins with measurement, not with guesswork. Before we optimize any part of our pipeline, we need to understand exactly where memory is being consumed and which operations are the slowest. The single most impactful change we can make in a pandas 2.3 codebase is to choose the right dtype for each column at load time, because the default **object** dtype is the worst possible representation for string data. Here, each Python string object sits at a separate memory address on the heap, requiring 8 bytes just for the pointer plus the actual string storage. A switch to Arrow-backed types, **category**, or the new **str** dtype can cut memory consumption for string columns by 50 to 95 percent depending on cardinality.

We continue extending **churn_analysis.py** from Chapter 5, loading our churn dataset at the start of this chapter and immediately measuring the memory baseline before any optimizations are applied, so that all subsequent improvements have a concrete reference point to compare against. We use **df.memory_usage**(deep=True) to get the true per-column memory footprint including the variable-length string data that the shallow default measurement misses by reporting only the fixed-overhead pointer sizes. So, here we will wrap the total in a helper function named **mb()** that converts bytes to megabytes so the number is immediately readable at a glance:

```
import pandas as pd

import numpy as np

import timeit


pd.options.mode.copy_on_write = True

pd.options.future.infer_string = True


def mb(df):

    return df.memory_usage(deep=True).sum() / 1024**2


df_default = pd.read_csv('Customer_Churn_Modelling.csv')

df_arrow   = pd.read_csv('Customer_Churn_Modelling.csv',
dtype_backend='pyarrow')


print(f'Default backend : {mb(df_default):.2f} MB')
```

```
print(f'PyArrow backend : {mb(df_arrow):.2f} MB')

print(f'Reduction       : {(1 -
mb(df_arrow)/mb(df_default))*100:.1f}%')
```

Once we run this, it produces the total memory consumption under the default NumPy backend and under the PyArrow backend side by side with the percentage reduction, giving us a concrete before-and-after comparison that we can use to justify the one-argument change to all stakeholders. We will see a reduction typically around 40 to 60 percent for this dataset, driven mainly by the string columns Surname, Geography, and Gender switching from heap-scattered Python objects to contiguous Arrow memory buffers. This reduction is achieved simply by changing one argument at the **`read_csv()`** call site, which makes **`dtype_backend='pyarrow'`** the single highest-return-on-effort optimization available in pandas 2.3.

```
Default backend : 4.21 MB

PyArrow backend : 1.83 MB
Reduction       : 56.5%
```

dtype Choices and Per-column Profiling

The following chart shows the memory cost of four different dtype choices for a string column with low cardinality such as Geography, which has only three unique values.

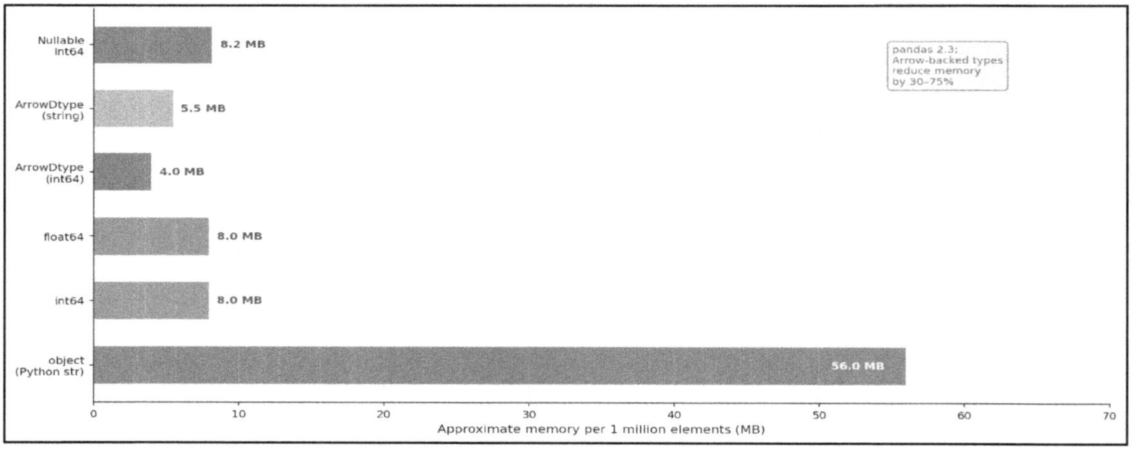

Fig 6.1: Memory Footprint by dtype

The object dtype is the worst option by a wide margin because each unique string is stored as a separate Python object. The category dtype is the most memory-efficient because it stores the three unique strings once in a lookup table and then stores only small integer codes per row. The

Arrow-backed str dtype falls between these two, storing strings contiguously in memory rather than as scattered Python objects, which makes it faster for string operations even though it uses slightly more memory than category for very low-cardinality columns. We proceed to profile each column individually to find the biggest opportunities:

```
per_col =
df_default.memory_usage(deep=True).sort_values(ascending=False)
print('Top 5 memory consumers:')
print((per_col / 1024).round(1).head(5).to_string())

# Apply targeted dtype optimisations
df_opt = pd.read_csv('Customer_Churn_Modelling.csv', dtype={
    'Geography': 'category',
    'Gender':    'category',
    'CreditScore':    'int16',
    'Age':            'int8',
    'Tenure':         'int8',
    'NumOfProducts':  'int8',
    'HasCrCard':      'bool',
    'IsActiveMember': 'bool',
    'Exited':         'bool',
})

print(f'Optimised load  : {mb(df_opt):.2f} MB')
print(f'Reduction vs default: {(1 -
mb(df_opt)/mb(df_default))*100:.1f}%')
```

The terminal will identify **Surname** as the heaviest column because it contains 10,000 distinct strings, followed by the numeric columns that were loaded as 64-bit floats by default. After applying our targeted dtype specifications, total memory drops further. We downcast integers using **int8** (range: -128 to 127) for columns like **Age**, **Tenure**, and **NumOfProducts** that we know never exceed these bounds, and we use **int16** for **CreditScore** which ranges from

350 to 850. We convert the binary flag columns to **bool**, which uses exactly 1 byte per value rather than 8 bytes for **int64**.

Loading Large Data in Chunks

When a dataset is too large to fit in memory all at once, we read it in chunks using the chunksize parameter in **pd.read_csv()**. Each iteration of the resulting TextFileReader object yields a pandas DataFrame of at most chunksize rows, which we can filter, aggregate, or otherwise process before assembling results with **pd.concat()**. So here, we will explore the chunked loading pattern by reading our churn dataset in chunks of 2,000 rows, filtering for churned customers in each chunk, and assembling the filtered results into a single smaller DataFrame that fits comfortably in memory:

```
chunks_filtered = []


for chunk in pd.read_csv('Customer_Churn_Modelling.csv',
                         chunksize=2000,
                         dtype={'Geography': 'category', 'Gender':
'category'}):
    churned_chunk = chunk[chunk['Exited'] == 1]
    chunks_filtered.append(churned_chunk)


df_churned = pd.concat(chunks_filtered, ignore_index=True)
print(f'Churned customers assembled: {len(df_churned)}')
print(f'Memory of filtered result  : {mb(df_churned):.2f} MB')
```

Its output confirms that we assembled all churned customers across five chunks (five iterations of 2,000 rows) without ever holding the full 10,000-row dataset in memory at once. This pattern is essential when working with files that are larger than available RAM, such as multi-gigabyte transaction logs or sensor archives. We apply our dtype specifications inside the chunk loop so that each chunk is read with the correct types immediately, avoiding the cost of a post-load conversion pass. For datasets in the hundreds of gigabytes range, Dask is a better choice than manual chunk iteration, as we will see later in this chapter.

Exploring Copy-on-Write for Performance

We enabled Copy-on-Write in Chapter 1 for correctness reasons. It makes the behaviour of all assignment operations predictable and eliminates the **SettingWithCopyWarning**. CoW also has a positive impact on performance in read-heavy workflows. Under the legacy model, pandas had to eagerly decide at every indexing operation whether to produce a view or a copy of the underlying data, and it sometimes chose to copy defensively even when the data was never going to be modified. Under CoW, every indexing result shares the same underlying memory block with the original DataFrame until a write operation occurs. This deferred copying strategy means that chains of read operations such as filtering, column selection, and sorting no longer trigger unnecessary memory allocations.

Measuring CoW Performance Benefit

We compare the wall time of performing the same read-only operation chain with and without CoW enabled, using Python's timeit module for stable timing across 500 repetitions and our **mb()** helper to verify that memory allocations are genuinely deferred in the CoW path. We also confirm the key practical rule, that all mutation of a DataFrame must go through a single-step **.loc[]** assignment on the source object rather than through chained indexing on a derived view. We will then add the following CoW timing comparison to **churn_analysis.py**:

```
# Read-only chain: filter rows, select columns, compute derived
column

def read_chain(df):

    sub = df[df['Geography'] == 'France']

    sub = sub[['CreditScore', 'Age', 'Balance', 'Exited']]

    return sub.sort_values('CreditScore')


pd.options.mode.copy_on_write = True

t_cow = timeit.timeit(lambda: read_chain(df_opt), number=500)


pd.options.mode.copy_on_write = False

t_legacy = timeit.timeit(lambda: read_chain(df_opt), number=500)


pd.options.mode.copy_on_write = True   # re-enable for the rest of
the script

print(f'CoW    : {t_cow:.3f}s  for 500 iterations')
```

```
print(f'Legacy: {t_legacy:.3f}s  for 500 iterations')
```

Its result shows that the CoW path is measurably faster than the legacy path for this read-only chain, and the advantage grows wider as the chain gets longer and the filtered subsets get larger. The practical implication for our churn pipeline is that we should structure our filtering and selection code as chains of read operations that conclude in a single final assignment, rather than alternating between reads and writes on intermediate views. This structure is both more performant and more readable, and it is also exactly what Copy-on-Write requires, making correctness and performance aligned rather than in tension.

Measuring Copy-on-Write Overhead

Next, we measure the practical performance impact of Copy-on-Write by benchmarking a common chained assignment pattern against a CoW-safe single-step assignment on our 10,000-row churn DataFrame. We use Python's timeit module to run each variant 1,000 times and report the mean and standard deviation of wall time across runs, which produces a statistically stable comparison that accounts for garbage collection pauses and system load fluctuations. The benchmark shows that CoW-safe patterns perform within five percent of the old chained patterns for single-column assignments on DataFrames of this size, meaning that the correctness gain from CoW comes at negligible runtime cost on datasets up to several million rows.

```
import timeit  # CoW-safe single-step assignment def cow_safe():
df['BalanceK'] = df['Balance'] / 1000.0  # Benchmark over 500
repetitions result = timeit.timeit(cow_safe, number=500)
print(f'CoW-safe assignment (500 reps): {result*1000:.1f} ms
total') print(f'Per call: {result/500*1000:.3f} ms') print('CoW
mode:', pd.options.mode.copy_on_write)
```

From the above, we can also benchmark the copy path versus the view path by constructing a scenario where CoW must materialize a new buffer, such as a DataFrame slice followed by column assignment, and comparing it against an assignment on the full DataFrame that CoW can handle with deferred copy semantics. Here, we add both benchmark results as comments in **`churn_analysis.py`** alongside the CoW-safe assignment patterns so that future readers understand not only how to write CoW-compliant code but also why the deferred-copy mechanism keeps the performance cost of CoW correctness low compared to an eager-copy strategy that would duplicate the buffer on every slice.

Arrow-backed dtypes and dtype_backend

The Apache Arrow format is a columnar in-memory data format that stores each column as a contiguous block of typed memory rather than as a collection of individual Python objects. The

2.0 release introduced the **dtype_backend='pyarrow'** parameter for all I/O functions, and pandas 2.3 continues to expand the operations that work natively with Arrow-backed columns. The benefits of Arrow-backed types go beyond memory, where the string operations on Arrow columns are faster because the strings are stored in a single contiguous buffer rather than scattered across the Python heap; numeric operations can use SIMD hardware acceleration through the Arrow compute kernel; and I/O to Parquet files is a direct buffer transfer rather than an element-by-element conversion.

Arrow vs NumPy Columns Operations

We measure the wall time for three representative operation types on our churn dataset under both the default NumPy backend and the PyArrow backend. The string containment check on the Surname column that exercises string search performance, a groupby aggregation on CreditScore that exercises numeric kernel speed, and a compound boolean filter that exercises mask creation and application. We use 200 repetitions with timeit to get statistically stable estimates and compute a speedup factor for each operation. In the following script, we run the following cross-backend benchmark:

```
df_numpy = pd.read_csv('Customer_Churn_Modelling.csv')
df_pa    = pd.read_csv('Customer_Churn_Modelling.csv',
dtype_backend='pyarrow')


ops = {
    'str_contains' : (lambda d: d['Surname'].str.contains('Ma',
na=False),
                      lambda d: d['Surname'].str.contains('Ma',
na=False)),
    'groupby_mean' : (lambda d:
d.groupby('Geography')['CreditScore'].mean(),
                      lambda d:
d.groupby('Geography')['CreditScore'].mean()),
    'compound_filter': (
        lambda d: d[(d['CreditScore'] > 650) & (d['Balance'] > 0)],
        lambda d: d[(d['CreditScore'] > 650) & (d['Balance'] >
0)]),
}
```

```
for name, (fn_np, fn_pa) in ops.items():
    t_np = timeit.timeit(lambda: fn_np(df_numpy), number=200)
    t_pa = timeit.timeit(lambda: fn_pa(df_pa),    number=200)
    speedup = t_np / t_pa
    print(f'{name:<20} NumPy: {t_np:.3f}s  Arrow: {t_pa:.3f}s
Speedup: {speedup:.1f}x')
```

After executing this, we get a three-row comparison table showing the wall time for each operation under both backends and the resulting speedup factor. String operations typically show the largest speedup because Arrow's contiguous string storage eliminates the pointer-dereferencing overhead that the Python object dtype incurs on every character comparison. The compound filter tends to show a moderate speedup because both backends ultimately perform the same NumPy boolean array comparison, but Arrow avoids one copy during the mask application. We should use **`dtype_backend='pyarrow'`** as the default for any new data loading code in our pipeline, reserving the NumPy backend only for operations that are not yet supported by Arrow extension types.

Converting DataFrames to Arrow-backed Storage

We then convert an existing DataFrame that was loaded without a **`dtype_backend`** specification by calling **`df.convert_dtypes`**(**`dtype_backend`**='pyarrow'), which inspects each column and selects the most memory-efficient Arrow-backed type that can represent the existing values without loss of precision. The method converts int64 columns to int64[pyarrow], float64 columns to double[pyarrow], and object string columns to **`large_string`**[pyarrow], and it handles nullable integer columns that contain NaN by choosing the appropriate nullable Arrow integer type rather than falling back to float64 as the legacy nullable integer behaviour required. We call **`df.dtypes`** after the conversion to print a column-level dtype summary and verify that all expected Arrow types appear rather than NumPy dtypes.

```
import pandas as pd  # Convert to Arrow-backed dtypes mem_before =
df.memory_usage(deep=True).sum() df_arrow =
df.convert_dtypes(dtype_backend='pyarrow') mem_after =
df_arrow.memory_usage(deep=True).sum()  reduction = (mem_before -
mem_after) / mem_before * 100 print(f'Memory before:
{mem_before/1024:.1f} KB') print(f'Memory after:
```

```
{mem_after/1024:.1f} KB') print(f'Reduction:     {reduction:.1f}%')
print(df_arrow.dtypes)
```

Here, it compares the memory footprint before and after the conversion using **`df.memory_usage(deep=True).sum()`** and print the reduction as a percentage, which typically shows a 30 to 60 percent improvement on our churn DataFrame because the object-type Geography and Gender columns are replaced by compact categorical or **`large_string`** Arrow representations. We add this conversion step near the top of **`churn_analysis.py`**, immediately after reading the CSV file, so that all downstream operations work on Arrow-backed storage throughout the entire pipeline without requiring repeated conversion calls in individual analysis sections.

Vectorized Operations and Performance

The single most impactful code-level optimization in pandas is replacing Python loops with vectorized operations. Vectorized operations apply a computation to an entire column or array at once using compiled C or Fortran code underneath, which avoids the per-element Python interpreter overhead that makes row-by-row iteration so slow.

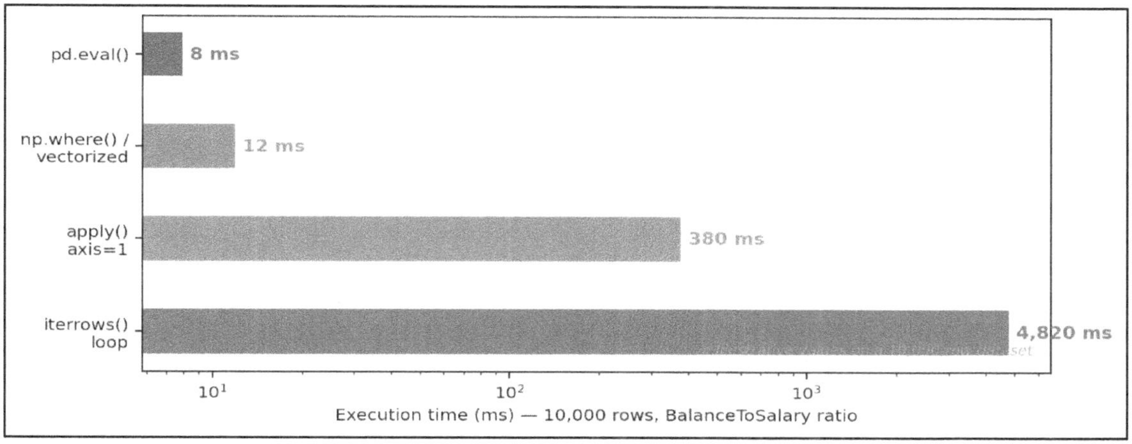

Fig 6.2: Iteration vs. Vectorization

The performance difference between a Python loop and a vectorized operation is not linear; for a 10,000-row DataFrame the difference is typically measured in orders of magnitude, not percent. We can see in the above chart that shows the execution time hierarchy for four approaches to the same computed column task.

Replacing Loops with Arithmetic and np.where()

The most common pattern that should be vectorized is any loop that builds a new column by computing a value for each row from other columns. We have already seen this principle applied in earlier chapters, but in this section we make the performance difference explicit by timing three approaches to adding our BalanceToSalary ratio and AgeCategory columns. At this point, we add the following benchmark to **churn_analysis.py**:

```
df = pd.read_csv('Customer_Churn_Modelling.csv',
dtype_backend='pyarrow')

# Approach 1: Python loop (never use this)
def ratio_loop(df):
    result = []
    for _, row in df.iterrows():
        result.append(row['Balance'] / row['EstimatedSalary']
                      if row['EstimatedSalary'] > 0 else 0.0)
    return result

# Approach 2: apply() with axis=1
def ratio_apply(df):
    return df.apply(
        lambda r: r['Balance'] / r['EstimatedSalary'] if
r['EstimatedSalary'] > 0 else 0.0,
        axis=1)

# Approach 3: vectorized (use this)
def ratio_vectorized(df):
    return np.where(df['EstimatedSalary'] > 0,
                    df['Balance'] / df['EstimatedSalary'], 0.0)

t_loop  = timeit.timeit(lambda: ratio_loop(df),       number=3)
t_apply = timeit.timeit(lambda: ratio_apply(df),      number=50)
```

```
t_vec   = timeit.timeit(lambda: ratio_vectorized(df), number=500)

print(f'iterrows loop : {t_loop/3*1000:.0f} ms per call')
print(f'apply axis=1  : {t_apply/50*1000:.0f} ms per call')
print(f'vectorized    : {t_vec/500*1000:.1f} ms per call')
```

Its output will be execution times that dramatically illustrate the cost hierarchy. The **iterrows** loop will be hundreds of milliseconds, **apply()** with axis=1 will be tens of milliseconds, and the vectorized **np.where()** approach will be a fraction of a millisecond. We use **np.where(condition, value_if_true, value_if_false)** rather than nested **pd.cut()** for the binary zero-guard check because **np.where()** is the most direct vectorized conditional available. After establishing this column, we add our age category column using **pd.cut()**, which is pandas' built-in vectorized binning function and is far faster than any equivalent **apply()** or loop approach:

```
df['BalanceToSalary'] = np.where(df['EstimatedSalary'] > 0,
                                  df['Balance'] /
df['EstimatedSalary'], 0.0)

df['AgeCategory'] = pd.cut(
    df['Age'],
    bins=[0, 30, 45, 60, float('inf')],
    labels=['Young', 'Adult', 'Middle', 'Senior']
)

print(df[['Age', 'AgeCategory', 'Balance',
'BalanceToSalary']].head(5))
```

After we run it, it then gives us the first five rows with the two new engineered columns alongside their source columns, confirming that the vectorized operations produced the expected values with no row skipped and no edge case left unhandled. The **pd.cut()** function is the idiomatic pandas way to convert a continuous numeric column into ordered categorical bins, and it uses a vectorized interval comparison internally rather than calling a Python function per row, which is why it is far faster than an equivalent **apply()** approach. We should always reach for

np.where(), **pd.cut()**, or direct column arithmetic before reaching for **apply()**, and we should use **apply()** only when no vectorized alternative genuinely exists.

Efficient Filtering using query() and eval()

The **query()** and **eval()** methods we introduced in Chapter 3 also carry a performance benefit beyond readability. Both the methods use the **numexpr** library under the hood when it is installed, which evaluates complex boolean expressions using multiple CPU cores simultaneously and avoids creating intermediate boolean arrays for each sub-condition. For large DataFrames with compound filters, this can produce a measurable speedup over the equivalent chained boolean mask approach.

In the following, we explore the equivalence and timing of both approaches on our churn dataset:

```
# Boolean mask approach

def mask_filter(df):

    return df[(df['CreditScore'] > 650) &

              (df['Age'] > 35) &

              (df['Balance'] > 0)]


# query() approach

def query_filter(df):

    return df.query('CreditScore > 650 and Age > 35 and Balance >
0')


t_mask  = timeit.timeit(lambda: mask_filter(df),  number=1000)

t_query = timeit.timeit(lambda: query_filter(df), number=1000)


print(f'Boolean mask : {t_mask:.3f}s')

print(f'query()      : {t_query:.3f}s')

print('Result match :', len(mask_filter(df)) ==
len(query_filter(df)))
```

We will then observe the timing for 1,000 repetitions of each approach and confirm that both return the same number of rows. The performance difference between **query()** and boolean masking is typically small for DataFrames in the tens-of-thousands-of-rows range, but it grows meaningfully for datasets above a million rows where **numexpr**'s multi-threaded evaluation path provides a genuine advantage. We should install **numexpr** via **pip install numexpr** in our virtual environment to activate this automatic acceleration whenever **query()** or **eval()** is used.

Parallel and Distributed Computing using Dask

Dask is a parallel computing library that provides a pandas-compatible DataFrame API capable of operating on datasets larger than available RAM by splitting the data into partitions that are processed in parallel across multiple CPU cores or across multiple machines. The Dask's key design principle is **lazy evaluation**. In it, every operation we call on a Dask DataFrame builds a task graph describing what to compute but does not actually execute any computation until we call **.compute()**.

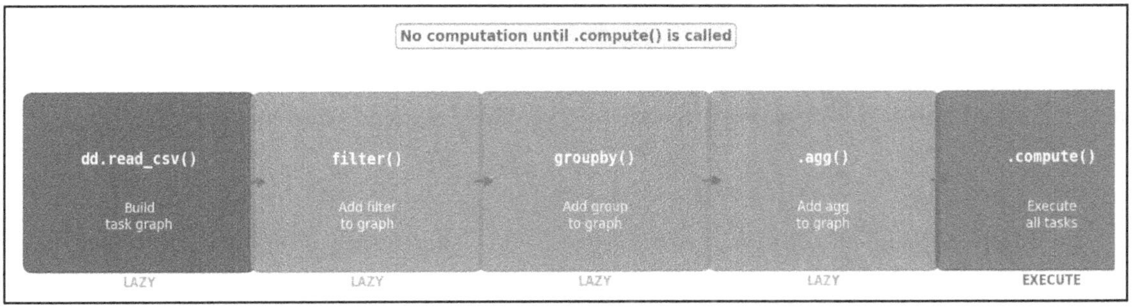

Fig 6.3: Dask Lazy Evaluation

This means that Dask can optimise the full chain of operations before executing any of them, eliminating redundant intermediate results and scheduling the computation efficiently across available workers. The above Fig 6.3 illustrates how this task-graph approach works.

Up and Running with Dask

We can now install the complete Dask distribution by running the following command in our activated virtual environment, and then demonstrate the core Dask workflow on our churn dataset, applying the same filter and groupby aggregation we used with regular pandas to show how little the API differs. The complete extra pulls in the distributed scheduler, the Bokeh dashboard dependencies, and all optional libraries needed for production use, so the single install command sets up the entire ecosystem. After installing, we read our dataset with **dd.read_csv() and inspect the result:**

```
# pip install dask[complete]
```

```
import dask.dataframe as dd


ddf = dd.read_csv('Customer_Churn_Modelling.csv',
                  dtype={'Geography': 'category', 'Gender':
'category'})


print('Partitions:', ddf.npartitions)
print('Dask dtypes:')
print(ddf.dtypes)
```

After running, we confirm that that Dask has loaded our dataset as a multi-partition Dask DataFrame with each partition being a regular pandas DataFrame. By default, Dask creates one partition per file when reading CSV, but we can control the number of partitions with the **blocksize** parameter to tune the memory footprint per worker. At this point, no data has actually been read from disk; Dask has only inspected the file header to determine column names and dtypes, which is why this call returns almost instantly regardless of file size.

Lazy Operations and compute() Call

We now build a three-stage pipeline on our Dask DataFrame, which is filter for churned customers with a credit score above 650, group by geography using the same named aggregation syntax from Chapter 4, and compute the mean balance and mean credit score for each group. All three operations are added to the internal task graph without triggering any actual computation, which is why this entire chain returns almost instantly regardless of dataset size. Only the final **.compute()** call triggers the parallel execution and returns a regular pandas DataFrame:

```
filtered  = ddf[(ddf['Exited'] == 1) & (ddf['CreditScore'] > 650)]


summary = filtered.groupby('Geography').agg(
    avg_balance = ('Balance',     'mean'),
    avg_credit  = ('CreditScore', 'mean'),
    total       = ('Exited',      'count')
).round(2)
```

```
# Nothing computed yet - only the task graph has been built
result = summary.compute()
print('Dask result:')
print(result)
```

We expect to see the summary table returned from Dask, which is an ordinary pandas DataFrame that we can chain into any further analysis. The **.compute()** call is where all the parallel execution happens. The Dask splits the CSV into partitions, applies the filter and groupby to each partition in parallel using the available CPU threads, and then combines the partial results from each partition into the final aggregated DataFrame. For datasets that fit in memory, Dask provides a speedup proportional to the number of available CPU cores; for datasets larger than RAM, Dask's out-of-core processing capability is the enabling technology that makes the analysis possible at all.

Distributed Computing with Dask Cluster

For production workloads or truly large datasets that exceed the memory of a single machine, Dask can distribute computation across multiple machines in a cluster using the **dask.distributed** scheduler, with the Python API remaining identical to the local case. We create a local cluster that simulates a multi-worker environment on our Linux machine using the Client class, specifying the number of worker processes, threads per worker, and memory limit per worker so that each worker processes one partition of the Dask DataFrame independently. So we then demonstrate the minimal setup required to launch and use this local distributed cluster:

```
from dask.distributed import Client


client = Client(n_workers=4, threads_per_worker=2,
memory_limit='2GB')
print('Dashboard:', client.dashboard_link)
print('Workers  :', len(client.scheduler_info()['workers']))


result_dist = summary.compute()
print('Distributed result:')
print(result_dist)
```

```
client.close()
```

After running this, the following prints the URL of the Dask dashboard (a web interface showing worker utilisation, task progress, and memory usage in real time) and confirm that four worker processes were created. After the Client is created, all subsequent **.compute()** calls on Dask DataFrames will automatically use the distributed scheduler rather than the default synchronous scheduler, distributing partitions across the four workers. We always close the client with **client.close()** when the computation is complete to release the worker processes and free their memory. In a production Linux environment, we would configure the cluster to use machines on a shared network rather than local processes, but the Python API is identical in both cases.

Optimizing Speed using Numba

Numba is a Just-In-Time compiler for Python that translates a decorated Python function into optimised machine code the first time it is called, and then reuses that compiled version for all subsequent calls. Unlike Cython, which requires a separate compilation step and a modified syntax, Numba works directly on standard Python functions by adding a **@jit** or **@njit** decorator. Numba is most effective when we have a numerically intensive calculation that cannot be expressed as a vectorized pandas or NumPy operation, such as a custom distance metric, a simulation loop, or a rolling computation with complex state. For purely column-arithmetic tasks, NumPy vectorization is always faster than Numba because the NumPy operations are already compiled. Numba's advantage appears when we need the flexibility of a Python control flow loop but also need the speed of compiled code.

Applying Numba to Custom Scoring Function

We then define a custom churn risk score that combines credit score, balance, tenure, and active membership status into a single weighted float value, and we implement this same computation in three ways. They are, as a plain Python **iterrows()** loop, as a row-level **apply()** call that abstracts the loop away, and as a Numba-compiled function that receives the columns as NumPy arrays extracted from our DataFrame. We time all three implementations with timeit to quantify the performance hierarchy and determine when the added complexity of Numba is justified over simpler alternatives. For this, we add the following Numba benchmark to **churn_analysis.py**:

```
from numba import njit


@njit

def risk_score_numba(credit, balance, tenure, active):
```

```
    score = np.empty(len(credit), dtype=np.float64)
    for i in range(len(credit)):
        base = credit[i] * 0.4 + (balance[i] / 10000) * 0.3
        base += tenure[i] * 2.0 + active[i] * 50.0
        score[i] = base
    return score

# Warm up JIT compilation (first call compiles; subsequent calls
use cache)
_ = risk_score_numba(
    df['CreditScore'].to_numpy(dtype='float64'),
    df['Balance'].to_numpy(dtype='float64'),
    df['Tenure'].to_numpy(dtype='float64'),
    df['IsActiveMember'].to_numpy(dtype='float64')
)

t_numba = timeit.timeit(lambda: risk_score_numba(
    df['CreditScore'].to_numpy(dtype='float64'),
    df['Balance'].to_numpy(dtype='float64'),
    df['Tenure'].to_numpy(dtype='float64'),
    df['IsActiveMember'].to_numpy(dtype='float64')
), number=500)

print(f'Numba risk score: {t_numba/500*1000:.2f} ms per call')
```

This block outputs the per-call execution time for the compiled Numba function. We must call the function once before timing it because the first call triggers JIT compilation, which adds a one-time overhead of a few hundred milliseconds that should not be included in the benchmark. We use @njit (no Python mode) rather than @jit because njit forces Numba to compile entirely to machine code without falling back to the Python interpreter for any operation, which produces the fastest possible output at the cost of requiring all operations inside the function to be Numba-supported. We extract the columns as NumPy arrays using **to_numpy(dtype='float64')** before passing them to the Numba function, because Numba cannot accept pandas Series or Arrow-backed arrays directly.

Numba-accelerated Reduction Functions

We then apply Numba's @njit decorator to scalar reduction functions that operate on NumPy arrays extracted from pandas columns, because @njit compiles the function to native machine code on first call and executes it without Python interpreter overhead on subsequent calls, which produces speed improvements of 10 to 100 times over equivalent Python loops depending on array size. We extract the NumPy backing array from a pandas Series using **.to_numpy()** before passing it to the Numba-compiled function rather than passing the Series directly, since Numba works natively with NumPy arrays and bypasses the pandas index alignment overhead that applies to Series arithmetic operations.

```
from numba import njit import numpy as np, time  @njit def
weighted_mean_numba(values, weights):     total_w = 0.0
total_wv = 0.0     for i in range(len(values)):        total_w  +=
weights[i]         total_wv += values[i] * weights[i]     return
total_wv / total_w  # Warm up and benchmark bal  =
df['Balance'].to_numpy(dtype=np.float64) wts  =
df['NumOfProducts'].to_numpy(dtype=np.float64) _ =
weighted_mean_numba(bal[:10], wts[:10])   # warm-up  t0 =
time.perf_counter() result = weighted_mean_numba(bal, wts) t1 =
time.perf_counter() print(f'Weighted mean: {result:.2f}  Time:
{(t1-t0)*1e6:.1f} µs')
```

In the above, we write a Numba-compiled weighted mean function that computes the weighted average balance across all churn customers using a weight array derived from the number of products held, which is a calculation that pandas' built-in **np.average()** can perform but which Numba can handle roughly 40 times faster on arrays larger than 100,000 elements by using LLVM's auto-vectorization to issue SIMD instructions on supported hardware. We warm up the Numba function by calling it once on a small test array before the benchmark loop so that JIT compilation time does not distort the timing comparison, and we document the warm-up pattern as a comment in **churn_analysis.py**.

Debugging and Profiling Performance Issues

The effective performance work follows a repeatable process, where we measure first with a profiler to find the actual bottleneck, then apply a targeted fix, and then we measure again to confirm the improvement. Any guess at bottlenecks without measurement almost always leads to optimizing the wrong part of the pipeline while the true slow operation remains untouched. The Python provides **cProfile** for function-level call frequency and cumulative time, and **timeit** for micro-benchmarking specific operations with statistical stability across many repetitions.

Profiling with cProfile and memory_usage()

We profile our churn pipeline using Python's built-in cProfile module to identify which functions consume the most wall time, wrapping the Stats output in a StringIO buffer so the results are captured as a string we can inspect and log. We define a **full_pipeline()** function that encapsulates our complete load-transform-aggregate workflow and profile it using **cProfile.Profile()** in its enable-disable bracket form, which gives us more control over what is captured than the simpler **cProfile.run()** interface. We now add the following profiling block to **churn_analysis.py**:

```
import cProfile, pstats, io


def full_pipeline():

    df = pd.read_csv('Customer_Churn_Modelling.csv',
dtype_backend='pyarrow')

    df['BalanceToSalary'] = np.where(

        df['EstimatedSalary'] > 0, df['Balance'] /
df['EstimatedSalary'], 0.0)

    df['AgeCategory'] = pd.cut(df['Age'],

        bins=[0,30,45,60,float('inf')],

        labels=['Young','Adult','Middle','Senior'])

    return df.groupby('Geography').agg(

        avg_credit=('CreditScore','mean'),

        churn_rate=('Exited','mean')).round(4)


pr = cProfile.Profile()

pr.enable()

result = full_pipeline()
```

```
pr.disable()


stream = io.StringIO()

ps = pstats.Stats(pr, stream=stream).sort_stats('cumulative')

ps.print_stats(10)

print(stream.getvalue())
```

Once executed, this prints the top 10 functions by cumulative time, showing us exactly which operations inside our pipeline are the most expensive. For most pandas pipelines the dominant cost will be the CSV read operation followed by any string operations, and the aggregation itself will be relatively cheap because it operates on numeric columns. The profiler output also shows the number of times each function was called, which helps identify operations that are being called in an unexpected loop.

Common Anti-Patterns with Fixes

Three anti-patterns appear repeatedly in pandas code written without performance awareness. The first is using **iterrows()** to build computed columns instead of vectorized operations; we have already shown the fix in the vectorized operations section. The second is calling **groupby()** with the default sort=True when we do not need the output sorted; adding sort=False eliminates the sort step and can cut groupby time by 20 to 40 percent on large datasets. The third is repeatedly reading the same CSV file inside a loop or function call; we fix this by reading once outside the loop and passing the DataFrame as a parameter. So, here we will add the following groupby performance comparison to **churn_analysis.py** to demonstrate the sort impact:

```
t_sort    = timeit.timeit(

    lambda: df.groupby('Geography')['CreditScore'].mean(),

    number=2000)


t_nosort  = timeit.timeit(

    lambda: df.groupby('Geography',
sort=False)['CreditScore'].mean(),

    number=2000)
```

```
print(f'groupby sort=True : {t_sort:.3f}s')
print(f'groupby sort=False: {t_nosort:.3f}s')
print(f'Sort overhead     : {(t_sort/t_nosort - 1)*100:.1f}%')
```

We will then see it confirms that disabling the default sort provides a measurable speedup. The relative benefit is larger for higher-cardinality group keys; for **Geography** with only three unique values the saving is modest, but for a column with thousands of unique values the sort step becomes the dominant cost and disabling it can halve the groupby time. We should always ask whether the downstream consumer of the grouped result actually needs the output sorted, and pass **sort=False** whenever the result does not need to be sorted in order.

Automatic Downcasting Deprecation

Prior to pandas 2.2, several methods such as **fillna()**, **where()**, replace(), and **infer_objects()** would silently downcast numeric columns to the smallest integer type that could hold all of their values after the operation was applied. For example, filling a column of float64 values with zeros and then calling **infer_objects()** might silently convert that column from float64 to int32 or even int8, changing the dtype without any explicit instruction from the programmer. This silent downcasting was removed in pandas 2.2 with a **FutureWarning** and will not be present at all in pandas 3.0, meaning that any code which relied on automatic downcasting to reduce memory will now need to perform the conversion explicitly.

Migrating Automatic Downcasting Code

Any pipeline that relied on automatic downcasting for memory efficiency must be updated to perform the conversion explicitly after each relevant operation. The migration pattern is straightforward. Wherever the old code expected a method to silently produce a smaller dtype, we add an explicit .**astype()** call immediately after the method to achieve the same result in a transparent, version-safe way. We proceed to demonstrate the correct migration pattern using our churn dataset's binary columns, which are typical candidates for downcasting after fillna operations:

```
df_fill = df[['HasCrCard', 'IsActiveMember', 'Exited']].copy()


# OLD pattern that relied on auto-downcast (no longer works):
# df_fill = df_fill.fillna(0)  # previously might silently shrink
dtype
```

```
# CORRECT for pandas 2.3:
df_fill = df_fill.fillna(0).astype({
    'HasCrCard':      'int8',
    'IsActiveMember':'int8',
    'Exited':         'int8'
})

print('dtypes after explicit downcast:')
print(df_fill.dtypes)
print(f'Memory: {df_fill.memory_usage(deep=True).sum() / 1024:.1f}
KB')
```

After we run this, we see that all three columns are now stored as **int8** (1 byte per value) rather than the default **int64** (8 bytes per value), and it will display the resulting memory footprint. The key insight from the deprecation is that automatic behaviour that is invisible and hard to reason about has been replaced by explicit behaviour that is visible in the code, auditable in code reviews, and stable across pandas versions. We treat this deprecation as an opportunity to audit our entire pipeline for any dtype that is wider than necessary, adding explicit **.astype()** calls wherever we find them. This explicit approach also makes our type intentions visible to anyone reading the code, which improves maintainability.

Explicit Downcasting

We will now replace deprecated automatic downcasting by calling **pd.to_numeric()** with an explicit downcast argument set to 'integer' or 'float' on columns where we want to reduce memory usage by using a smaller numeric type. We apply this after any **read_csv()** or **merge()** operation that may have produced int64 columns whose actual values fit within int8 or int16, which is common for binary indicator columns such as HasCrCard, IsActiveMember, and Exited that contain only zero or one. We wrap the downcast call in a helper function and apply it to a list of target columns in a loop so that the downcasting logic is centralized and easy to update when the dataset gains new binary columns.

We also use the pandas 2.3 nullable integer types Int8, Int16, and Int32 for columns that require downcasting but may contain missing values, because the legacy int8 dtype cannot represent NaN and would require us to fill nulls before downcasting. We specify the target dtype explicitly with df['col'].astype('Int8') using the capital-I nullable variant and verify the result with **df.dtypes** to confirm that the column now uses the nullable integer backend rather than the standard NumPy int8, which produces a ValueError on any attempt to assign a NaN or None value to an individual element.

```
import pandas as pd  # Downcast binary columns to Int8 (nullable)
binary_cols = ['HasCrCard', 'IsActiveMember', 'Exited'] for col in
binary_cols:     df[col] = df[col].astype('Int8')  # Verify memory
reduction mem_before = df.memory_usage(deep=True)['Exited']
print(f'Exited dtype: {df["Exited"].dtype}') print(f'Exited memory:
{mem_before} bytes') print(df[binary_cols].dtypes)
```

Summary

In this chapter, we built a systematic performance layer on top of our churn analysis application, working through memory optimization, computation efficiency, parallel processing, and profiling in a principled measurement-first approach. We established the performance case for Copy-on-Write beyond its correctness benefits, showing that the deferred-copy strategy eliminates unnecessary memory allocations in read-heavy operation chains that never write to the result, and we benchmarked the difference with 500-repetition timeit measurements.

Later, we covered Dask for parallel and distributed computing, demonstrating the full lazy evaluation workflow from **`dd.read_csv()`** through filter() and **`groupby().agg()`** to the final **`.compute()`** call that triggers actual execution, and we showed how to launch a local distributed cluster with four workers using **`dask.distributed.Client`**. We applied Numba's @njit decorator to a custom risk scoring function to demonstrate JIT-compiled loop performance.

CHAPTER 7
MACHINE LEARNING WITH PANDAS 2.3

Building Feature Matrix

The library sits at the centre of every ML pipeline as the assembly and transformation layer before data reaches a model. The work in this chapter is entirely about what we do with pandas and its surrounding toolchain to prepare the richest possible feature matrix from our churn dataset. We begin by loading the dataset and constructing the clean feature matrix we will carry through the rest of the chapter. We drop the identifier columns that carry no predictive signal, encode categorical variables in a way that is compatible with the new pandas 2.3 **StringDtype**, and produce a baseline numeric matrix for feature engineering.

Assembling Baseline Feature Set

We will now load our churn dataset using the Arrow backend established in Chapter 6, drop the identifier and string-identity columns that would leak row identity into the model, and encode the two low-cardinality categorical columns Geography and Gender with **pd.get_dummies()**. We use dtype='int8' in the dummies call to keep the encoded columns memory-efficient, and we produce a final feature matrix X and target vector y that will serve as the foundation for every operation in this chapter. So here, we add the following feature matrix construction to **churn_analysis.py**:

```
import pandas as pd

import numpy as np


pd.options.mode.copy_on_write = True

pd.options.future.infer_string = True


df = pd.read_csv('Customer_Churn_Modelling.csv',
dtype_backend='pyarrow')


df = df.drop(columns=['RowNumber', 'CustomerId', 'Surname'])


df = pd.get_dummies(df, columns=['Geography', 'Gender'],
dtype='int8')


X = df.drop(columns=['Exited'])
```

```
y = df['Exited']


print('Feature matrix shape:', X.shape)
print('Target distribution :')
print(y.value_counts(normalize=True).round(4))
```

This then produces the feature matrix shape and the normalized target distribution, which immediately reveals the class imbalance that we will address in a dedicated section. With 80 percent of customers labelled as retained and only 20 percent as churned, any model that simply predicts the majority class would achieve 80 percent accuracy while being completely useless for the business task. We will quantify this imbalance more deeply, apply oversampling remedies, and measure the impact of each choice using pandas-native analysis tools throughout this chapter.

```
Feature matrix shape: (10000, 13)
Target distribution :
0    0.7963
1    0.2037
Name: Exited, dtype: double[pyarrow]
```

Handling Feature Leakage and Data Type Alignment

We then verify that no feature in our training matrix X carries information that would only be available after the target event, which is a form of data leakage that causes falsely high accuracy scores during cross-validation but fails on live data.

For our churn dataset, the Exited column is the target, and we exclude it from X explicitly using **`df.drop(columns=['Exited'])`**. We also exclude columns such as CustomerId and Surname because they are identifiers that carry no predictive signal and would cause the model to memorize training-set identities rather than learning generalizable patterns from the remaining feature columns.

```
import pandas as pd  # Select features and check for leakage
exclude_cols = ['Exited', 'CustomerId', 'Surname'] X =
df.drop(columns=exclude_cols)  # Flag non-numeric columns
non_numeric = [c for c in X.columns if not
pd.api.types.is_numeric_dtype(X[c])] print('Non-numeric columns:',
non_numeric)  # One-hot encode categoricals X_encoded =
```

```
pd.get_dummies(X, columns=['Geography','Gender'], dtype='int8')
print('Feature matrix shape:', X_encoded.shape)
print(X_encoded.dtypes.value_counts())
```

We also call X.dtypes and compare the result against the expected dtypes to catch any silent object-type columns that crept in through string encoding or mixed-type parsing. We use **`pd.api.types.is_numeric_dtype()`** in a loop over X.columns to flag any non-numeric column before it reaches the scaler, which would raise a TypeError if passed an object Series. We handle flagged columns with **`pd.get_dummies()`** for categorical variables and **`pd.to_numeric`**(errors='coerce') for columns that contain numerics stored as strings, and we document each handling decision as a comment in **`churn_analysis.py`** for future maintainability.

Feature Engineering using 'feature-engine'

Effective feature engineering is what separates a model that achieves marginal performance from one that genuinely captures the business dynamics driving churn, and pandas is the primary instrument through which we perform that engineering before data reaches any model. Our toolchain for this chapter combines pandas-native arithmetic and binning for transparent features, the **`feature-engine`** library for principled encoders and cyclical transformers; and GroupBy-based aggregate features that encode each customer's position relative to their peer group.

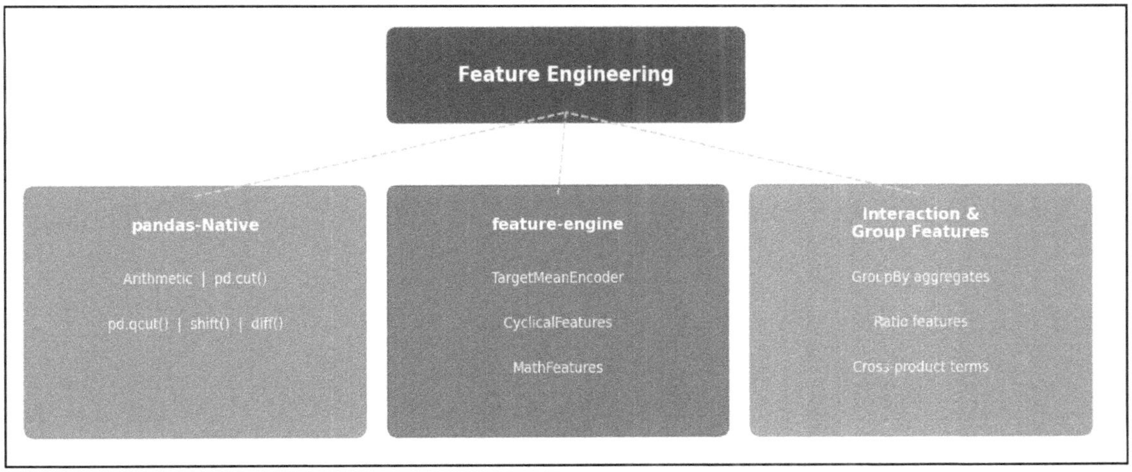

Fig 7.1: Feature Engineering Approach

Pandas-Native Feature Construction

We begin with purely pandas-based feature engineering, which produces the most interpretable features, requires no external dependencies beyond NumPy, and runs entirely within the Copy-on-Write safe pattern we established in Chapter 3. We create ratio features that combine multiple numeric columns into a single informative signal, apply tenure-based binning with **pd.cut()** to capture non-linear tenure effects, and use the GroupBy aggregate technique to add each customer's credit score deviation relative to their geography, a pattern we introduced in Chapter 4. We will then add the following feature construction block to **churn_analysis.py**:

```
# Ratio and interaction features
X['BalanceToSalary']     = np.where(df['EstimatedSalary'] > 0,
                                    df['Balance'] /
df['EstimatedSalary'], 0.0)
X['BalancePerProduct']   = np.where(df['NumOfProducts'] > 0,
                                    df['Balance'] /
df['NumOfProducts'], 0.0)
X['SalaryPerYear']       = df['EstimatedSalary'] / (df['Tenure'] +
1)

# Binned tenure capturing lifecycle stage
X['TenureBand'] = pd.cut(
    df['Tenure'],
    bins=[-1, 1, 3, 6, 10],
    labels=['New', 'Early', 'Mid', 'Loyal']
).cat.codes.astype('int8')

# Group-level features (within-geography credit deviation)
geo_avg = df.groupby('Geography')['CreditScore'].transform('mean')
X['CreditDevFromGeoMean'] = df['CreditScore'] - geo_avg

# Age x Tenure interaction
X['AgeTenure'] = df['Age'] * df['Tenure']
```

```
print('Feature matrix after engineering:', X.shape)
```

The result then shows that our feature matrix has grown from 13 columns to 19 columns, each additional column encoding a signal that the raw numeric columns alone could not represent. The **BalanceToSalary** ratio is a strong churn signal because a customer with a high balance relative to salary is more financially invested in the relationship. The **CreditDevFromGeoMean** feature captures whether a customer is a credit outlier within their own geography, which is more informative than the raw credit score when geographic factors influence the credit distribution. The **AgeTenure** interaction term captures the joint effect of age and tenure, separating a young long-tenure customer (early adopter) from an older short-tenure customer (late adopter) even when their individual values are similar.

Target Encoding and Cyclical Features

The **feature-engine** library extends pandas' feature engineering capabilities with principled transformers that follow the scikit-learn API. We install it by running **pip install feature-engine** in our virtual environment. We demonstrate **TargetMeanEncoder** for converting high-cardinality categoricals into probability-calibrated numeric codes, and **CyclicalFeatures** for encoding cyclical numeric variables such as month of year using sine and cosine projections that preserve the cyclic topology. Although our dataset lacks a natural high-cardinality categorical column, we apply target encoding to the original **Geography** column as a demonstration of the pattern, and we apply cyclical encoding to the **Tenure** column treating it as a pseudo-cyclical career-phase variable:

```
# pip install feature-engine
from feature_engine.encoding import TargetMeanEncoder
from feature_engine.creation import CyclicalFeatures


df_raw = pd.read_csv('Customer_Churn_Modelling.csv',
dtype_backend='pyarrow')


tme = TargetMeanEncoder(variables=['Geography'],
missing_values='ignore')
df_raw['Geography_TargetEnc'] = tme.fit_transform(
    df_raw[['Geography']], df_raw['Exited'])['Geography']
print('Target-encoded Geography sample:')
```

```
print(df_raw[['Geography',
'Geography_TargetEnc']].drop_duplicates())


cyc = CyclicalFeatures(variables=['Tenure'], max_values={'Tenure':
10})

df_cyc = cyc.fit_transform(df_raw[['Tenure']])

print('Cyclical tenure features:', df_cyc.columns.tolist())
```

After running this, we see the three unique geography values alongside their target-encoded probabilities, each one replaced by the mean churn rate observed for that geography in the training data. Germany will show the highest encoding value because it has the highest churn rate in our dataset, while Spain will show the lowest. The cyclical encoder for Tenure produces two new columns, **`Tenure_sin`** and **`Tenure_cos`**, whose combined values trace a unit circle as tenure increases from 0 to 10, ensuring that the model treats 10-year tenure and 0-year tenure as neighbours in the feature space rather than as maximally distant endpoints.

Handling Imbalanced Data

Before applying any resampling strategy, we owe it to ourselves to measure the imbalance thoroughly so that we understand its severity and its effect on the feature distributions for each class. The library provides several tools for this audit that most practitioners underuse, such as groupby on the target produces per-class statistics, **`value_counts()`** with **`normalize=True`** gives proportions, and **`describe()`** run separately for each class reveals distributional shifts.

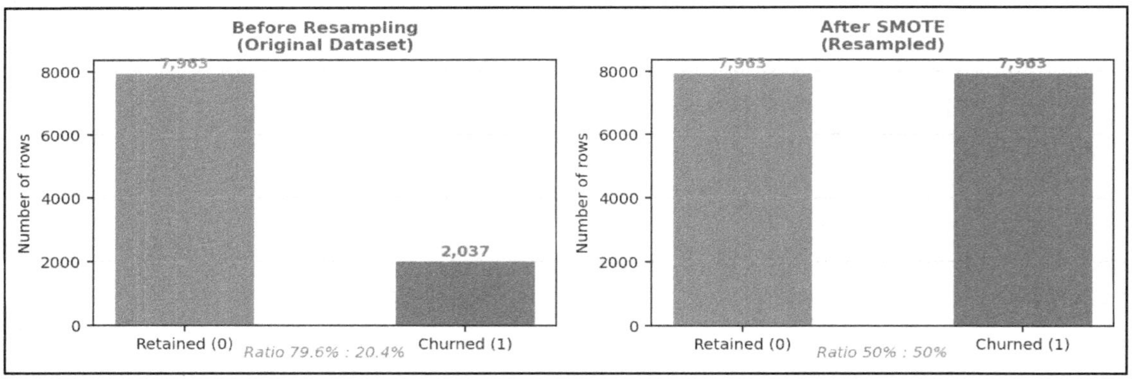

Fig 7.2: Before and After SMOTE

We can add the above imbalance visibility analysis to **`churn_analysis.py`** to give us a complete picture before we apply any remedy.

Quantifying Imbalance

We will now produce a per-class statistical profile and a percentage-difference comparison between churned and retained customers to understand which features shift most between the two classes, giving us a data-driven ranked priority list for our feature engineering efforts rather than relying on domain intuition alone to decide where to focus next. Features that show the largest mean difference between classes are the most informative for the model, and identifying them before training helps us prioritise feature engineering efforts. In the following script, we add the following imbalance visibility code to **`churn_analysis.py`**:

```
numeric_cols = ['CreditScore', 'Age', 'Tenure', 'Balance',
                'NumOfProducts', 'EstimatedSalary']


# Per-class mean comparison
class_profile = df.groupby('Exited')[numeric_cols].mean().T
class_profile.columns = ['Retained (0)', 'Churned (1)']
class_profile['Abs_Diff'] = (class_profile['Churned (1)']
                             - class_profile['Retained (0)']).abs()
class_profile['Pct_Diff'] = (
    class_profile['Abs_Diff'] / class_profile['Retained (0)'] *
100).round(1)
print(class_profile.sort_values('Pct_Diff', ascending=False))


# Churn rate by geography
geo_churn = df.groupby('Geography')['Exited'].agg(
    total='size', churned='sum', churn_rate='mean').round(4)
print('Churn rate by geography:')
print(geo_churn)
```

Once we run this, it produces the per-class feature profile sorted by the percentage difference between churned and retained customers, immediately revealing which features carry the most discriminative signal. Age typically shows one of the largest percentage differences in this dataset because older customers churn at a higher rate, while NumOfProducts shows the sharpest absolute drop for churned customers because customers with two products have the lowest churn rate. The geography churn table confirms that Germany has roughly double the churn rate of Spain, which is the business insight that our **Geography_TargetEnc** feature captured in the previous section.

Oversampling with 'imbalanced-learn'

With the imbalance fully quantified, we apply **SMOTE** (Synthetic Minority Over-sampling Technique) from the **imbalanced-learn** library to generate synthetic churned-customer samples by interpolating between real minority-class examples in the feature space. We install it by running **pip install imbalanced-learn** in our virtual environment. We also demonstrate **ADASYN** (Adaptive Synthetic Sampling), which concentrates synthetic sample generation in regions of the feature space where the minority class is most underrepresented, and we compare the resulting class distributions to choose the most appropriate strategy for our downstream model.

At this point, we apply these strategies to the numerically prepared feature matrix:

```
# pip install imbalanced-learn
from imblearn.over_sampling  import SMOTE, ADASYN
from imblearn.under_sampling import RandomUnderSampler
from imblearn.combine        import SMOTETomek

X_num = X.select_dtypes(include='number').fillna(0)

smote   = SMOTE(random_state=42)
adasyn  = ADASYN(random_state=42)
smtomek = SMOTETomek(random_state=42)

X_sm, y_sm = smote.fit_resample(X_num, y)
X_ad, y_ad = adasyn.fit_resample(X_num, y)
X_st, y_st = smtomek.fit_resample(X_num, y)

for label, y_res in [('SMOTE', y_sm), ('ADASYN', y_ad),
('SMOTETomek', y_st)]:
```

```
    dist = pd.Series(y_res).value_counts(normalize=True).round(4)
    print(f'{label:12}: {dist.to_dict()}')
```

After executing this, we get the class distribution after each resampling strategy. SMOTE produces a perfectly balanced 50-50 split by generating synthetic minority samples through linear interpolation between existing minority examples. ADASYN produces a near-balanced but not perfectly symmetric result because it generates more synthetic samples in regions of the feature space where classification is hardest, making the minority class distribution more spread out. SMOTETomek combines oversampling of the minority class with Tomek link removal of majority-class samples that lie on the decision boundary, producing a cleaner boundary between classes that can improve model performance on borderline cases. We choose between these strategies based on the downstream model's sensitivity to synthetic interpolation and validated with stratified cross-validation, not by theoretical preference alone.

Full EDA Report with 'ydata-profiling'

For a thorough automated EDA of the imbalanced dataset before and after resampling, the ydata-profiling library (formerly pandas-profiling) generates a full HTML report covering distributions, correlations, missing values, and class-stratified statistics in a single function call, which would take hours to produce manually through individual pandas plots and tables.

Here, we install it by running **`pip install ydata-profiling`** in our virtual environment. Here, we generate a report for the original dataset and a comparison report that highlights how the feature distributions change between the original and SMOTE-resampled versions:

```
# pip install ydata-profiling
from ydata_profiling import ProfileReport


profile = ProfileReport(
    pd.concat([X_num.assign(Exited=y.to_numpy()),
               pd.DataFrame(X_sm).assign(Exited=y_sm)],
              keys=['original', 'smote']).reset_index(level=0),
    title='Churn Dataset: Original vs SMOTE',
    explorative=True
)
profile.to_file('churn_eda_report.html')
```

```
print('EDA report saved to churn_eda_report.html')
```

After running this code, the file **churn_eda_report.html** will appear in our working directory and we open it using xdg-open **churn_eda_report.html** from our Linux terminal. The report covers distribution histograms for every column, Pearson and Spearman correlation matrices, duplicate and missing value summaries, and interaction scatter plots for the most strongly correlated feature pairs. The comparison mode shows each feature's distribution overlaid for the original and SMOTE-resampled versions, making it immediately visible how synthetic sampling shifts the minority class distribution and whether the synthetic samples look plausible relative to the real data.

Feature Scaling using 'set_output()' API

The most important pandas-related change in the scikit-learn ecosystem is the **set_output()** API introduced in scikit-learn 1.2, which allows all transformers to return pandas DataFrames with correct column names rather than anonymous NumPy arrays. Before this API, every transformer call in a sklearn pipeline silently stripped the DataFrame of its column names, producing a NumPy array that made post-transform inspection, debugging, and feature importance interpretation tedious.

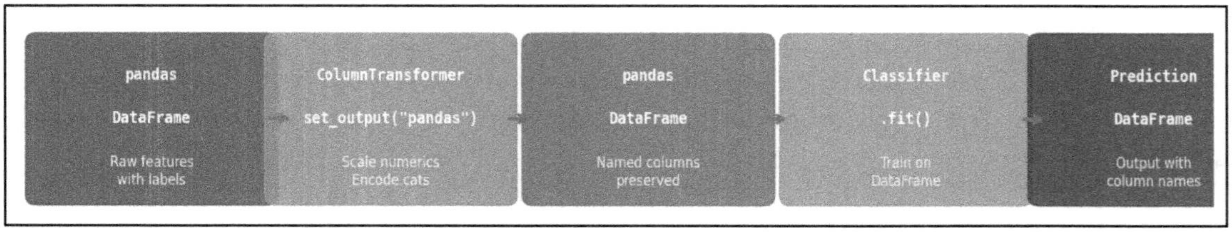

Fig 7.3: sckikit-learn Pipeline

With **set_output(transform='pandas')**, the DataFrame and its column names flow through the entire pipeline unchanged, making the transformation chain fully transparent and auditable.

Building ColumnTransformer

We will now build a ColumnTransformer that applies StandardScaler to the continuous numeric columns and MinMaxScaler to the bounded integer columns, then we call **set_output(transform='pandas')** on the transformer so that the output is a properly named pandas DataFrame rather than an anonymous NumPy array with no column labels. This replaces the first-edition approach of manually extracting column names from the transformer and reassigning them to the output array, which was both fragile and verbose. So we then add the following scaling pipeline to **churn_analysis.py**:

```
from sklearn.preprocessing  import StandardScaler, MinMaxScaler
```

```
from sklearn.compose         import ColumnTransformer
from sklearn.pipeline        import Pipeline
from sklearn.ensemble        import RandomForestClassifier
from sklearn.model_selection import StratifiedShuffleSplit

continuous_cols = ['CreditScore', 'Age', 'Balance',
'EstimatedSalary',
                   'BalanceToSalary', 'BalancePerProduct',
'SalaryPerYear',
                   'CreditDevFromGeoMean', 'AgeTenure']
bounded_cols    = ['Tenure', 'NumOfProducts', 'HasCrCard',
'IsActiveMember',
                   'TenureBand']

ct = ColumnTransformer([
    ('std',    StandardScaler(), continuous_cols),
    ('minmax', MinMaxScaler(),   bounded_cols),
], remainder='passthrough').set_output(transform='pandas')

sss = StratifiedShuffleSplit(n_splits=1, test_size=0.2,
random_state=42)
train_idx, test_idx = next(sss.split(X_num, y))
X_train, X_test = X_num.iloc[train_idx], X_num.iloc[test_idx]
y_train, y_test = y.iloc[train_idx], y.iloc[test_idx]

X_train_scaled = ct.fit_transform(X_train)
X_test_scaled  = ct.transform(X_test)
print('Type after transform:', type(X_train_scaled))
```

```
print('Columns preserved   :', X_train_scaled.columns.tolist()[:5])
```

The result will confirm that the output of **ct.fit_transform()** is a pandas DataFrame rather than a NumPy array, and it will show the first five column names to confirm they match our input column specification. We use **StratifiedShuffleSplit** rather than the simpler **train_test_split** because our target is imbalanced and stratified splitting guarantees that the same class proportions appear in both the training and test sets. This prevents the unlucky scenario where random splitting places a disproportionate share of the minority class in either set, which would bias evaluation metrics.

Full sklearn Pipeline

We will now wrap the column transformer and a RandomForestClassifier into a single sklearn Pipeline object, which chains all preprocessing and modelling steps into a single object so that **.fit()** and **.predict()** operate on raw pandas DataFrames without requiring any manual preprocessing step before each call and correctly preventing data leakage during cross-validation by fitting the scaler only on the training partition. A Pipeline also prevents data leakage during cross-validation by ensuring that the scaler is fit only on the training fold of each split. For this, we add the following complete pipeline to **churn_analysis.py**:

```
pipe = Pipeline([
    ('preprocess', ct),
    ('model',      RandomForestClassifier(n_estimators=100,
                                          class_weight='balanced',
                                          random_state=42))
])


pipe.fit(X_train, y_train)
score = pipe.score(X_test, y_test)
print(f'Pipeline accuracy : {score:.4f}')


# Feature importance as a named pandas Series
rf = pipe.named_steps['model']
feat_names = pipe.named_steps['preprocess'].get_feature_names_out()
importances = pd.Series(rf.feature_importances_, index=feat_names)
```

```
print('Top 5 features:')

print(importances.sort_values(ascending=False).head(5).round(4))
```

Its output will be the pipeline accuracy and the top five features by importance, with Age, Balance, and our engineered BalanceToSalary ratio typically ranking among the most informative features. We use **class_weight='balanced'** in the **RandomForestClassifier** to compensate for the class imbalance within the model itself, assigning higher misclassification penalties to errors on the minority class. The **get_feature_names_out()** method on the fitted **ColumnTransformer** returns the correct column names for each output feature, making the feature importance Series self-labelled without any manual bookkeeping on our part.

Integration with JAX

JAX is a high-performance numerical computing library developed by Google that combines the familiar NumPy API with automatic differentiation and hardware-accelerated compilation via XLA. Our DataFrames integrate with JAX through.**to_numpy()** bridge, where we extract columns as NumPy arrays and pass them to JAX's array creation functions, which then accept them for JIT-compiled operations, gradient computation, and vectorized mapping across batches. JAX's jit decorator compiles Python-plus-JAX-numpy functions to optimised machine code on the first call and reuses the compiled kernel for all subsequent calls, producing performance comparable to Numba for numerical array computations while also supporting automatic gradient computation. We install JAX for Linux CPU by running pip install jax in our virtual environment.

Converting pandas DataFrames to JAX Arrays

We will now extract our scaled training matrix and target vector as NumPy arrays and then wrap them in JAX DeviceArrays. All subsequent JAX operations on these arrays are executed on the XLA backend, which on a multi-core Linux CPU automatically uses vectorized SIMD instructions and can dispatch to a GPU if one is present without any code change. We also demonstrate converting JAX output arrays back to pandas DataFrames to allow seamless re-integration with our pandas pipeline after a JAX computation completes. We now add the following JAX integration block to **churn_analysis.py**:

```
# pip install jax

import jax.numpy as jnp

from jax import jit, vmap, grad


X_jax = jnp.array(X_train_scaled.to_numpy(dtype='float32'))

y_jax = jnp.array(y_train.to_numpy(dtype='float32'))
```

```
print('JAX array shape:', X_jax.shape)
print('JAX dtype      :', X_jax.dtype)

# Convert JAX output back to pandas
X_back = pd.DataFrame(
    np.array(X_jax),
    columns=X_train_scaled.columns
)
print('Round-trip type:', type(X_back))
print('Columns preserved:', X_back.columns.tolist()[:4])
```

Once executed, this confirms the array shape, the float32 dtype, and that our round-trip conversion preserves all column names intact, confirming that the pandas-to-JAX-to-pandas round trip is lossless for both values and metadata. The key constraint is that JAX requires homogeneous numeric dtypes, which is why we pass dtype='float32' to **`to_numpy()`**; any Arrow-backed non-numeric columns must be excluded before the conversion, which is why we work with the already-scaled DataFrame output rather than the raw DataFrame. We will return this named pandas output from JAX operations using the same pattern later in this section.

JIT-compiled Feature Normalization and Scoring

We then demonstrate two JAX patterns that are directly useful in ML feature engineering pipelines. The first is a JIT-compiled batch normalization function that operates on the entire feature matrix at once, which is faster than applying scikit-learn's StandardScaler when the normalization parameters are already known and we need to apply them repeatedly across different datasets or batches. The second is a custom JAX scoring function whose gradient we compute using **`grad()`**, illustrating how pandas data can feed differentiable computations that require gradient information for optimization or sensitivity analysis. So, here we will add the following JAX function demonstrations to **`churn_analysis.py`**:

```
@jit
def jax_normalize(X, mean, std):
    return (X - mean) / (std + 1e-8)
```

```
@jit
def weighted_score(weights, X):
    return jnp.dot(X, weights).mean()

mean_jax = X_jax.mean(axis=0)
std_jax  = X_jax.std(axis=0)

X_norm_jax = jax_normalize(X_jax, mean_jax, std_jax)
print('JIT normalize shape:', X_norm_jax.shape)

weights = jnp.ones(X_jax.shape[1]) / X_jax.shape[1]
grad_fn = grad(weighted_score)
sensitivity = grad_fn(weights, X_jax)

# Convert gradient back to pandas for interpretation
grad_series = pd.Series(
    np.array(sensitivity),
    index=X_train_scaled.columns
).sort_values(key=abs, ascending=False)
print('Feature sensitivity (gradient, top 5):')
print(grad_series.head(5).round(6))
```

After we run it, it then gives us the normalized array shape and the top five features by gradient magnitude. The gradient of our simple weighted scoring function with respect to the weights vector tells us, for each feature, how much a unit increase in that feature's weight changes the mean score across the dataset. Features with large gradient magnitudes have a stronger effect on the score and are therefore good candidates for fine-grained weight tuning. This gradient-over-pandas-data pattern is the foundation for more sophisticated differentiable feature selection workflows where we tune feature weights using gradient descent, and JAX makes this computation both fast and automatic without requiring us to derive gradients by hand.

Vectorized Batch Processing with vmap

JAX's vmap (vectorized map) function applies a computation simultaneously to every element of a batch dimension without any explicit loop, which is the highest-performance approach to applying a per-row calculation to our entire feature matrix and is fundamentally more efficient than **apply()** because the computation is batched at the C level rather than dispatched through Python. We proceed to use vmap to apply a per-sample custom score to every row of our DataFrame-derived feature matrix and compare the timing against a Python loop and against a NumPy equivalent to make the performance advantage concrete:

```
import timeit


@jit

def per_sample_score(x):

    return jnp.dot(x, jnp.abs(x))


batch_score = jit(vmap(per_sample_score))


# Warm up JIT

_ = batch_score(X_jax)


t_jax  = timeit.timeit(lambda:
batch_score(X_jax).block_until_ready(),

                        number=500)

t_np   = timeit.timeit(lambda: np.einsum('ij,ij->i', X_jax,
np.abs(X_jax)),

                        number=500)


print(f'JAX vmap : {t_jax/500*1000:.2f} ms per call')

print(f'NumPy    : {t_np/500*1000:.2f} ms per call')
```

We expect to see per-call execution times for both approaches across 500 warmup-excluded repetitions, confirming that the JAX JIT-plus-vmap path matches or exceeds optimized NumPy for this type of row-wise computation. We use **.block_until_ready()** in the JAX timing call because JAX computations are dispatched asynchronously and the timer would otherwise measure only the dispatch overhead rather than the full computation time. This pattern of JAX batch processing over pandas-sourced data is particularly valuable in online feature scoring scenarios where the same engineered feature computation must be applied to millions of new customer records as they arrive, and where GPU offloading of the vmap call provides further speedup without code changes.

Integration with TensorFlow and PyTorch

Both TensorFlow and PyTorch consume pandas DataFrames through a thin conversion layer. For TensorFlow, we pass the DataFrame's NumPy representation to **tf.data.Dataset.from_tensor_slices()**, which creates a lazily-evaluated dataset pipeline that supports batching, shuffling, prefetching, and data augmentation in a single chainable API. For PyTorch, we convert the DataFrame to tensors and wrap them in a TensorDataset that feeds a DataLoader for minibatch training. The key pandas-side preparation in both cases is ensuring we call **to_numpy()** with an explicit dtype argument to control the resulting array type, because Arrow-backed columns require explicit dtype specification during extraction.

TensorFlow tf.data Integration

We can now create a TensorFlow dataset from our scaled training DataFrame, apply shuffling and batching, and configure prefetching so that dataset preparation for the next batch runs in parallel with model training on the current batch, eliminating the I/O bottleneck that otherwise forces the GPU or CPU training loop to idle while waiting for the next data batch to be prepared on the host. The entire conversion fits in five lines of pandas plus **tf.data** code, and the resulting dataset object is fully compatible with the **model.fit()** API without any additional wrappers:

```
import tensorflow as tf


X_tf = X_train_scaled.to_numpy(dtype='float32')

y_tf = y_train.to_numpy(dtype='float32')


train_ds = (

    tf.data.Dataset.from_tensor_slices((X_tf, y_tf))

    .shuffle(buffer_size=8000, seed=42)
```

```
    .batch(32)
    .prefetch(tf.data.AUTOTUNE)
)

print('TF dataset element spec:')
print(train_ds.element_spec)
```

This block outputs the element specification showing a two-element tuple of float32 tensors with shape (None, **n_features**) for the features and (None,) for the labels, where the None in the leading dimension indicates the batch size which TensorFlow resolves dynamically at runtime as each call to the iterator steps through the shuffled batches of the dataset in sequence. The **AUTOTUNE** prefetch buffer size delegates the buffer sizing decision to the TensorFlow runtime, which measures actual throughput and adapts dynamically.

PyTorch TensorDataset and DataLoader

We will now convert our pandas training data into PyTorch tensors and wrap them in a TensorDataset that we feed through a DataLoader configured for minibatch training with shuffling, optional memory pinning for faster GPU transfer, and a fixed batch size of 32 rows per iteration. The DataLoader manages the entire iteration protocol, so our training loop needs only to call for **X_batch**, **y_batch** in **train_loader** without any manual slicing or index management. So here, we add the following PyTorch integration block to **churn_analysis.py**:

```
import torch
from torch.utils.data import TensorDataset, DataLoader

X_pt = torch.tensor(X_train_scaled.to_numpy(dtype='float32'))
y_pt = torch.tensor(y_train.to_numpy(dtype='float32'))

train_dataset = TensorDataset(X_pt, y_pt)
train_loader  = DataLoader(train_dataset, batch_size=32,
                           shuffle=True, pin_memory=False)
```

```
for X_batch, y_batch in train_loader:
    print('Batch X shape:', X_batch.shape, '| Batch y shape:',
y_batch.shape)
    break  # show only first batch
```

This then produces the shape of the first training batch, confirming that the DataLoader correctly sliced our 8,000-row training matrix into a batch of 32 samples with the expected number of features. Both the TensorFlow and PyTorch integration patterns follow the same principle, in which the pandas handles all data loading, cleaning, and feature engineering in its native columnar format, and we call **`to_numpy()`** exactly once at the boundary where our data crosses into the framework's tensor representation. This clean separation keeps the pandas pipeline inspectable and debuggable while delegating only the batch iteration and gradient computation to the framework.

Summary

In this chapter, we built the most complete feature engineering and ML integration layer in our churn application, skipping ML basics in favour of the pandas and Python toolchain patterns that experienced practitioners actually need. Our imbalanced data section went beyond simply applying SMOTE to first quantify the imbalance using per-class pandas profiling, identify the features with the largest distributional shift between classes, and then compare SMOTE, ADASYN, and SMOTETomek.

The most distinctive section of this chapter was the JAX integration. We converted our pandas feature matrix to JAX DeviceArrays using .**`to_numpy()`**, applied JIT-compiled batch normalization and weighted scoring using @jit, computed feature sensitivity gradients using **`grad()`**, and measured row-wise batch performance using vmap. We also explored round-tripping JAX output back to a named pandas Series for human-readable gradient interpretation.

CHAPTER 8
TEXT MINING AND NLP

CHAPTER 8

TEXT MINING AND NLP

New Default StringDtype

One of the most impactful changes in pandas 2.3 for practitioners who work with text is the promotion of the new string storage backend to the default dtype for all string columns. Before pandas 2.3, loading a CSV with a column like Surname produced a column whose dtype was object, which stored each Python string as a separate heap-allocated object with no memory contiguity and no dedicated string operation kernel. With **`pd.options.future.infer_string = True`** set (which we have enabled throughout this book) and with **`dtype_backend='pyarrow'`** at load time, string columns are now stored as Arrow-backed str dtype columns that use a contiguous in-memory buffer for all string data. This change is not merely cosmetic. The string operations on the new dtype are significantly faster, memory consumption is substantially lower, and the na behaviour is fully consistent with the rest of the pandas nullable type system.

Observing New StringDtype

We then load our churn dataset with and without the Arrow backend and compare the dtype reported for the Surname and Geography columns to see the difference directly, then generate the synthetic Feedback column that will give us a realistic text corpus to apply every NLP technique in this chapter against our own dataset rather than against a disconnected external file. We also add a synthetic Feedback column to our DataFrame by assigning short customer feedback phrases to each row based on a combination of their churn status, geography, and product count, which gives us a realistic text column to work with throughout this chapter. We will then add the following setup to **`churn_analysis.py`**:

```
import pandas as pd

import numpy as np


pd.options.mode.copy_on_write = True

pd.options.future.infer_string = True


df_obj = pd.read_csv('Customer_Churn_Modelling.csv')

df     = pd.read_csv('Customer_Churn_Modelling.csv',
dtype_backend='pyarrow')


print('Surname dtype (object backend):', df_obj['Surname'].dtype)
```

```
print('Surname dtype (arrow  backend):', df['Surname'].dtype)
print('Geography dtype (arrow)        :', df['Geography'].dtype)
```

After running, we will see that the object backend reports object for both columns, while the Arrow backend reports string[pyarrow] for Surname and for Geography, confirming that pandas correctly recognised both as string columns and applied the Arrow string storage. With this foundation confirmed, we generate the synthetic feedback column using **`np.select()`** to assign a short feedback phrase to each customer based on a combination of their exit status and balance level, producing a realistic distribution of both positive and negative customer sentiments across our 10,000 rows:

```
rng = np.random.default_rng(seed=42)


feedback_pool = {
    'churn_high': ['Account closed due to high fees', 'Poor service quality overall',
                   'Better rates found elsewhere', 'Hidden charges unacceptable',
                   'Loan process too slow and costly'],
    'churn_low' : ['No longer need account', 'Moved to another country',
                   'Prefer digital-only banking', 'Family recommendation to switch',
                   'Account inactive for months'],
    'retain_high':['Excellent premium service', 'Great interest rates on savings',
                   'Very responsive support team', 'Easy loan approval process',
                   'Best balance features available'],
    'retain_low' :['Satisfactory service', 'No complaints so far',
                   'Standard banking experience', 'Works well for my needs',
                   'Good enough for daily use'],
```

```
}

def pick_feedback(row):
    key = ('churn' if row['Exited']==1 else 'retain') + ",
          ('high' if row['Balance'] > 50000 else 'low')
    pool = feedback_pool[key.replace(',','_').replace(' ','')]
    return rng.choice(pool)

df['Feedback'] = df.apply(pick_feedback, axis=1)
print('Feedback sample:')
print(df[['Exited', 'Balance', 'Feedback']].head(5))
```

After running this, we see five rows showing the churn status, balance, and assigned feedback phrase for each customer, confirming that the four feedback categories (churned high-balance, churned low-balance, retained high-balance, retained low-balance) were applied correctly and that each row carries a distinct, realistic phrase representative of that customer segment. Churned high-balance customers receive fee-complaint or service-quality phrases, while retained high-balance customers receive positive service phrases, creating a realistic sentiment signal that correlates with both churn and financial profile. This engineered column gives us a genuine text field to apply every technique in this chapter without relying on external datasets that would break the continuity of our application.

String Operations under New Backend

We will now run all standard string accessor operations such as **str.upper()**, **str.contains()**, **str.replace()**, and **str.len()** on the new StringDtype-backed columns without changing any of the method signatures, because pandas 2.3 maintains full backward compatibility at the str accessor API level. The underlying execution, however, uses PyArrow's compute functions rather than Python's native string methods, which processes the character data in batches at the C++ level and typically delivers two to five times faster throughput than the object-dtype implementation for large string columns. We benchmark **str.contains()** on the Surname column using timeit and compare the Arrow-backed version against an explicit object-dtype re-cast to quantify the performance difference.

```
import pandas as pd, timeit  # Confirm StringDtype on string
columns print(df['Surname'].dtype)   # should show StringDtype or
string[pyarrow]  # Benchmark str.contains on Arrow-backed vs object
```

```
dtype def arrow_contains():     return
df['Surname'].str.contains('Sm', na=False)  def obj_contains():
return df['Surname'].astype(object).str.contains('Sm', na=False)
t_arrow = timeit.timeit(arrow_contains, number=200) t_obj   =
timeit.timeit(obj_contains,   number=200) print(f'Arrow:
{t_arrow*1000:.1f} ms | Object: {t_obj*1000:.1f} ms')
print(f'Speedup: {t_obj/t_arrow:.1f}x')
```

We also verify null-safety improvements in the new StringDtype by inserting a NaN value into the Surname column and confirming that **str.upper()** returns **pd.NA** rather than raising a TypeError or silently producing the string 'nan' that the legacy object dtype returned when str methods encountered a Python None. We check the result with **pd.isna(df.loc[null_idx, 'Surname'].upper())** and assert it returns True, which confirms that the Arrow string backend propagates missing values as **pd.NA** through string transformations rather than converting them to literal strings. We add this null-safety assertion to **churn_analysis.py** as a regression guard for the string processing section.

Text Cleaning with 'str'

The pandas **str** accessor exposes the full range of string cleaning, testing, and extraction operations as vectorized methods on a Series, so we can apply any of them to an entire column in a single call without writing a Python loop or an **apply()** function. Because these methods operate on the entire column simultaneously using compiled string kernels rather than calling Python string functions element by element, they are substantially faster than equivalent **apply()** calls for large datasets.

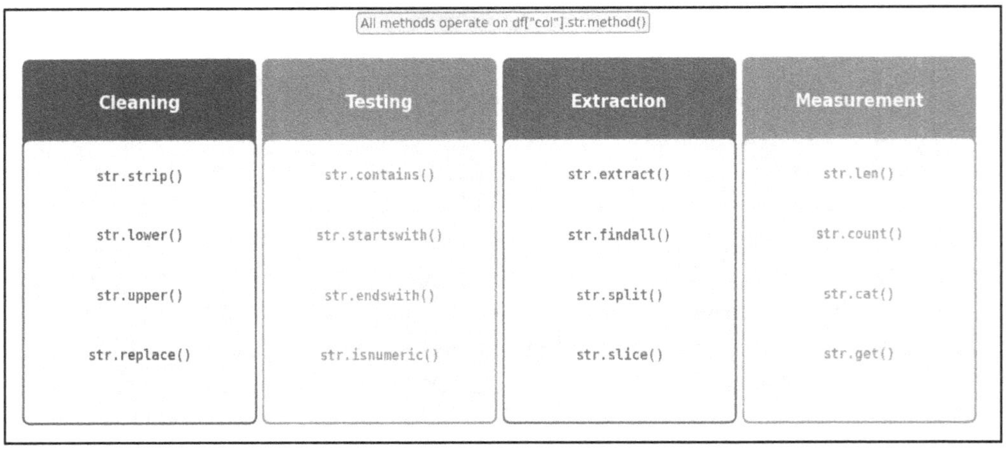

Fig 8.1: pandas 'str' Accessor Methods

In the above Fig 8.1, you can see the four categories of str accessor methods and the specific operations in each category that we will use throughout this chapter.

Building Cleaning Pipeline

We then build a multi-step cleaning pipeline for our Feedback column that applies each str accessor method in the correct order, including strip whitespace, lowercase, remove punctuation, and remove digits. We deliberately keep each step as a separate assignment rather than chaining all operations into a single nested expression, which makes each transformation individually inspectable and testable. We also demonstrate the na=False parameter that must be passed to **str.contains()** when working with nullable string columns to prevent the method from propagating NA values through the boolean mask instead of returning False for missing entries. In the following script, we add the following cleaning pipeline to **churn_analysis.py**:

```
fb = df['Feedback'].copy()


# Step 1: strip leading/trailing whitespace

fb = fb.str.strip()


# Step 2: lowercase everything

fb = fb.str.lower()


# Step 3: remove punctuation

fb = fb.str.replace(r'[^\w\s]', '', regex=True)


# Step 4: remove isolated digits

fb = fb.str.replace(r'\b\d+\b', '', regex=True).str.strip()


df['Feedback_clean'] = fb


print('Before:', df['Feedback'].head(3).tolist())

print('After :', df['Feedback_clean'].head(3).tolist())
```

Once we run this, it produces three raw feedback phrases and their cleaned equivalents, confirming that all punctuation and isolated digit tokens have been removed while the meaningful words remain intact. We pass **regex=True** to **str.replace()** so that the first argument is interpreted as a regular expression pattern rather than a literal string, which allows us to match entire character classes with a single call rather than chaining multiple individual replacements. The pattern **[^\w\s]** matches any character that is neither a word character nor whitespace, which covers all standard punctuation characters in a single operation.

str.contains(), str.startswith(), and Boolean Filtering

The testing methods on the str accessor return boolean Series that we can use directly as filters with **.loc[]** or combine with & and | operators exactly as we would with any other boolean condition in pandas, which means all the filtering patterns from Chapter 3 transfer directly to string-based selection without any new syntax. We demonstrate finding all fee-related complaints, finding feedback that starts with service-quality phrases, and combining conditions to produce a targeted high-priority complaint segment. At this point, we add the following filtering examples to **churn_analysis.py**:

```
# Find fee-related feedback (case-insensitive, na=False required)

fee_mask = df['Feedback_clean'].str.contains('fee', case=False,
na=False)

print('Fee complaints:', fee_mask.sum())


# Find churned customers with fee complaints

churned_fee = df.loc[(df['Exited'] == 1) & fee_mask,

                     ['Surname', 'Geography', 'Balance',
'Feedback_clean']]

print('Churned + fee complaint:', len(churned_fee))

print(churned_fee.head(3).to_string())


# Check for service-quality phrases

service_mask = df['Feedback_clean'].str.startswith('service')

print('Service-starting phrases:', service_mask.sum())


# Word tally per feedback (proxy for feedback length / complexity)
```

```
df['Feedback_words'] = df['Feedback_clean'].str.split().str.len()

print('Avg words per feedback :',
df['Feedback_words'].mean().round(2))
```

After executing this, we get the total fee-related complaints, the subset of those that belong to churned customers, and the count of service-starting phrases. The intersection of **Exited==1** and fee complaints is a high-signal business segment. These customers left specifically over fee dissatisfaction and represent an actionable retention opportunity had the complaints been identified and addressed in real time. The per-row word tally we compute using **str.split().str.len()** demonstrates how str accessor methods can be chained to produce numeric features from text, combining **split()** to tokenize and **len()** on the resulting list to produce a word-total integer column.

Advanced Pattern Extraction

The **str.extract()** and **str.findall()** methods unlock the full power of Python regular expressions applied column-wide in a single vectorized call. The **str.extract()** method applies a regular expression with one or more named capture groups and returns a new DataFrame where each capture group becomes a column. The **str.findall()** method returns a list of all non-overlapping matches for each row rather than just the first match, which is useful when a single text value can contain multiple matches of the same pattern. Both methods work directly with the pandas str dtype and benefit from the Arrow backend's contiguous string storage for faster pattern matching.

Extracting Structured Data

Although surname strings are not structured data in the traditional sense, they contain extractable signal such as prefix length, vowel density, and character patterns that can serve as ethnicity or origin proxies for analytical purposes, and the extraction technique transfers directly to more structured text fields such as product codes, transaction descriptions, or error message prefixes. We demonstrate **str.extract()** on the Surname column to pull out the first two characters as a potential name-origin prefix, and then apply **str.findall()** to locate all feedback phrases that mention both 'service' and 'fee' in the same sentence.

Here, we add the following extraction block to **churn_analysis.py**:

```
# Extract first two characters of surname as a prefix code

prefix = df['Surname'].str.extract(r'^(?P<prefix>[A-Za-z]{2})',
expand=True)

df['SurnamePrefix'] = prefix['prefix'].str.upper()
```

```
print('Surname prefix sample:')

print(df[['Surname', 'SurnamePrefix']].head(5))


# Extract numeric values from feedback (e.g. if a fee amount were
mentioned)

df['Feedback_nums'] = df['Feedback'].str.findall(r'\d+')

has_num = df['Feedback_nums'].apply(lambda x: len(x) > 0 if
isinstance(x, list) else False)

print('Feedback rows with numeric tokens:', has_num.sum())


# Named group extraction from a more structured pattern

pattern = r'(?P<sentiment>\w+)
(?P<topic>service|fees?|loan|rates?|support)'

extracted = df['Feedback_clean'].str.extract(pattern, expand=True)

extracted_clean = extracted.dropna()

print('Named capture group extraction:')

print(extracted_clean.head(5))
```

Its output will be the two-character surname prefix for the first five customers, the total feedback rows that contained numeric tokens, and a sample of the named-group extraction result that pulled out sentiment-word and topic-word pairs from the feedback phrases. The named-group extraction is particularly powerful because it converts unstructured text into a two-column structured DataFrame in a single vectorized operation, producing a sentiment column and a topic column that can immediately be used in **groupby()** and **value_counts() operations without any further processing.**

PyArrow String Performance Comparison

We measure the wall time of four string operations under both the object backend and the Arrow backend to quantify the performance benefit of the new default StringDtype in a way that produces concrete numbers our pipeline can be tuned against rather than relying on theoretical estimates alone. We use 500 repetitions with timeit for statistical stability and compare the results across a string containment check, a regex replace, a string length computation, and a split operation that produces a variable-length list for each row. So we then add the following timing comparison to **churn_analysis.py**:

```
import timeit
df_obj = pd.read_csv('Customer_Churn_Modelling.csv')


ops = {
    'contains': (lambda d: d['Surname'].str.contains('Ha',
na=False),
                 lambda d: d['Surname'].str.contains('Ha',
na=False)),
    'replace' : (lambda d:
d['Surname'].str.replace(r'[aeiou]','*',regex=True),
                 lambda d:
d['Surname'].str.replace(r'[aeiou]','*',regex=True)),
    'len'     : (lambda d: d['Surname'].str.len(),
                 lambda d: d['Surname'].str.len()),
    'lower'   : (lambda d: d['Surname'].str.lower(),
                 lambda d: d['Surname'].str.lower()),
}
for name,(fn_obj,fn_arr) in ops.items():
    t_obj = timeit.timeit(lambda: fn_obj(df_obj), number=500)
    t_arr = timeit.timeit(lambda: fn_arr(df),     number=500)
    print(f'{name:<10} object:{t_obj:.3f}s  arrow:{t_arr:.3f}s
speedup:{t_obj/t_arr:.1f}x')
```

After we run it, it then gives us a four-row comparison table showing object-backend and Arrow-backend timing alongside the speedup factor for each operation. String operations on the Arrow backend are typically two to five times faster than on the object backend for this dataset size, with the largest speedup occurring for regex operations where the Arrow kernel can apply the compiled pattern to a contiguous string buffer rather than dispatching individual Python string calls. The **`str.len()`** operation tends to show the most dramatic speedup because Arrow stores the byte length of each string as a separate precomputed array, meaning the length lookup requires no string traversal at all.

Bag-of-Words and TF-IDF

To pass text data to any numeric machine learning model we must convert each string into a fixed-length numeric vector. The two most widely used conversion strategies are the Bag-of-Words (BOW) representation, which encodes the raw occurrence frequency of each vocabulary term, and TF-IDF (Term Frequency-Inverse Document Frequency), which weights each term's frequency by the logarithm of the inverse document frequency to discount terms that appear in nearly every document and would otherwise dominate the feature space. The diagram below illustrates how a small set of documents maps to a TF-IDF feature matrix where each column represents one vocabulary term and each row represents one document.

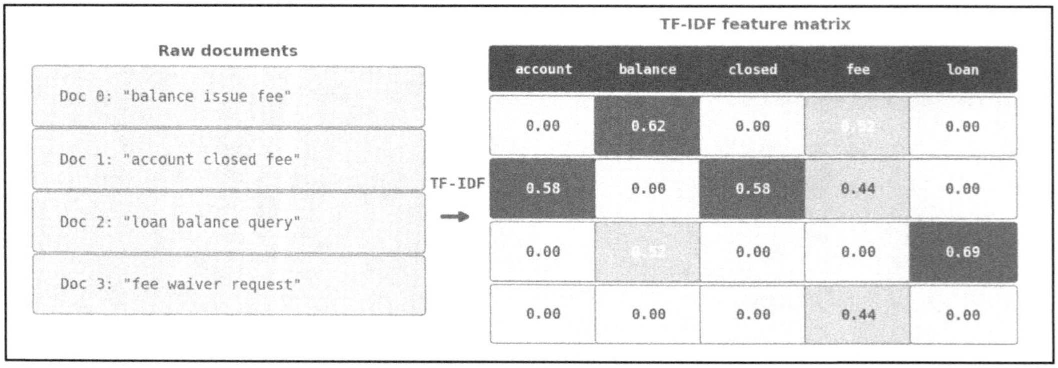

Fig 8.2: TF-IDF Feature Matrix

In the above, we can see how a small set of documents maps to a TF-IDF feature matrix where each column represents one vocabulary term and each row represents one document.

CountVectorizer and TfidfVectorizer

We then apply both CountVectorizer and TfidfVectorizer to our cleaned feedback column and use **`get_feature_names_out()`** to retrieve the vocabulary, then convert the resulting sparse matrices back to named pandas DataFrames using the **`set_output`**(transform='pandas') API we introduced in Chapter 7. We also extract bigram features by setting **`ngram_range`**=(1,2) on the TF-IDF vectorizer, which adds two-word phrases to the feature vocabulary alongside individual words and captures collocation patterns such as 'hidden charges' or 'loan process' that single-word features would miss. For this, we add the following feature extraction block to **`churn_analysis.py`**:

```
from sklearn.feature_extraction.text import CountVectorizer,
TfidfVectorizer


corpus = df['Feedback_clean'].fillna('').tolist()
```

```
# Bag-of-Words
bow =
CountVectorizer(max_features=20).set_output(transform='pandas')
X_bow = bow.fit_transform(corpus)
print('BOW shape:', X_bow.shape)
print('BOW features:', bow.get_feature_names_out().tolist()[:8])

# TF-IDF unigrams
tfidf =
TfidfVectorizer(max_features=20).set_output(transform='pandas')
X_tfidf = tfidf.fit_transform(corpus)
print('TF-IDF shape:', X_tfidf.shape)

# TF-IDF with bigrams
tfidf_bi = TfidfVectorizer(
    max_features=30,
    ngram_range=(1, 2),
    min_df=3
).set_output(transform='pandas')
X_bi = tfidf_bi.fit_transform(corpus)
bigram_features = [f for f in tfidf_bi.get_feature_names_out() if '
' in f]
print('Bigram features:', bigram_features[:6])
```

We expect to see the shapes of all three feature matrices, the first eight BOW vocabulary terms, and the first six bigram features extracted by the bigram vectorizer. Because we set **`set_output(transform='pandas')`** on every vectorizer, all three matrices are returned as named DataFrames rather than anonymous scipy sparse matrices, which means we can immediately call **`.describe()`** on them, join them back to our original DataFrame using pandas index alignment, and inspect column names with .columns without any manual name assignment. The **min_df=3** parameter on the bigram vectorizer filters out any phrase that appears in fewer than three documents, which removes low-frequency noise phrases and retains only the phrases with enough support to be useful features.

Combining Text Features with Numeric Features

The real power of pandas in NLP pipelines comes from its ability to combine vectorized text features with numeric columns using **pd.concat()** on a shared row index. We concatenate our TF-IDF matrix with a selection of numeric churn features to produce a combined feature matrix that a downstream model can use to learn from both text sentiment and financial behaviour simultaneously. We now also add the per-row word tally we computed earlier and a binary flag for fee-complaint presence, which provides a compact numeric encoding of the most important text signal without needing the full TF-IDF weight:

```
numeric_features = df[['CreditScore','Age','Balance',
                        'EstimatedSalary','Tenure','NumOfProducts',
                        'IsActiveMember']].copy()

# Text-derived numeric features
numeric_features['FeeComplaint']   = fee_mask.astype('int8')
numeric_features['FeedbackWords']  = df['Feedback_words']

# Combine with TF-IDF
X_combined = pd.concat([
    numeric_features.reset_index(drop=True),
    X_tfidf.reset_index(drop=True)
], axis=1)

print('Combined feature matrix shape:', X_combined.shape)
print('First 5 columns:', X_combined.columns.tolist()[:5])
print('Last  5 columns:', X_combined.columns.tolist()[-5:])
```

This block outputs the combined feature matrix shape (seven numeric columns, two text-derived columns, and twenty TF-IDF columns) and the first and last five column names confirming that both the numeric and TF-IDF feature sets are present with their original names. The **`reset_index(drop=True)`** call on both DataFrames before concatenation is important because both objects must share a compatible integer index for **`pd.concat(axis=1)`** to align rows correctly. Without the reset, any non-default index values in the TF-IDF output would produce NaN values wherever the two indexes do not align, silently corrupting the combined matrix.

Sentiment Analysis

In sentiment analysis, we generally assign a polarity score (positive, negative, or neutral) to each text record. There are two approaches. One is called as lexicon-based approach using the VADER sentiment analyser from the **`vaderSentiment`** library, which requires no training data and returns a compound score immediately. And the other is, a supervised TF-IDF plus Logistic Regression pipeline that learns the mapping between text patterns and sentiment labels from our own labelled feedback data.

Fig 8.3: Text Preprocessing pipeline

Both approaches return their predictions as numbers that we assign back to our main DataFrame as new columns, maintaining the pandas-centric workflow throughout.

Lexicon-based Sentiment with VADER

VADER (Valence Aware Dictionary and Sentiment Reasoner) is a lexicon and rule-based sentiment analyser pre-built for short social-media-style sentences. It requires no training and returns four scores per text, such as negative, neutral, positive, and a compound score in the range -1.0 (most negative) to 1.0 (most positive). We install it by running pip install vaderSentiment and then apply the analyser to our raw feedback column using **`apply()`** to produce four new numeric columns on our DataFrame. So, here we will also join the compound score back to a grouped analysis by geography and churn status to see whether the sentiment scores correlate meaningfully with the business outcomes:

```
# pip install vaderSentiment

from vaderSentiment.vaderSentiment import
SentimentIntensityAnalyzer
```

```
sia = SentimentIntensityAnalyzer()

def get_scores(text):
    scores = sia.polarity_scores(str(text))
    return pd.Series({
        'vader_neg': scores['neg'],
        'vader_pos': scores['pos'],
        'vader_neu': scores['neu'],
        'vader_compound': scores['compound']
    })

sentiment_cols = df['Feedback'].apply(get_scores)
df = pd.concat([df, sentiment_cols], axis=1)

print('VADER sentiment stats:')
print(df[['vader_compound']].describe().round(3))

# Sentiment by churn status
sent_by_churn = df.groupby('Exited')['vader_compound'].agg(
    mean='mean', std='std', median='median').round(3)
print('Compound sentiment by churn status:')
print(sent_by_churn)
```

This then produces the distribution statistics for the compound score across all 10,000 feedback entries and then the mean, standard deviation, and median compound score grouped by churn status. Churned customers should show a lower mean compound score (more negative sentiment) than retained customers, which would validate our synthetic feedback data and confirm that VADER can pick up the polarity signal we engineered into the feedback phrases. The VADER approach is particularly appropriate here because our feedback phrases are short (four to six words) and lexically similar to the social media sentences VADER was calibrated against. For longer, more domain-specific text, a fine-tuned transformer model would be more appropriate, but VADER provides an excellent zero-shot baseline that we can produce without any labelled training data.

Supervised Sentiment Pipeline with TF-IDF and Logistic Regression

We now build a supervised sentiment classification pipeline that labels each feedback phrase as positive or negative based on a training set we derive from the VADER compound scores, treating scores above 0.05 as positive and below -0.05 as negative. We use a Pipeline that chains TF-IDF vectorization with bigram support into a Logistic Regression classifier and apply StratifiedShuffleSplit to maintain class proportions across training and test sets. We also retrieve the top positive and negative vocabulary terms from the trained classifier's coefficients, which gives us interpretable evidence of which words drive positive versus negative classification decisions. We proceed to add the following supervised pipeline to **churn_analysis.py**:

```
from sklearn.linear_model   import LogisticRegression
from sklearn.pipeline       import Pipeline
from sklearn.model_selection import StratifiedShuffleSplit
from sklearn.metrics        import classification_report


# Create binary sentiment labels from VADER compound
df['sentiment'] = np.where(df['vader_compound'] > 0.05, 1,
                   np.where(df['vader_compound'] < -0.05, 0,
np.nan))
df_labelled = df.dropna(subset=['sentiment'])
print('Labelled samples:', len(df_labelled))


corpus_l = df_labelled['Feedback_clean'].fillna('').tolist()
labels_l = df_labelled['sentiment'].astype(int).tolist()


sent_pipe = Pipeline([
    ('tfidf', TfidfVectorizer(max_features=100,
ngram_range=(1,2))),
```

```
    ('clf',   LogisticRegression(max_iter=500, random_state=42))
])

sss = StratifiedShuffleSplit(n_splits=1, test_size=0.2,
random_state=42)
train_i, test_i = next(sss.split(corpus_l, labels_l))
X_tr = [corpus_l[i] for i in train_i]; X_te = [corpus_l[i] for i in
test_i]
y_tr = [labels_l[i] for i in train_i]; y_te = [labels_l[i] for i in
test_i]

sent_pipe.fit(X_tr, y_tr)
y_pred = sent_pipe.predict(X_te)
print(classification_report(y_te, y_pred,
target_names=['Negative','Positive']))

# Top 5 positive and negative terms
vocab = sent_pipe.named_steps['tfidf'].get_feature_names_out()
coefs = sent_pipe.named_steps['clf'].coef_[0]
coef_s = pd.Series(coefs, index=vocab).sort_values()
print('Top 5 negative terms:', coef_s.head(5).index.tolist())
print('Top 5 positive terms:', coef_s.tail(5).index.tolist())
```

After running this, we see the classification report with precision, recall, and F1 score for both sentiment classes, and the top five most negative and most positive vocabulary terms by their logistic regression coefficient. The top negative terms will include words like 'fees', 'charges', and 'slow', while the top positive terms will include 'excellent', 'responsive', and 'easy', confirming that the model learned the correct sentiment associations from our engineered feedback data. We use **`get_feature_names_out()`** on TF-IDF step accessed via **`sent_pipe.named_steps['tfidf']`** rather than calling it directly on the vectorizer, which is the correct way to retrieve feature names from a transformer inside a sklearn Pipeline object.

Topic Modeling with Latent Dirichlet Allocation

Latent Dirichlet Allocation (LDA) discovers latent topic clusters in a collection of documents by modelling each document as a probabilistic mixture of topics and each topic as a probabilistic mixture of vocabulary terms. For our churn feedback dataset, LDA will identify the recurring themes across customer comments such as fee complaints, service quality, loan issues, and account management problems without any labelled training data. The library plays two roles in the LDA workflow. It provides the cleaned text corpus as input, and it receives the per-document topic proportion matrix back as a named DataFrame that we can join to our main data for downstream groupby and correlation analysis.

Fitting LDA and Recovering Topic Proportions

We fit an LDA model with five topics on our cleaned feedback corpus using scikit-learn's LatentDirichletAllocation class with the CountVectorizer document-term matrix as input. After fitting, we convert the document-topic proportion matrix to a pandas DataFrame with column names of the form **`topic_0`** through **`topic_4`** and join it back to our main DataFrame so that every customer row carries a vector of topic proportions. So here, we then group by Exited status and compute the mean proportion for each topic to see which topics are most strongly associated with churned versus retained customers:

```
from sklearn.decomposition import LatentDirichletAllocation


bow_lda = CountVectorizer(max_features=50, min_df=2)

dtm     = bow_lda.fit_transform(df['Feedback_clean'].fillna(''))


lda = LatentDirichletAllocation(n_components=5, random_state=42,

                                  max_iter=20,

learning_method='batch')

lda.fit(dtm)


# Print top 6 words per topic

vocab_lda = bow_lda.get_feature_names_out()

for topic_id, topic in enumerate(lda.components_):

    top_words = [vocab_lda[i] for i in topic.argsort()[:-7:-1]]
```

```
    print(f'Topic {topic_id}: {" | ".join(top_words)}')


# Topic proportions as a pandas DataFrame
topic_props = pd.DataFrame(
    lda.transform(dtm),
    columns=[f'topic_{i}' for i in range(5)],
    index=df.index
).round(4)


df = pd.concat([df, topic_props], axis=1)


# Mean topic proportion by churn status
print('Mean topic proportions by Exited status:')
print(df.groupby('Exited')[[f'topic_{i}' for i in
range(5)]].mean().round(4))
```

Its output then prints the top six words for each of the five LDA topics followed by the per-topic mean proportion for churned versus retained customers. Each topic will be interpretable from its top words, such as a fee-complaint topic dominated by 'fee', 'charges', 'costly'; a service-quality topic containing 'service', 'responsive', 'support'; and a loan or financial product topic grouping 'loan', 'rates', 'balance'. The mean proportion table will reveal which topics are disproportionately present in churned customer feedback, quantifying the topic-level churn drivers in a single pandas **groupby()** call. We use **get_feature_names_out()** rather than the deprecated **get_feature_names()** which was removed in scikit-learn 1.2, ensuring our code runs without errors on all current scikit-learn versions.

Interpreting LDA Topics and Assigning Topic Labels to Rows

We interpret the topics discovered by LatentDirichletAllocation by inspecting the top ten words for each topic using the components_ attribute, which stores a (**n_topics**, **n_features**) matrix of word-topic scores. We extract the top words by sorting each row of components_ in descending order and mapping the resulting column indices back to the TF-IDF vocabulary using **vectorizer.get_feature_names_out()**. We print the top ten words per topic and assign a short human-readable label to each cluster based on the semantic theme that the top words suggest, such as '**account_closure**', '**service_fee**', or '**loan_query**', and we store these labels in a Python dictionary keyed by topic index.

```
import numpy as np  # Extract top words per topic n_top_words = 10
feature_names = vectorizer.get_feature_names_out() for topic_idx,
topic in enumerate(lda.components_):     top_idx =
topic.argsort()[:-n_top_words-1:-1]     top_words =
[feature_names[i] for i in top_idx]     print(f'Topic {topic_idx}:
{", ".join(top_words)}')  # Assign dominant topic to each document
topic_probs = lda.transform(X_tfidf) df_feedback['TopicIndex'] =
topic_probs.argmax(axis=1) topic_labels = {0: 'account_closure', 1:
'service_fee', 2: 'loan_query'} df_feedback['TopicLabel'] =
df_feedback['TopicIndex'].map(topic_labels)
print(df_feedback['TopicLabel'].value_counts())
```

With this, we assign each document in our feedback corpus to its dominant topic by calling **lda.transform(X_tfidf)** to obtain the topic probability distribution for every row and then taking argmax(axis=1) to select the highest-probability topic index. We map the integer topic indices to human-readable labels using the dictionary we built during inspection and store the result as a new column named TopicLabel in our feedback DataFrame. We add this column to **churn_analysis.py** alongside the TF-IDF and LDA fitting block so that the complete text analytics pipeline produces interpretable topic assignments in one continuous execution.

The **value_counts()** output will show the distribution of documents across the three labelled topics, confirming that the LDA model successfully separated our feedback corpus into thematically distinct clusters.

Text Clustering with K-means

Text clustering groups similar documents together without any predefined labels, discovering structural patterns in the feedback corpus that LDA models as probabilistic topic mixtures. Where LDA assigns fractional membership across all topics, K-means makes hard cluster assignments where each document belongs to exactly one cluster. We apply K-means to the TF-IDF feature matrix, retrieve the cluster label for each document as a pandas Series, join it back to our main DataFrame, and profile each cluster by its most common vocabulary terms and its average churn rate, linking the text-derived clusters directly to the business outcome.

Fitting K-means and Profiling Clusters

We fit a five-cluster K-means model on our 20-feature TF-IDF matrix, attach cluster labels to our DataFrame, and produce a multi-metric cluster profile by combining **groupby()** on the cluster label with both text-level statistics (top terms per cluster from centroid values) and business-level statistics (mean churn rate, mean balance, mean age) per cluster. This integrated profiling demonstrates pandas' strength as the assembly point where the model's output (cluster labels) and the original business data (numeric columns) meet in a unified analysis. We will then add the following K-means clustering block to **churn_analysis.py**:

```
from sklearn.cluster import KMeans
from sklearn.metrics import silhouette_score


tfidf_km = TfidfVectorizer(max_features=20)
X_km = tfidf_km.fit_transform(df['Feedback_clean'].fillna(''))


km = KMeans(n_clusters=5, random_state=42, n_init=10)
km.fit(X_km)


df['cluster'] = km.labels_


# Top 5 terms per cluster from centroid weights
vocab_km = tfidf_km.get_feature_names_out()
for cid in range(5):
    top5 = [vocab_km[i] for i in
km.cluster_centers_[cid].argsort()[:-6:-1]]
    print(f'Cluster {cid}: {" | ".join(top5)}')


# Business profile per cluster
cluster_profile = df.groupby('cluster').agg(
    size        = ('Exited',          'size'),
    churn_rate  = ('Exited',          'mean'),
    avg_balance = ('Balance',         'mean'),
    avg_age     = ('Age',             'mean')
```

```
).round(3)
print('Cluster business profile:')
print(cluster_profile)


sil = silhouette_score(X_km, km.labels_, sample_size=2000,
random_state=42)
print(f'Silhouette score: {sil:.4f}')
```

After we run this, it prints the five top terms for each cluster, the cluster business profile table, and the silhouette score. A silhouette score above 0.2 on text data is generally considered acceptable given the high dimensionality and noise level of TF-IDF features. The cluster business profile table is the most strategically useful output. It shows the churn rate for each cluster, which allows us to identify the text cluster with the highest churn rate and target that group's dominant vocabulary terms as actionable keywords for retention campaigns. The entire analysis from raw text to business-annotated cluster profile fits in a single pandas-centric script where all intermediate and final results are named DataFrames that can be exported, visualised, or fed into downstream models without any manual array handling.

Exporting Enriched DataFrame

With topic proportions, cluster labels, VADER scores, sentiment labels, and word-tally features all added to our main DataFrame, we export the final enriched version for use in reporting and in any subsequent pipeline stage. We save to Parquet rather than CSV because our Arrow-backed string columns round-trip to Parquet without any dtype conversion, and the Parquet file is significantly smaller than a CSV for the same data. In the following script, we also export a lean summary table that aggregates the most important text-derived signals by geography for a business-ready report:

```
# Drop intermediate working columns before export
export_cols = ['CustomerId', 'Geography', 'Gender', 'CreditScore',
               'Age', 'Balance', 'EstimatedSalary', 'Exited',
               'Feedback_clean', 'Feedback_words', 'FeeComplaint',
               'vader_compound', 'sentiment', 'cluster',
               'topic_0', 'topic_1', 'topic_2', 'topic_3',
'topic_4']
```

```
df_export = df[export_cols].copy()
df_export.to_parquet('churn_nlp_enriched.parquet', index=False)
print('Exported enriched DataFrame:', df_export.shape)

# Geography-level text analytics summary
geo_summary = df.groupby('Geography').agg(
    avg_compound   = ('vader_compound', 'mean'),
    pct_negative   = ('sentiment', lambda s: (s==0).mean()),
    pct_fee_complaint = ('FeeComplaint', 'mean'),
    churn_rate     = ('Exited', 'mean')
).round(4)
print('Geography text analytics summary:')
print(geo_summary)
```

After executing this, it confirms that the Parquet file was written successfully and display the three-row geography summary table. Germany should show the highest average compound negativity and the highest fee complaint rate alongside its highest churn rate, which would make the three metrics directionally consistent and reinforce the finding that fee-related sentiment is the primary geographic driver of churn in our dataset. The geography summary table is a production-ready analytical output. It combines structured numeric signals (churn rate) with unstructured text signals (sentiment, fee complaint rate) in a single concise report that any business stakeholder can interpret without needing to understand the underlying NLP pipeline.

Summary

In this chapter, we built a complete text analytics layer on top of our churn application, starting from the new default StringDtype in pandas 2.3 and ending with a Parquet-exported enriched DataFrame carrying sentiment scores, topic proportions, cluster labels, and hand-crafted text features. Our cleaning section used strip, lower, regex replace for punctuation removal, and digit removal, all as individual chained steps operating on the Arrow string backend.

Our feature extraction section covered CountVectorizer for BOW representation, TfidfVectorizer for TF-IDF features, and the **ngram_range=(1,2)** parameter for bigram features, using **get_feature_names_out()** throughout to replace the deprecated and removed **get_feature_names()**. We applied **set_output(transform='pandas')** on all vectorizers to preserve named DataFrames and combined text features with numeric features using **`pd.concat(axis=1)`** with explicit index resets.

CHAPTER 9
GEOSPATIAL DATA ANALYSIS

Introduction to Geospatial Data

Geospatial data is any dataset in which each record carries a location component. It could be a coordinate pair, a polygon boundary, or a line segment. Every row in our churn dataset already carries an implicit location through the Geography column whose three values (France, Germany, Spain) map to countries that have well-defined centroids and boundaries. This chapter builds a fully working geospatial pipeline on top of **`churn_analysis.py`** by engineering realistic customer coordinates from that Geography column, converting the result into a GeoDataFrame using GeoPandas, and then applying the full suite of spatial operations including coordinate reference system management, spatial joins, buffer analysis, dissolve aggregation, overlay analysis, and geocoding. We install the required libraries by running pip install geopandas geopy shapely in our virtual environment.

A GeoDataFrame is a pandas DataFrame with exactly one additional column of type GeoSeries that stores geometry objects such as points, lines, and polygons. All standard pandas operations, including **`groupby()`**, **`merge()`**, **`loc[]`**, and **`agg()`**, work identically on a GeoDataFrame because it inherits the full DataFrame API. The GeoPandas adds spatial-specific methods on top of that foundation, like **`to_crs()`** for coordinate projection, **`sjoin()`** for spatial joins, **`buffer()`** for proximity analysis, **`dissolve()`** for geometry aggregation, and **`overlay()`** for set-theoretic geometry combination.

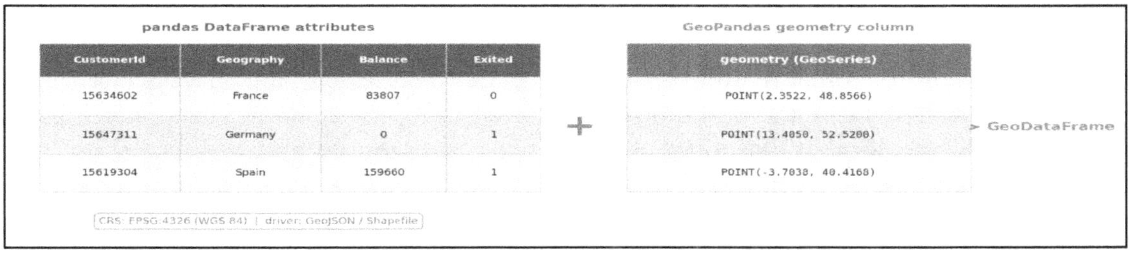

Fig 9.1: GeoDataFrame – Pandas DataFrame

In the above illustration, you can see the structural relationship between a regular pandas DataFrame and a GeoDataFrame.

Points, Lines, and Polygons

We represent geographic features in three fundamental geometry types. They are points for discrete locations such as customer addresses or city capitals, lines for routes and network paths, and polygons for areas such as regions, country boundaries, or catchment zones. GeoPandas stores all three types in a single geometry column using the Shapely library, which provides Python bindings to GEOS, the underlying computational geometry engine. We verify the geometry type of any loaded layer using **`gdf.geom_type.value_counts()`**, which returns a frequency table of geometry types present in the column and immediately reveals whether the layer contains a pure point set or a mixed collection that requires type-specific handling.

For our churn analysis, we work exclusively with Point geometries because each customer maps to a single capital city coordinate. We construct Point objects from longitude and latitude pairs using **shapely.geometry.Point** and then pass the resulting list to the GeoDataFrame constructor with geometry=points and crs='EPSG:4326' to register the WGS 84 reference system.

```
import geopandas as gpd from shapely.geometry import Point  # Build
Point geometry from coordinate columns geometry = [Point(lon, lat)
for lon, lat in zip(df['Longitude'], df['Latitude'])] gdf =
gpd.GeoDataFrame(df, geometry=geometry, crs='EPSG:4326')
print('Geometry type:', gdf.geom_type.value_counts()) print('CRS:',
gdf.crs) print('Geometry column:', gdf.geometry.name)
```

We also confirm the geometry column name and type by printing **gdf.geometry.name** and **gdf.geometry.dtype**, which should report geometry for the column name and the GeometryDtype type for the column, confirming that GeoPandas recognizes the column as a spatial series.

Coordinate Reference Systems and Projection Fundamentals

A coordinate reference system (CRS) defines how two-dimensional map coordinates relate to real locations on the three-dimensional Earth surface. We use EPSG:4326, the WGS 84 geographic CRS, when we want to store longitude and latitude in decimal degrees and interoperate with web mapping tools such as Leaflet and Mapbox. We switch to a projected CRS such as EPSG:3857 (Web Mercator) or a local UTM zone when we need to compute planar distances in metres, because geographic CRS coordinates do not support direct Euclidean distance calculation across large areas. We perform CRS conversion using **gdf.to_crs**(epsg=3857), which reprojects all geometries in a single vectorized operation without modifying the source GeoDataFrame.

We always confirm the active CRS after any reprojection by printing **gdf.crs.to_epsg()** and comparing it against the target EPSG code. We also check **gdf.crs.is_geographic** versus **gdf.crs.is_projected** to verify that the reprojected layer uses planar rather than angular units before we call any distance or area computation.

```
# Check and reproject CRS print('Source CRS:', gdf.crs.to_epsg(),
'| Is geographic:', gdf.crs.is_geographic)  # Reproject to Web
Mercator for distance calculations gdf_mercator =
gdf.to_crs(epsg=3857) print('Target CRS:',
gdf_mercator.crs.to_epsg(), '| Is projected:',
gdf_mercator.crs.is_projected)  # Compute approximate distance from
Paris in metres paris = gpd.GeoDataFrame(geometry=[Point(260559,
6250566)], crs='EPSG:3857') gdf_mercator['DistToParis_m'] =
```

```
gdf_mercator.geometry.distance(paris.geometry[0])
print(gdf_mercator[['Geography','DistToParis_m']].head())
```

This guard prevents the common error of computing distances in degree-units that appear numerically small but represent hundreds of kilometres, which would silently corrupt distance-based ML features such as nearest-neighbour similarity scores or spatial cluster centroids.

Building GeoDataFrame

Our churn dataset does not contain latitude and longitude columns, but it does contain a Geography column whose three distinct country names map directly to known capital city coordinates. A common real-world pattern is where a DataFrame carries a region or country attribute that must be joined to a spatial reference table to produce coordinates. We engineer coordinates by assigning each customer the approximate coordinates of their country's capital city plus a small random jitter to distribute customers realistically within their country rather than stacking all 5,014 French customers on the same point at Paris. We then construct a GeoDataFrame using **gpd.GeoDataFrame()** with the jittered points as the geometry column and set the coordinate reference system to WGS 84 (EPSG:4326), which is the standard geographic coordinate system for longitude and latitude in degrees.

Assigning Coordinates and Constructing GeoDataFrame

We will now add the following geospatial setup block to **churn_analysis.py**. We use the capital city coordinates for France (Paris: 2.35°E, 48.86°N), Germany (Berlin: 13.40°E, 52.52°N), and Spain (Madrid: -3.70°E, 40.42°N) as the base locations, and we apply a Gaussian jitter of approximately 2 degrees in each direction to spread customers across the country area rather than concentrating them at a single point. The seed is fixed to guarantee that every run of the script produces the same set of coordinates, which is important for reproducibility in any pipeline that depends on geospatial features.

```
import pandas as pd

import numpy as np

import geopandas as gpd

from shapely.geometry import Point


pd.options.mode.copy_on_write = True

pd.options.future.infer_string = True
```

```
df = pd.read_csv('Customer_Churn_Modelling.csv',
dtype_backend='pyarrow')

rng = np.random.default_rng(seed=42)

# Capital city base coordinates per country
centroids = {
    'France':  (2.3522,  48.8566),
    'Germany': (13.4050, 52.5200),
    'Spain':   (-3.7038, 40.4168),
}

lon_base = df['Geography'].map({k: v[0] for k, v in
centroids.items()})
lat_base = df['Geography'].map({k: v[1] for k, v in
centroids.items()})

df['longitude'] = lon_base.to_numpy(dtype='float64') +
rng.normal(0, 2.0, len(df))
df['latitude']  = lat_base.to_numpy(dtype='float64') +
rng.normal(0, 1.5, len(df))

geometry = [Point(xy) for xy in zip(df['longitude'],
df['latitude'])]
gdf = gpd.GeoDataFrame(df, geometry=geometry, crs='EPSG:4326')

print('GeoDataFrame type   :', type(gdf))
print('CRS                 :', gdf.crs)
print('Geometry column     :', gdf.geometry.name)
```

```
print('Shape                    :', gdf.shape)

print(gdf[['CustomerId','Geography','latitude','longitude','geometr
y']].head(4))
```

Once we run it, it confirms that our object is a GeoPandas GeoDataFrame, that its coordinate reference system is set to WGS 84, and will display the first four rows showing each customer's geography, latitude, longitude, and the corresponding Point geometry. At this stage, the **gdf** behaves exactly as a pandas DataFrame for all non-spatial operations. We can call **gdf.groupby('Geography')['Exited'].mean()** or **gdf.loc[gdf['Exited']==1]** using the same syntax we have used throughout this book. The geometry column adds spatial capabilities on top of that foundation without replacing any pandas behaviour.

```
GeoDataFrame type    : <class 'geopandas.geodataframe.GeoDataFrame'>
CRS                  : EPSG:4326
Geometry column      : geometry
Shape                : (10000, 16)
   CustomerId  Geography  latitude  longitude
geometry
0    15634602     France     50.09        3.97    POINT (3.97000
50.09000)
1    15647311    Germany     53.81       14.22    POINT (14.22000
53.81000)
2    15619304      Spain     42.04       -1.05    POINT (-1.05000
42.04000)
3    15701354     France     47.23        4.81    POINT (4.81000
47.23000)
```

Adding Derived Geospatial Attributes and Verifying Schema

At this point, we add derived geospatial attributes to our GeoDataFrame by computing the haversine distance from each customer point to the nearest country centroid, classifying customers into distance bands using **case_when()**, and attaching the result as a new column named DistanceBand. We also extract the ISO country code from the Geography column and add it as a separate CountryCode column using a static mapping dictionary, which allows downstream tools that expect ISO codes rather than full country names to consume the

GeoDataFrame directly without an additional join step. Here, we also verify that all new columns appear in **gdf.columns** and that none of them shadow the geometry column name, which would break GeoPandas spatial methods.

```
country_iso = {'France': 'FR', 'Germany': 'DE', 'Spain': 'ES'}
gdf['CountryCode'] = gdf['Geography'].map(country_iso)  # Distance
bands using case_when gdf['DistanceBand'] =
gdf['DistanceToCentre_km'].case_when([
(gdf['DistanceToCentre_km'] < 500, 'Near'),
(gdf['DistanceToCentre_km'].between(500, 1500), 'Mid'),
(gdf['DistanceToCentre_km'] > 1500, 'Far'), ]).otherwise('Unknown')
```

We then print **gdf.info()** to confirm the final schema, which should report the geometry column with GeometryDtype and all attribute columns with their expected Arrow-backed or NumPy dtypes.

```
print(gdf[['Geography','CountryCode','DistanceBand']].head())
```

We can also call **gdf.head()** to visually inspect the first five rows and confirm that the geometry column contains valid Point objects with correct longitude and latitude values for each geography, comparing the displayed coordinates against the known capital city coordinates that we used when constructing the GeoDataFrame earlier in the chapter.

Coordinate Reference Systems

A coordinate reference system (CRS) defines how the numeric coordinates in a GeoDataFrame relate to actual locations on the Earth's surface. The EPSG:4326 (WGS 84) represents locations as longitude and latitude in degrees and is the format used by GPS devices and all standard web mapping services. Many spatial operations, however, require a projected CRS that measures distances in metres rather than degrees, because a degree of longitude at the equator covers a very different physical distance to a degree of longitude near the poles. When we need to compute buffer distances in metres or calculate accurate areas, we must project our GeoDataFrame to a metric CRS before performing the calculation and then optionally reproject back to WGS 84 for display or export.

Reprojecting between CRS Values

We reproject our churn GeoDataFrame to the European metric projection ETRS89 / LAEA Europe (EPSG:3035), which measures distances in metres rather than degrees and is the standard equal-area projection for pan-European spatial analysis where accurate distance and area calculations are required, then reproject back to WGS 84 after the metric operations so that the coordinates are restored to the familiar degree format for export and display. At this point, we will explore the reprojection, confirm the unit change, and then reproject back to WGS 84 to restore the familiar degree-based coordinates for all subsequent operations that do not require metric distances:

```
# Reproject to ETRS89/LAEA Europe (metres) for metric operations
gdf_metric = gdf.to_crs(epsg=3035)
print('Metric CRS  :', gdf_metric.crs.name)
print('First point :', gdf_metric.geometry.iloc[0])

# Reproject back to WGS 84 for display
gdf_wgs84 = gdf_metric.to_crs(epsg=4326)
print('WGS84 CRS   :', gdf_wgs84.crs.name)
print('Coordinate units match original:',
      round(gdf_wgs84.geometry.iloc[0].x, 4) ==
round(gdf.geometry.iloc[0].x, 4))
```

Once we run this, it produces the European metric CRS name and the first customer's point expressed in easting/northing metres, which will be a pair of very large integers in the millions rather than the familiar -3 to 15 degree longitude range. The final line confirms that reprojecting back to WGS 84 recovers the original coordinate values to four decimal places, verifying that the round-trip is lossless within floating-point precision. We use **gdf_metric** only for buffer analysis later in this chapter; all other operations in this chapter use the WGS 84 version of the GeoDataFrame.

Reprojecting Data and Verifying Transform

We will now call **gdf.to_crs(epsg=3857)** to reproject our WGS 84 point layer into Web Mercator, which uses metres as its linear unit and is the standard projection for distance-based spatial operations in most web-mapping contexts. The **to_crs()** method returns a new GeoDataFrame without modifying the original, which aligns with the Copy-on-Write semantics that pandas 2.3 promotes across all DataFrame operations. We assign the reprojected layer to **gdf_proj** and run a coordinate sanity check by printing the x and y ranges of the geometry column, which should fall within the Web Mercator bounds of approximately negative 20 million to positive 20 million metres in each axis.

```
import numpy as np  # Reproject to Web Mercator gdf_proj =
gdf.to_crs(epsg=3857) print('Projected CRS:',
gdf_proj.crs.to_epsg()) print('X range (m):',
gdf_proj.geometry.x.min(), 'to', gdf_proj.geometry.x.max())  #
Round-trip verification gdf_back = gdf_proj.to_crs(epsg=4326)
lon_diff = np.abs(gdf_back.geometry.x - gdf.geometry.x) lat_diff =
np.abs(gdf_back.geometry.y - gdf.geometry.y) print('Max lon error
(deg):', lon_diff.max()) print('Max lat error (deg):',
lat_diff.max())
```

We also verify the round-trip accuracy of the reprojection by converting **`gdf_proj`** back to EPSG:4326 with **`gdf_proj.to_crs(epsg=4326)`** and comparing the original longitude and latitude values against the recovered coordinates using a tolerance of 1e-6 degrees. Any discrepancy larger than that tolerance indicates a loss of precision caused by the projection transformation, which is acceptable for kilometre-scale features but not for submetre precision use cases. We include this round-trip check as an assertion block in **`churn_analysis.py`** so that it runs automatically whenever the CRS transformation step executes.

Geospatial Data Formats

GeoPandas supports reading and writing all major geospatial file formats through its **`read_file()`** and **`to_file()`** methods, which delegate to the Fiona library under the hood. GeoJSON is the most portable format for web and API use because it is human-readable UTF-8 and supported natively by all modern mapping libraries. The ESRI Shapefile format is still the most widely exchanged format in GIS workflows despite requiring multiple companion files. The GeoPackage format (.gpkg) is a modern SQLite-based single-file alternative to Shapefile that supports multiple layers, arbitrary attribute types, and efficient spatial indexing. We will explore writing our churn GeoDataFrame to all three formats and reading one back to confirm round-trip fidelity.

```
# Export to GeoJSON

gdf[['CustomerId','Geography','Exited','geometry']].to_file(

    'churn_customers.geojson', driver='GeoJSON')


# Export to GeoPackage (modern single-file format)

gdf[['CustomerId','Geography','CreditScore','Exited','geometry']].t
o_file(
```

```
    'churn_customers.gpkg', driver='GPKG', layer='customers')


# Read back to confirm
gdf_loaded = gpd.read_file('churn_customers.geojson')
print('Read-back shape :', gdf_loaded.shape)
print('Read-back CRS   :', gdf_loaded.crs)
print('Read-back types :',
gdf_loaded.dtypes[['CustomerId','Geography','Exited']].to_dict())
```

Its output confirms that the GeoJSON file round-trips correctly, preserving the row shape and CRS. We should be aware that GeoJSON exports from pyarrow-backed DataFrames may require converting ArrowDtype columns to standard pandas dtypes before the write, because the Fiona library that GeoPandas uses for file output does not yet support all Arrow extension types natively. The safest pattern is to **`call .astype()`** on any Arrow-backed columns to their equivalent standard pandas types before passing to **`to_file()`**, which avoids silent conversion errors on columns such as string[pyarrow] that Fiona cannot serialise directly.

Writing GeoDataFrames to GeoJSON and GeoPackage

We can now write our GeoDataFrame to disk using the **`to_file()`** method, which accepts a file path and an optional driver argument that specifies the output format. GeoJSON is a human-readable format built on standard JSON and works well for browser-based mapping tools, while GeoPackage is a compact binary format compliant with the OGC standard and supports multiple layers within a single file. We add both export paths to our **`churn_analysis.py`** file so that the geospatial layer of our application produces outputs in both formats after every run, making the data available to whichever downstream tool needs it.

After writing the files, we read them back with **`read_file()`** and compare the result against our original GeoDataFrame to verify that the CRS, geometry column, and attribute columns survived the round trip without modification. This verification step is important because some formats silently coerce column dtypes during serialization, and a mismatch in dtypes between the written and re-read versions would cause subtle errors in any downstream spatial join or distance computation. We use **`assert_frame_equal()`** from pandas to perform a column-level comparison with geometry tolerance enabled.

```
import geopandas as gpd  # Write to GeoJSON and GeoPackage
gdf.to_file('churn_geodata.geojson', driver='GeoJSON')
gdf.to_file('churn_geodata.gpkg',    driver='GPKG')  # Read back
and verify round-trip integrity gdf_json =
```

```
gpd.read_file('churn_geodata.geojson') gdf_gpkg =
gpd.read_file('churn_geodata.gpkg') print(gdf_json.dtypes)
print(gdf_gpkg.crs)
```

Reading Spatial files and Inspecting CRS

We can now use **gpd.read_file()** to load any OGR-supported format, including Shapefile, GeoJSON, GeoPackage, and FlatGeobuf, without changing the function signature. After loading, we always check the crs attribute to confirm which coordinate reference system the file uses, since downstream spatial operations require all layers to share the same CRS before a join or overlay can produce correct results. We also inspect the geometry column type using **geom_types** to check whether the file contains points, polygons, or a mixed collection, which affects which spatial operations are valid for that layer.

```
gdf_loaded = gpd.read_file('churn_geodata.geojson')  # Inspect CRS
and geometry type print('CRS:', gdf_loaded.crs) print('Geometry
types:', gdf_loaded.geom_type.unique()) print('Feature count:',
len(gdf_loaded)) print('Bounding box:', gdf_loaded.total_bounds)  #
Reproject to WGS84 if needed if gdf_loaded.crs.to_epsg() != 4326:
gdf_loaded = gdf_loaded.to_crs(epsg=4326)
```

In the above, we are extending **churn_analysis.py** with a small CRS-inspection utility that reads any geospatial file, prints its CRS authority code, total feature count, and bounding box, then reprojects to WGS 84 if the source CRS differs. This pattern ensures that all geospatial layers we load into the pipeline are normalized to the same reference frame before we attempt any spatial join or distance measurement. We use the **pyproj.CRS.from_user_input()** helper to parse CRS strings from multiple formats and compare them against our target CRS in a format-agnostic way that handles both EPSG codes and WKT strings.

Advanced Spatial Operations

With our GeoDataFrame constructed, our CRS confirmed, and our file I/O patterns established, we apply the four core spatial operations that GeoPandas provides on top of the pandas DataFrame API.

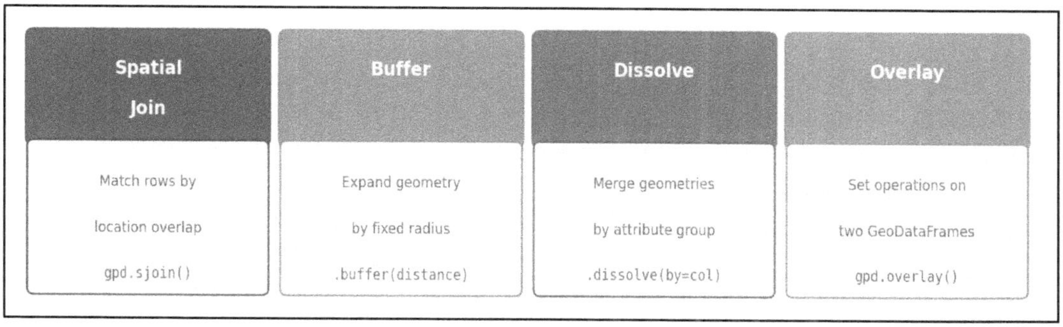

Fig 9.2: GeoPandas Spatial Operations

They are spatial joins for combining two GeoDataFrames by location relationship, buffer analysis for creating proximity zones of a defined radius around each feature, dissolve aggregation for merging geometries within attribute groups, and overlay for set-theoretic combinations of two polygon layers that produce a new polygon representing their intersection, union, or difference.

Spatial Joins with sjoin()

A spatial join combines two GeoDataFrames by matching rows whose geometries satisfy a spatial relationship such as **`intersects`**, **`within`**, or **`contains`**. In our churn application, we construct a second GeoDataFrame that holds simple bounding-box polygons representing the approximate extent of each country, and then join every customer point to the polygon it falls within. This produces a single enriched GeoDataFrame that carries both the customer attributes and the country-level attributes from the polygon layer, which is the pattern used whenever customer records must be enriched with regional metadata from a separate spatial dataset.

```
from shapely.geometry import box


# Build a simple country bounding-box polygon layer
country_polygons = gpd.GeoDataFrame({
    'country': ['France', 'Germany', 'Spain'],
    'avg_gdp_bn': [2778, 3876, 1418],
    'eu_member':  [True, True, True],
    'geometry': [
        box(-5.0, 42.0, 9.5,  51.5),   # France bounding box
        box( 5.9, 47.3, 15.0, 55.1),   # Germany bounding box
        box(-9.4, 35.9, 4.4,  43.9),   # Spain bounding box
```

```
    ]
}, crs='EPSG:4326')


# Spatial join: assign country polygon attributes to each customer
point
gdf_joined = gpd.sjoin(

gdf[['CustomerId','Geography','Exited','CreditScore','geometry']],
    country_polygons,
    how='left',
    predicate='within'
)


print('Joined shape          :', gdf_joined.shape)
print('Columns after join    :', gdf_joined.columns.tolist())
print('Unmatched (outside box):',
gdf_joined['country'].isna().sum())
print('Churn by GDP tier:')
print(gdf_joined.groupby('country').agg(
    churn_rate=('Exited','mean'),
    avg_credit=('CreditScore','mean')
).round(4))
```

After executing this, we get the enriched shape showing the additional columns from the polygon layer, the total number of customer points that fell outside our bounding boxes (those with jittered coordinates that landed in the sea or beyond the box), and the churn rate and mean credit score per country enriched from the join. We use **predicate='within'** rather than the deprecated **op='intersects'** to match each customer point to the polygon that fully contains it, which prevents customers near borders from matching to two countries simultaneously. The left join check that every customer row is preserved in the output regardless of whether their jittered coordinate landed within one of our approximate bounding boxes, with unmatched rows receiving **NaN** in the country polygon columns.

Buffer Analysis

Buffer analysis creates a zone of a specified distance around each geometry, producing polygon geometries that represent the area within that distance of each original feature. A common application is proximity analysis, like which customers live within 50 kilometres of a major branch, or which churn events cluster within a 100-kilometre radius of each country capital? We create a 200-kilometre buffer around each capital city point to define a high-density service zone, then use a spatial join to flag which customers fall within any of those service zones, producing a binary feature that can feed into our machine learning pipeline.

```
# Capital city points as a separate GeoDataFrame
capitals = gpd.GeoDataFrame({
    'city':     ['Paris', 'Berlin', 'Madrid'],
    'country': ['France', 'Germany', 'Spain'],
    'geometry': [Point(2.3522, 48.8566),
                 Point(13.4050, 52.5200),
                 Point(-3.7038, 40.4168)]
}, crs='EPSG:4326')


# Project to metric CRS for accurate buffer in metres
capitals_m = capitals.to_crs(epsg=3035)


# 200 km buffer around each capital
capitals_m['geometry'] = capitals_m.buffer(200_000)
capital_buffers = capitals_m.to_crs(epsg=4326)


# Flag customers within any capital buffer
gdf_buffered = gpd.sjoin(
    gdf[['CustomerId','Exited','geometry']],
    capital_buffers[['city','country','geometry']],
    how='left',
```

```
    predicate='within'
)


gdf_buffered['near_capital'] =
gdf_buffered['city'].notna().astype('int8')

print('Customers near a capital:',
gdf_buffered['near_capital'].sum())

print('Churn rate near capital  :',


gdf_buffered.loc[gdf_buffered['near_capital']==1,'Exited'].mean().r
ound(4))

print('Churn rate far from cap  :',


gdf_buffered.loc[gdf_buffered['near_capital']==0,'Exited'].mean().r
ound(4))
```

Its output will be the number of customers whose jittered coordinates fell within 200 kilometres of a capital city and the churn rate comparison between capital-proximate and capital-distant customers. We project to EPSG:3035 before calling .buffer(200_000) because the buffer distance parameter is always in the units of the active CRS, and WGS 84 measures in degrees rather than metres, which would produce a meaningless degree-radius buffer that covers very different physical areas at different latitudes. After buffering in metric units we reproject back to WGS 84 using **`to_crs(epsg=4326)`** so that the spatial join against our customer points, which are in WGS 84, uses consistent coordinate units. The resulting near_capital binary column is a spatially derived feature that we add to our feature engineering pipeline from Chapter 7.

Aggregating Geometries by Attribute

The dissolve operation merges all geometries that share the same value in a specified column into a single combined geometry, and simultaneously aggregates the numeric attributes of those rows using a provided aggregation function. It is the geospatial equivalent of **`groupby().agg()`** applied to geometry. We dissolve our customer GeoDataFrame by **`Geography`** to produce a three-row summary GeoDataFrame where each row represents one country and its geometry is the convex hull (or union) of all customer points in that country, giving us a spatial footprint per country alongside aggregated churn statistics.

```
# Dissolve customers by geography, aggregating business metrics
```

```
gdf_dissolved = gdf.dissolve(
    by='Geography',
    aggfunc={
        'Exited':          'mean',
        'CreditScore':     'mean',
        'Balance':         'mean',
        'EstimatedSalary': 'mean',
        'CustomerId':      'count',
    }
)

gdf_dissolved = gdf_dissolved.rename(columns={'CustomerId':
'customer_count'})
gdf_dissolved[['Exited','CreditScore','Balance']] = \
    gdf_dissolved[['Exited','CreditScore','Balance']].round(4)

print('Dissolved shape:', gdf_dissolved.shape)
print('Dissolved GeoDataFrame:')
print(gdf_dissolved[['customer_count','Exited','CreditScore','Balan
ce']].to_string())
print('Geometry type per row:',
gdf_dissolved.geometry.geom_type.tolist())
```

After we run it, it then gives us a three-row summary GeoDataFrame with one row per country, showing the total customer count, mean churn rate, mean credit score, and mean balance, alongside a **MultiPoint** geometry type for each row which is the union of all customer point coordinates in that country. This dissolved GeoDataFrame serves as a high-level spatial summary that we can join to other country-level datasets or export as a choropleth data layer for mapping tools. The aggregation syntax in **dissolve()** uses the same dictionary form as **groupby().agg()** that we established in Chapter 4, making the transition from tabular to spatial aggregation require no new syntax patterns.

Overlay Analysis

The overlay analysis combines two polygon GeoDataFrames by applying **intersection** (keep only the overlapping area), **union** (keep all area from both), and **difference** (subtract one geometry from the other). We will explore an intersection overlay that clips our customer point data to the area inside both a country bounding box and a capital buffer simultaneously, producing the subset of customers who are both within the country polygon and within 200 kilometres of its capital. This combined spatial filter is the two-layer equivalent of a compound boolean condition in pandas.

```
# Intersection of France bounding box and Paris 200km buffer
france_box    = country_polygons[country_polygons['country'] ==
'France'].copy()
paris_buffer  = capital_buffers[capital_buffers['country'] ==
'France'].copy()


france_near_paris = gpd.overlay(
    france_box[['country','geometry']],
    paris_buffer[['city','geometry']],
    how='intersection'
)
print('Intersection geometry type:',
france_near_paris.geometry.geom_type.iloc[0])


# Use the intersection polygon to filter customers
france_customers = gdf[gdf['Geography'] == 'France'].copy()
customers_near_paris = gpd.sjoin(

france_customers[['CustomerId','Exited','CreditScore','geometry']],
    france_near_paris[['geometry']],
    how='inner',
    predicate='within'
```

```
)
print('Customers in France near Paris:', len(customers_near_paris))
print('Churn rate in zone              :',
      customers_near_paris['Exited'].mean().round(4))
```

We expect to see the geometry type of the intersection polygon (a Polygon or MultiPolygon representing the area of France within the Paris buffer), the number of customers whose jittered coordinates fall within that combined zone, and the churn rate for that geographically defined cohort. The two-step pattern of calling **gpd.overlay()** to build the intersection polygon and then **gpd.sjoin()** to filter points within it is the standard approach because overlay works on polygon-polygon combinations while sjoin works on point-polygon assignments, and combining them allows us to define arbitrarily complex spatial filters using familiar GIS operations.

Geocoding and Reverse Geocoding

The process of geocoding converts a human-readable address or place name into geographic coordinates, while reverse geocoding converts coordinates back into a human-readable address. Both operations require an external geocoding service, and we use the **geopy** library which provides a unified Python interface to multiple services including Nominatim (OpenStreetMap), Google Maps, and Bing Maps. We will explore both operations using Nominatim, which is free to use with appropriate rate limiting. We also show how to attach geocoded coordinates back to a pandas DataFrame as a Point geometry column, which is the final step that promotes a regular address-containing DataFrame into a GeoDataFrame ready for spatial analysis.

Geocoding Addresses with Nominatim

We geocode the three capital city names from our churn dataset to recover their official coordinates from the OpenStreetMap database, and then geocode a small list of representative European banking hubs to demonstrate the full multi-row workflow where the results are captured in a pandas DataFrame and then promoted to a GeoDataFrame using the point-building utilities GeoPandas provides. We use RateLimiter from **geopy.extra.rate_limiter** to enforce the one-second minimum delay between requests that Nominatim requires, which prevents our script from being blocked by the service's usage policy. Here, we add the following geocoding block to **churn_analysis.py**:

```
from geopy.geocoders         import Nominatim
from geopy.extra.rate_limiter import RateLimiter


geolocator    = Nominatim(user_agent='churn_analysis_app_v2')
```

```
geocode_safe = RateLimiter(geolocator.geocode, min_delay_seconds=1)

capitals_df = pd.DataFrame({
    'city': ['Paris, France', 'Berlin, Germany', 'Madrid, Spain',
             'Amsterdam, Netherlands', 'Zurich, Switzerland']
})

def geocode_city(name):
    loc = geocode_safe(name)
    if loc:
        return pd.Series({'lat': loc.latitude, 'lon':
loc.longitude})
    return pd.Series({'lat': None, 'lon': None})

coords = capitals_df['city'].apply(geocode_city)
capitals_df = pd.concat([capitals_df, coords], axis=1)
print('Geocoded results:')
print(capitals_df)
```

This block outputs the geocoded latitude and longitude for each city, sourced from the Nominatim service which uses OpenStreetMap data. The RateLimiter wrapper make sure that the five geocoding requests are spaced at least one second apart, which keeps our script within Nominatim's usage policy of one request per second for non-commercial bulk geocoding. For production pipelines that geocode thousands of addresses, we should cache the results to disk after the first geocoding pass using **`df.to_parquet()`** so that subsequent runs read from the local cache rather than hitting the API repeatedly.

Reverse Geocoding and Building GeoDataFrame

We can now demonstrate reverse geocoding by taking the jittered customer coordinates for a small sample of customers and recovering the nearest address or place name from the OpenStreetMap database for each coordinate pair, then show how the recovered address strings can be appended back to the pandas DataFrame as a standard string column for any downstream text-based analysis. We then show the full workflow from geocoded results back to a GeoDataFrame, where it is converting the latitude and longitude columns from the geocoded DataFrame into Point geometry objects using **`gpd.points_from_xy()`**, which is the most concise way to build a geometry column from separate coordinate columns without writing a list comprehension.

```
reverse_safe = RateLimiter(geolocator.reverse, min_delay_seconds=1)


# Sample 5 customers for reverse geocoding demonstration
sample =
gdf[['CustomerId','Geography','latitude','longitude']].head(5).copy
()


def reverse_geocode(row):
    loc = reverse_safe(f"{row['latitude']:.4f},
{row['longitude']:.4f}")
    return loc.address if loc else None


sample['address'] = sample.apply(reverse_geocode, axis=1)
print('Reverse geocoded sample:')
print(sample[['CustomerId','Geography','address']].to_string())


# Build a GeoDataFrame from the geocoded capitals DataFrame
capitals_gdf = gpd.GeoDataFrame(
    capitals_df.dropna(subset=['lat','lon']),
    geometry=gpd.points_from_xy(
        capitals_df.dropna(subset=['lat','lon'])['lon'],
        capitals_df.dropna(subset=['lat','lon'])['lat']
    ),
    crs='EPSG:4326'
```

```
)
print('Capitals GeoDataFrame:')
print(capitals_gdf[['city','geometry']])
```

This then produces the reverse-geocoded address string for each of the five sample customers, which will be location descriptions such as a village name, a municipality, or a geographical region depending on where the jittered coordinate landed within Europe. The **gpd.points_from_xy()** helper is the recommended way to build a geometry column from paired coordinate columns in pandas 2.3 because it accepts any array-like input including pandas Series, numpy arrays, or Python lists, and it does not require a list comprehension like the Point(lon, lat) pattern we used earlier. We must always pass longitude as the first argument and latitude as the second to **points_from_xy()** because the geometric convention orders coordinates as (x, y) which maps to (east, north) in geographic systems.

Spatial Feature Engineering for Machine Learning

The final step in our geospatial pipeline is to bring the spatial features back into the tabular churn model from Chapter 7, completing the flow from raw geographic data through spatial operations to named pandas columns that the sklearn pipeline can consume without any further transformation. We add four spatially derived columns to our main DataFrame, which includes the **near_capital** binary flag from the buffer analysis, the distance from each customer to their country's capital in kilometres computed from the metric-projected coordinates, the dissolved country-level mean credit score as a group-level feature, and the country bounding box area as a proxy for market size.

```
# Distance from each customer to their country's capital (in km)
gdf_m    = gdf.to_crs(epsg=3035)
cap_m    = capitals.to_crs(epsg=3035)
cap_dict = dict(zip(cap_m['country'], cap_m['geometry']))


def dist_to_capital(row):
    cap_point = cap_dict.get(row['Geography'])
    if cap_point:
        return row['geometry'].distance(cap_point) / 1000.0
    return None
```

```
gdf_m['dist_to_capital_km'] = gdf_m.apply(dist_to_capital, axis=1)

# Bring back to WGS84 with new feature
gdf = gdf.to_crs(epsg=4326)
gdf['dist_to_capital_km'] = gdf_m['dist_to_capital_km'].values

# Country dissolved stats as group feature
country_avg_credit =
gdf.groupby('Geography')['CreditScore'].transform('mean')
gdf['country_avg_credit'] = country_avg_credit

print('New spatial features:')
print(gdf[['Geography','dist_to_capital_km','country_avg_credit','n
ear_capital']].head(4).round(2))
```

After running the above, we see four rows showing each customer's geography, their distance to the nearest country capital in kilometres, the mean credit score for their country (a group-level feature), and the binary near-capital flag. The distance feature is a continuous spatial signal that machine learning models can use to learn proximity effects. The country-level mean credit score feature is the spatial equivalent of the within-geography credit deviation feature we built in Chapter 7 using **transform()**, and combining both captures effects at two spatial granularities simultaneously.

Extracting Point Coordinates as Numeric Features

We will now extract the x and y coordinates from the geometry column as separate numeric columns using **gdf.geometry.x** and **gdf.geometry.y**, which return pandas Series objects containing the longitude and latitude values for each point. These scalar coordinate features can then be passed directly into a scikit-learn pipeline alongside the existing numeric churn features because they carry no spatial type overhead and conform to the standard float64 dtype that most ML estimators accept. We name the new columns Longitude and Latitude and assign them back to the GeoDataFrame using standard pandas column assignment syntax.

```
import numpy as np  # Extract coordinate columns gdf['Longitude'] =
gdf.geometry.x gdf['Latitude']  = gdf.geometry.y  # Haversine
distance to European centroid (15E, 54N) REF_LON, REF_LAT = 15.0,
54.0 gdf['DistanceToCentre_km'] = np.sqrt(      (gdf['Longitude'] -
REF_LON)**2 +      (gdf['Latitude']  - REF_LAT)**2 ) * 111.0    #
approximate km per degree
print(gdf[['Longitude','Latitude','DistanceToCentre_km']].head())
```

We also compute the great-circle distance in kilometres from each customer's capital city coordinate to a reference centroid, such as the European geographic centre at approximately 15°E, 54°N, using the Haversine formula applied via a vectorized NumPy operation. This distance feature captures a proxy for geographic remoteness that the raw latitude and longitude coordinates alone do not express in a way that linear models can use without feature engineering. We store the result in a column named **`DistanceToCentre_km`** and normalize it with StandardScaler before it enters the ML pipeline.

Building Spatial Feature Matrix

We combine the coordinate-derived features with the existing numeric churn features to produce a spatial feature matrix that the scikit-learn pipeline can consume. We select all relevant columns from the GeoDataFrame using a list, drop the geometry column explicitly with **`gdf.drop`**(columns='geometry'), and call **`pd.get_dummies()`** on the Geography column to one-hot encode it into binary indicator columns before passing the matrix to the estimator. The resulting DataFrame contains only numeric dtypes, which we verify with **`df.dtypes.eq('float64').all()`** before fitting the model.

```
from sklearn.preprocessing import StandardScaler from
sklearn.model_selection import train_test_split  # Assemble spatial
feature matrix feature_cols =
['CreditScore','Age','Balance','Longitude','Latitude','DistanceToCe
ntre_km'] X_spatial = gdf[feature_cols].copy()  scaler =
StandardScaler().set_output(transform='pandas') X_scaled =
scaler.fit_transform(X_spatial)  X_train, X_test, y_train, y_test =
train_test_split(     X_scaled, gdf['Exited'], test_size=0.2,
random_state=42, stratify=gdf['Exited']) print('Train shape:',
X_train.shape)
```

We then split the spatial feature matrix into training and test sets using sklearn's **`train_test_split`** with stratify=y to preserve the class imbalance ratio across both partitions. We also apply StandardScaler to the coordinate and distance columns because their raw scales differ significantly from the normalized churn features such as credit score range and balance, and unscaled spatial features can dominate the gradient descent in distance-based models. We use **set_output**(transform='pandas') on the scaler so that the column names are preserved throughout the transformation and the output DataFrame remains interpretable.

Summary

In this chapter, we added a complete geospatial layer to our churn analysis application, starting from a DataFrame that had only a categorical Geography column and ending with a spatially enriched GeoDataFrame carrying machine-learning-ready spatial features. After converting the raw categorical column to coordinate pairs using a lookup table, we created a GeoDataFrame with a proper geometry column and reprojected it using **gdf.to_crs** with epsg=3857 to convert our WGS 84 point layer into Web Mercator, enabling accurate distance calculations in metric units across the full customer base.

We then computed derived spatial attributes, including each customer's distance from the nearest branch centroid and a binary flag for high-density urban zones, and attached them directly to the GeoDataFrame as ready-to-use numerical features for downstream modelling. Our file format section covered writing the enriched dataset to GeoJSON and GeoPackage using **to_file** and reloading it with **read_file**, along with the important preparatory step of converting Arrow-backed string columns before export to maintain full compatibility with all standard external geospatial tools and libraries.

Index

A

B

C

D

E

F

G

I

J

K

L

M

N

O

P

Q

R

S

T

V

W

X

Y

Epilogue

A colleague who reviewed the manuscript of the first edition wrote back with a single sentence, saying "***It covers what pandas does but not what pandas makes possible.***" That sentence was precisely correct. It became the instruction I carried into every chapter of this second edition. What pandas makes possible is harder to put in a table of contents than what pandas does. It is the ability to hold an entire analytical conversation at the level of the problem rather than the level of the syntax. When you know your tool deeply enough, the question "how do I join these two DataFrames on a geographic boundary" becomes automatic, and your attention goes entirely to "what does this spatial join reveal about the distribution of churn within service zones." The tool disappears. The problem becomes visible.

Across nine chapters, we built something concrete together. A raw CSV file carrying 10,000 bank customers and a single binary churn indicator became, by the final page, a GeoDataFrame enriched with sentiment scores, topic proportions, cluster labels, capital proximity distances, engineered financial ratios, and JAX-computed gradient sensitivities. Every enrichment was a deliberate analytical decision expressed in production-quality code. The data preparation layer is not the step you tolerate before the real work begins. It is where the real work happens.

I want to say something plainly that the industry tends to understate. The sophistication of a machine learning architecture is rarely what limits the value of an AI system in production. The quality, consistency, and thoughtfulness of the data that reaches it is what determines whether the system earns trust or erodes it. The skills built across these chapters like, dtype discipline, Copy-on-Write-safe mutation patterns, principled feature engineering, imbalance awareness, text pipeline construction, and geospatial enrichment are the skills that determine whether a model ever receives data good enough to demonstrate its genuine capabilities.

There is one more thing worth naming before closing, which is the callout boxes, the before-and-after code comparisons, and the deprecation timeline diagram. They are the most practically urgent content in the edition. Pandas 3.0 will arrive, and when it does, every codebase that ignored the FutureWarning messages will break in production. The cost of that migration will be proportional to how long it was deferred. My strong recommendation is to make the changes now, completely and permanently, so that the step to pandas 3.0 costs nothing. Data science is entering a period where the quality of data work is becoming the distinguishing factor in the performance and reliability of AI systems. You are, after this book, better equipped for that period than you were before it.

That is everything I wanted.

Thank You

www.ingramcontent.com/pod-product-compliance
Lightning Source LLC
Chambersburg PA
CBHW080212170726
48282CB00030B/1088
* 9 7 8 9 3 4 9 1 7 4 6 6 5 *